Advance Praise For

THE PRESENT MOTHER

"Any parent who reads and practices the insights in this book will not only heal their own wounds from childhood, they will change things for their offspring for all generations to come."

> - Dr. Shefali Tsabary, PhD, New York Times bestselling author, *The Conscious Parent*, *Out of Control*, and *The Awakened Family*, featured on the OWN network in *Oprah's Lifeclass* and *Super Soul Sunday*

"Becoming a parent is just the beginning of our own becoming. *The Present Mother* is beautifully written, warm and comforting as it guides us into a spiritual process of seeing the sacredness of the relationship with our children and ourselves. Inspired by her own personal evolution, Catherine Weiss shares moving and sometimes challenging exercises that call us to question the truth of our negative thoughts that are often at the root of our reactions to our children. In her daily exercises we learn the value of being in the present moment, to accept and learn to love what is."

> - Barbara Nicholson and Lysa Parker, Co-Authors, *Attached at the Heart: Eight Proven Parenting Principles for Raising Connected and Compassionate Children*, Co-founders, Attachment Parenting International

"The difference between *The Present Mother* and other parenting books is radical: It gives mothers the tool to know what to do in every parenting situation before applying parenting skills learned from other parenting books. Indeed, it takes mothers out of thinking and straight into their own unequivocal knowing. This book of short lessons can either transform someone's life or get them started on transforming it. It is the work that most parents need, probably before any of the other parenting books!"

> - Karen M. Pietruszka, Parenting Communication Skills Specialist, B.A. in Psychology and Child Development, Boulder, CO

"This book is a blessing to all mothers – even those whose children are grown and have moved on. For all those mothers with grown kids, it is never too late to be a "present mother." It means we can be present with our partners and ex-partners, our grown kids and grandkids, neighbors, co-workers, everyone! I love the softness and sensitivity with which you address people who may be new to self-inquiry. And for those that are not new to it, there are simple gentle reminders. Your own personal experiences and examples are lovely and they make me feel so connected to you. Your vulnerability encourages openness from me as a reader and participant."

- Lyn Dean, single mother of two kids, both now in college, Denver, CO

"Catherine's book is a gift, not only for mothers but for the world."

-Bonnie Compton, APRN, BC, CPNP, Child & Adolescent Therapist, Parent Coach, Host of *Wholehearted Parenting Radio*

"Just the title of *The Present Mother* makes a strong statement and I relax just hearing it. Catherine Weiss's book offers real down to earth and practical guidance for taking responsibility for our own feelings as mothers and learning how to transcend and transform our judgments so that we can become more authentic with our children and ourselves."

- Peggy O'Mara, founder of *Mothering.com*, past publisher, editor and owner of *Mothering Magazine*, author of four books, featured in *The Wall Street Journal, USA Today, The Washington Post, Chicago Tribune, Mother Earth News, and Utne Reader*

"Catherine Weiss makes the hardest job on earth phenomenally easier with *The Present Mother* and establishes herself as a world class Life-Skills Educator."

- Mama Marlaine, Founder Parenting 2.0, Creator of the *Life Skills Report Card*

"I found *The Present Mother* to have really had me reaching down into my soul, reflecting on myself. It made me look to my inner self as I also thought of how my actions affected my everyday life. It is a book that you will find you walk away from with deep, heartfelt reflection."

- Stephanie Petters, Attachment Parenting International Resource Leader and API Reads Coordinator

The

PRESENT MOTHER

How to Deepen Your Connection with the Present Moment,
Yourself, and Your Child

~

Catherine Weiss

The Present Mother:

How to Deepen Your Connection with the Present Moment, Yourself, and Your Child

Copyright © 2016 by Catherine Weiss
Published by Catherine Weiss, LLC

The intent of the author of this book is to educate the reader in order to improve the mother-child relationship. If difficult memories or feelings begin to surface within you, please reach out for professional help. Catherine Weiss does not dispense medical advice, is not a healthcare professional, nor does she prescribe the use of any technique as a form of medical treatment. The author and the publisher assume no responsibility for your actions as a result of any information in this book.

Inspired in part from passages in the book *Byron Katie on Parents and Children* ©2006, Publisher: The Work of Byron Katie, ISBN: 1890246794

Library of Congress Cataloging-in-Publication Data
Weiss, Catherine, 1965-
The Present Mother: How to Deepen Your Connection with the Present Moment, Yourself, and Your Child / Catherine Weiss
ISBN-13: 978-0-9961400-1-0   ISBN-10: 0996140018

1. Parenting
2. Self-Help
3. Spirituality
4. Meditation

Bulk Ordering Information:
Quantity sales: Special discounts are available on quantity purchases by mothering organizations, associations, and others. Orders by U.S. trade bookstores and wholesalers, please contact catherine@thepresentmother.com

First Paperback Edition

Cover design by Evan Weiss, age 12
Author portrait © Bob Carmichael

To every mother-child relationship in the world

Gratitude

I am deeply and forever grateful for my husband, children, and parents, for they are the people who opened the door to everything in me that exists in this book. By being who they naturally are, they allowed me and encouraged me to use my actual experience of being a mother, wife, and daughter in order to bring this life-changing manuscript to you.

I also thank whatever the universal force of love is that moves in and through all of us every moment of every day. I feel like this book literally came to life because of that entity, whatever that is. It may sound strange but it literally feels like I didn't write this book…that energy of pure love and connection wrote it *through* me and I was the vehicle for delivering it.

Thank you dear mother-reader for your intention to be present with your child, not just in body, but also in mind and spirit. Your act of picking up this book tells me that there is a wonderful movement taking place within you and on our planet right now.

Thank you to my talented colleagues, editors, proofreaders, designers and friends who gave their time, talent, and recommendations for the good of this book, namely Michele Beach, Lyn Dean, Jessica Hall-Upchurch, Elizabeth Lanni, David Nelson, Mandy Nicolosi, David Ord, Stephanie Petters, Karen Pietruszka, Dr. Shefali Tsabary and Kathy Wetzel.

I am eternally grateful to the many scientists, doctors, teachers, authors, coaches, and mentors, whose works have helped me deepen my connection with the present moment, myself, and my family.

I have so much appreciation for the wise words of the 13th century poet, Rumi, because they have been such a guiding light in my mothering and in the writing of this book:

Out beyond ideas of wrongdoing and rightdoing, there is a field.
I'll meet you there.

When the soul lies down in that grass, the world is too full to talk about.
Ideas, language, even the phrase "each other" doesn't make any sense.

Contents

Foreword

We are on the brink of a new consciousness in parenting—a shift from imagining our children are in need of being "fixed" by us, or at the very least "molded," to realizing that the behavior issues we are increasingly seeing in young people ought to be a wake-up call to *us as parents* to face up to our own failure to "grow up" in terms of how we parent.

This new consciousness recognizes that unless parents become aware of their own emotional imprinting from childhood—including the stories they buy into such as "my parents spanked me and I turned out fine" or their unexamined beliefs about parenting such as "children need to be shown who's boss"—they inevitably load onto their offspring baggage that should never be a child's to bear.

The unconscious way we were parented—and the way we now parent—is the result of a huge crack in the foundations of our sense of who we are. This split in our understanding of ourselves occurred because the unique person each of us is in our essence—in our original, authentic self—wasn't fully supported. Instead, to one degree or another, it was crushed by the prevailing unconsciousness of family and society at the time.

When our original, authentic self wasn't nurtured as it should have been, we were left with a void, an emptiness, a hollow feeling at our center. No longer able to feel the joy of our true being, but instead experiencing a sense of something lacking, we needed to somehow plug the hole. This we did by beginning to *think* of ourselves a certain way, based largely on the opinions of others. What we thought of ourselves became a picture of ourselves we carry around in our head. Often referred to as our "ego," this self-image—this way of imagining ourselves—became a substitute for our lost ability to *feel* and simply *be* ourselves.

The ego we develop, which often has little in common with our true self, operates from a quite different mindset than the overflowing fullness that's intrinsic to our essence. Instead of growing up with an exuberant love of life, filled with joy and seeing abundance everywhere, we grow up feeling needy and therefore constantly seeking someone or something to end our neediness.

Enter our children. Powerless, completely dependent on us, and almost infinitely pliable, they are the perfect substitute for our missing self. The consequence is that, instead of honoring our children for who they are in their uniquely individual essence, we parent them from a sense of lack and a mindset of fear—a fear that they might not meet our expectations, once again leaving us feeling empty inside. This is why we are all so terrified that our children might not turn out "right."

And so it is that "discipline"—spelled out in control, compliance, and conformity—becomes the hallmark of parenting. We are *determined* that our children should satisfy our demands—the demands of our egoic substitute for our own missing essence.

Bringing our children up in the same unconscious way we were brought up, we end up hijacking their unique personalities—their individual brilliance—instead shaping them to fill our own sense of lack. Tragically, many of our children grow up with awareness of their original self all but obliterated which is why so many of us end up experiencing a midlife crisis of identity as we suddenly wake up to the fact that we really don't know ourselves at all.

Children cut off from their natural sense of delight no longer see the world as a place to be explored with curiosity and great excitement. As they are increasingly saddled with the expectations of family and society, they find themselves becoming immersed in the emotional pain that results from losing touch with their essence. Dysfunction, depression—even death at their own hand—are all too often the result.

Thankfully, a growing number of parents and educators are becoming aware of how unconsciously we have all parented for generations. As more of us wake up to how unconsciously we ourselves were parented, and how unconsciously we now parent our own children, books such as *The Present Mother* become vital companions.

Catherine shares her story with warmth, insight, and humility. In so doing, she shows us how self-inquiry can help us examine our past conditioning, our assumptions, and our unproductive fantasies of "how our children should be," thereby paving the way for us to be truly "present" for our children in a way few parents have ever been. Because she has tapped into the wellspring of her own essential and authentic life, she is able to be a wise guide for her readers.

A book like *The Present Mother* is especially valuable because it can help mitigate the effects of disconnection from our essence—particularly in the case of mothers, who have such a huge impact on children. It's vital that, in our day and age when our young people are in so much trouble, we shift into the higher state of consciousness to which Catherine points us. If we can transform the most elemental of all relationships, the mother-child bond, we can literally change our world.

Any parent who reads and practices the insights in this book will not only heal their own wounds from childhood, they will change things for their offspring for all generations to come.

Namaste,
Dr. Shefali Tsabary, PhD
Author of *The Conscious Parent*, *Out of Control* and *The Awakened Family*

Introduction

This might be the first parenting book you've ever read that is exclusively about you, dear mother. This book focuses on your thoughts, your enlightenment, and your presence with your child. As the doorway, we will be looking deeply into the challenges you experience in your mothering and seeing what's truly behind them. This isn't a book about how to raise your children, how to school your children, or what lifestyle to lead. Instead, this is 100% about you and the thoughts on your mind. The focus is on you because inside of you is the answer to every parenting question you've ever had.

Whether trusting yourself sounds like a foreign concept or not, this book will help you see that you *can* trust yourself all of the time, no matter how much doubt you have in yourself right now, or this book will remind you of the self-trust you already know and help you connect even more deeply to it. If you are already familiar with the work I present, this book will deepen your practice all the more, jumpstart it, and lead you to new insights. If you are new to it, you'll find it an incredibly valuable resource that will help you experience brand new ways of seeing things that you would have never dreamed of before. This will become experientially evident as you work your way through this book and its 40-day parenting workshop led by your own spiritual guide: yourself.

~

The *thought* which occurs at the exact moment of disconnection with your child *is the root cause* of the disconnection itself. This book guides you in the experience of questioning those thoughts that cause the disconnection. When you question them, and you see through the illusion of disconnection, you simply can't believe them anymore, and you are returned to your natural state of peace, wisdom and clarity. Your awareness of the love and connection with the present moment, your true self, and your child, is regained. You realize that you are already always present. In fact, you are presence itself.

In this intimate memoir, I share personal details of how being present has manifested in my life, what it looks like, and specific instructions for how you can do the same as you wish. I share how this has positively revolutionized me and my entire family. These profound changes make a daily positive impact on my children. I trust that these changes will positively impact all future generations in my family.

I've noticed time and time again in my own mothering life that my children seem to "copy" my ways of being. They are my mirror. And science backs that up. According to cellular biologist Bruce Lipton, PhD.[1] and other prominent physicians[2], a parent's beliefs - whether conscious or unconscious - are passed down to the child. I am passing down beliefs that will keep my children rooted in the ever perfect present moment, without guilt over their memory of the past, or fears of their imaginings of the future. I love that I pass down this new belief system to them. It is always possible for you to start or continue expanding these same kinds of positive changes in your life. I love that we all have that opportunity.

~

At some point in their young lives, children seem to do and say things that we feel we should try to control. They exert their strong will in all of its biological perfection. They are determined to get that thing they're trying to get and go in the direction they're trying to go. Sometimes, in our attempt to keep our children safe from real or perceived harm, or to try to give them what we see as the best for them, our desire to control or our worries about them result in an unwanted perceived disconnection from them.

Through my own experience of deeply understanding the root cause of this disconnection in myself, and from witnessing others who understand it as well, I've realized that it is, in reality, an *illusion*. It's an illusion because the love that binds us together is always here now and always connects us. In fact, our children and we are *one* - we are the same love, the same energy that animates both our bodies, the same divine presence living a human experience. When we identify with a thought that is incongruent with the here and now, we lose the awareness of that love. We lose it because we unconsciously believe the stressful thoughts that cause the perceived disconnection. Those stressful thoughts are always based in the past or the future. It's almost like a curtain on the stage of a play. The left curtain is the past; the right curtain is the future. When we're lost in memories of the past or imaginings of the future, the curtain is closed and you can't be fully present in the reality of your life in the here and now.

If you really stop and notice, the only moment that ever exists is now, and even now is gone in a second. Past and future only exist as a thought in the mind, never as what is seen

---

[1] Bruce Lipton, PhD, The Biology of Belief, 20017 https://www.brucelipton.com/books/biology-of-belief November 30, 2007).

[2] Gabor Mate, PhD, http://drgabormate.com/, for example.

through your eyes in the present. For the purpose of this book, however, I believe it will be useful now for me to share my memory of how my experience of being present came about.

My Story

For me, the ultimate realization of being present started with the birth of my two children. All the things that defined me before becoming a mother vanished when I poured all of my love into the human beings sent to me to love. I didn't care about the way my hair looked, the makeup I wore, the clothes I wore, how many degrees I had, how much money I made, or what other people thought of me. All at once, and over time, that all faded away. It was so beautifully breathtaking how love bloomed.

Along the way though, sometimes I would experience intense worry about my children, which seemed like it literally overtook me. Sometimes I would have a sudden, surprising negative reaction to something one of my children did. These reactions were not congruent with my love for them nor my intentions for the kind of mother I wanted to be. Then I would notice guilt in me, about my reactions. I could not understand where the reactions came from or why they were getting triggered so strongly. I had never reacted this way before. I felt deeply how those worries, frustrations, and guilty feelings kept me from being present with my children. My body was present, but my mind and spirit definitely were not.

Do you know those reactions I'm talking about? They are the ones that seemed to come out of nowhere. For me, they seemed to create all kinds of uncomfortable feelings between me and my child, and my partner. They seemed to create a lot of disconnection. Have you ever had worries about passing on unproductive habits and patterns to your child? I would worry so much about that. I would get a feeling sometimes, a mood, that just seemed to spring itself on me and I couldn't figure out why.

I've always been interested in self-realization and spirituality. When my kids were about one and two, I read *The Power of Now* and *A New Earth*, both by Eckhart Tolle. I loved both books, and still do. You may already know that Eckhart Tolle calls these episodes of disconnection and suffering the "pain body." After reading that, I tried to apply it to my mothering life in some way. I wanted my kids to know the power of now too. So, my kids, husband, and I gave a kid-friendly name to our "pain bodies" and identified them with a color and a shape. My son's was a red hammer, my daughter's was a purple triangle, mine was a purple tornado, and my husband's was a red weapon.

After the storm had passed from one of our "pain body" episodes, the kids and I would talk about our "shape." We would say how it occurred when we had our upsetting feelings and then we would notice that it was gone. I would ask the kids where their shape went and they would say something like "It's taking a nap" or "It went on a vacation." In this way, I helped myself and my kids become aware that our true selves were the awareness that could see and witness our "shape" - our "suffering." We were consciously noticing that the "suffering" was not us. In that way, I hope I helped them stay connected to their true selves. Once they could see the upset for what it was, it seemed to lose some of its power over them.

I was happy with this bit of awareness in our family for a while, although nothing but the whole thing would ultimately suffice for me. I wanted to know how I could stop myself from having these upsets and reactions in the first place. For a while I tried everything I could to avoid these "negative" experiences in myself. At the same time, I worried about when they would happen again, directed at my precious children and husband. I didn't want to pass on these behaviors to our children.

I wanted more than anything to be present with them, in the here and now, deeply connected, deeply rooted in love, without any worries about their future or any guilt over how I had reacted toward them in the past. My son used to say, "Mommy, *be* with me." I wanted to learn how to do that without my mind wandering off while I was with him. I wanted to realize the power of now, in how I was with both my children in every single moment. I wanted a way out of my anxiety and panic about them. I wanted to realize spiritual enlightenment. I wanted to stop getting irritated with them, stop bossing them around, stop yelling at them, and stop the war with reality that was happening in my mind. I wanted to know the real cause of my suffering, so I could begin anew. I wanted to be an enlightened human being as I raised my children.

When my children were about three and four, I discovered something that completely changed my life called self-inquiry. From the yogic tradition, and originating in 14th century India, self-inquiry is the most efficient and direct way of seeing the unreality of the ego - the "pain body" as Eckhart Tolle calls it - and releasing it. With our focused attention on the thoughts coming from the ego, we finally see it for what it really is: non-existent. An illusion. Then the "ego" literally disappears – falls away - from our awareness, and only our true, awakened state remains: pure awareness, presence, consciousness. This is spiritual awakening, or liberation from suffering.

~

There are many different types of self-inquiry methods, and of course, many different types of spiritual and personal growth practices and resources. I've been introduced to and experienced a multitude of them over the last 25 years. They all can help. The one I've found to help me be the most effective parent I can possibly be in the shortest amount of time is the self-inquiry process that I share with you in this book. Since 1987, millions of people around the world have used this process, first created by Byron Katie, and have reportedly found more happiness than they ever dreamed possible (when they use it consistently.) In my experience of doing this type of self-inquiry since 2007, it has also helped me realize the way to:

- Understand the root cause of your parenting challenges with complete clarity and begin again in truly enjoying being a parent;
- Work with your own thoughts so you can stop passing on any kind of pain to your child and instead, pass on what you want;

- Shed any guilt you feel over what you've said or done to your child in the past and repair your relationship so you can be a positive influence on your child again;
- Melt away your worries about your child and instead, have quick, easy, complete access to your wisdom, creativity, kindness and joy;
- Stop any doubts you have in your mothering abilities so you can more consistently be the powerful, loving leader you want to be for your child;
- Be a fully present mother in body, mind and spirit.

So, along the way in my parenting, whenever I noticed a reaction in me that was not what I truly wanted to do or say to my children, I would pick up a pen and paper, or call a friend, to facilitate me in my newfound, powerful self-inquiry process. I couldn't help but apply what I saw there to my mothering. After a while, I could quickly do self-inquiry at any time, by myself in my own mind, and could therefore be totally present *and* connected to my children during *any* situation. I don't know how I'll react one second from now, but if it's a reaction I'd rather not have, I now know how to quickly bring myself back to the present moment.

What Self-Inquiry Did for Me and My Family

Debbie Ford, author of the New York Times bestseller called *The Shadow Effect* said, "Like the lotus flower that is born out of mud, we must honor the darkest parts of ourselves and the most painful of our life's experiences, because they are what allow us to birth our most beautiful self." In all the years of working through the apparent mud myself, it wasn't until I started doing self-inquiry that I realized that the mud was created and thickened by *me* every time I believed a thought that wasn't true in the here and now. This all happened totally without my awareness, completely unconsciously...until self-inquiry. In other words, before self-inquiry, every time I didn't know to question a thought/belief/expectation/assumption that caused stress in me (which is always a thought based in past/future), the mind I have believed something about the present that wasn't even *true*. It can't help but do this until we realize what is actually happening. Once I realized I was the *creator* of the mud itself I laughed hysterically on and off for a few *years*. Seriously. How freeing it was!! It's the most incredible feeling one can ever have. It's enlightenment. It's liberation from suffering. Self-inquiry is the most direct, effective form of this birthing process. With self-inquiry, we liberate ourselves from the illusion of the mud and our most beautiful self is all that's left.

Self-inquiry has helped me and my family more than words can say. I literally cannot describe how much my life has been renewed. I am a completely different person now than I was 10 years ago. My perception of myself, other people, and life have completely changed for the better. I love, love, love every single solitary moment of life, including any stressful thought that would still arise in me. Sometimes I laugh hysterically (again) when a stressful thought arises because I see it for what it really is. I'm healthy, my marriage is healthy, my kids are healthy and the world is a beautiful place, *with* all of its circumstances and *with* all the experiences of motherhood. I've come to see the beauty in everything, including any stressful thoughts that could arise in myself or others because they are always the sign pointing us back home. I practice self-inquiry daily, sometimes 10-12 times a day in my mind, naturally, and it only takes a few seconds now. Some days, I experience no stressful thoughts at all. This is possible for everyone.

I've realized that the way that I'm being has an incredible impact on my children and spouse. *At the same time,* I've realized that we are ultimately not in control of the thoughts that arise in our mind. Our thoughts *think* us. I am also not in control of the divine love that emanates through me. It's just there - here, now - as it is in every person on the planet. So, if we unconsciously believe our stressful assumptions, judgments, beliefs and thoughts, then our feelings, words and actions manifest from them. That's why we sometimes say to ourselves in surprise, "Wow, did I really react that way?!"

However, when we notice those reactions in us that we would like to change, identify the stressful thoughts behind our reaction, write them down, and question them, the stressful thoughts fall away *all on their own*. Really. It truly feels like magic. You're not even doing the letting go of the stressful thoughts. You *can't* "let go" of a thought. It's there. You have to question it for *it* to let go of you. Those stress-inducing thoughts get debunked and rewired all on their own after we question them. It's science; it's brain development; it's neural pathway reprogramming in action, grounded in the truth, in reality, in what's real, right here and now. So, the thing we *can* control is whether or not we question the stressful thinking when we become aware of it. If we don't question the stressful thoughts, we will believe them and so will our kids. After we question those thoughts that block love and presence, we're free to parent in the here and now, responding to our child with love and kindness - our true nature - right in every moment, no matter what the circumstances.

Through self-inquiry, I realized that my children have within them the seed of enlightenment, just like me, just like my husband, just like you and your family. When I was present, and couldn't possibly fall for fearful, sad stories, I noticed my family couldn't either. I was no longer teaching suffering to my children. I am with them now, in mind and spirit, as well as body. Today, we all flow together from each beautiful present moment to the next, like floating down an awe-inspiring river. We create, laugh, learn, love, play, eat, sleep, and grow from each perfect moment to the next. Pure love has bloomed. It is the most beautiful way of being with your children, of being with your partner, of being a woman in this world. It's the most natural way too. And, it's the easiest, in my experience. It's not easy to suffer.

I've realized that I am pure awareness, pure consciousness, pure presence, divine love (and you are too), manifesting itself through living a human experience. I simply don't believe any stressful stories anymore. It's so freeing! When you're free of past and future, your bright loving light can shine, fully present, in the here and now, with your precious child. You are the beautiful, whole, peaceful, present, powerful, divine mother you wish to be. Mothering becomes easy to you, even blissful, and you get to bask in all of its breathtaking love.

~

The Nature of Thoughts

Have you ever stopped to consciously notice and witness your thoughts? If you haven't then you are believing your thoughts, whether you know it or not, and whether you like it or not. If you have paused to consciously witness them then you may have noticed that you don't actually *plan* to have a thought. It just *pops* into your mind within the present moment. Even the thought, "I'm going to plan to have a thought" comes out of nowhere (now here). We don't even actually *do* the thinking of a thought either. It just occurs without our having to do anything.

This may seem frightening at first. Actually though, this is very good news; it's the most empowering and liberating thing we can ever realize if we want to change anything about our lives. If you're conscious of your thoughts, you can question them when they cause you any stress, pain, or suffering of any kind. If stress is the result when you believe them, you can be sure that they are thoughts about the past or the future and never about this now moment. When you start noticing your stressful thoughts, you have the opportunity to either believe them or question them. There are no other choices when it comes to thoughts. You start seeing that the *you* that you *think* you are has *nothing* to do with your thoughts. Instead, you begin to notice that *you are the awareness that notices* the thoughts themselves.

~

The thoughts on your mind *are* flexible. You can work with them; you can change them - they aren't *you*. Questioning the thoughts on your mind is one of the most liberating activities you can ever do in your entire life. I didn't realize this by reading it in a book or hearing someone talk about it. I realized it through *experience*. The only way to ever truly *know* something is to experience it. I love inviting you to test this out for yourself as you experience your true self by reading and filling in the worksheets in this book. I love that you would have an open enough mind to recognize some bit of this as the truth that matches what you already know to be true within the deepest part of you. If so, you are recognizing, remembering, or beginning to detect the presence that is always here now.

~

Why I Wrote This Book

My intention in writing this book is that it will somehow help you transcend all of the stress you experience in your mothering into unwavering connection with your child, with yourself and with the precious present moment, where all love resides, no matter what your circumstances. I hope that it will inspire, guide, and assist you in your presence practice. I want it to help you become even more deeply aware of both your love for your child, which never goes away, *and* the stressful thoughts you unconsciously believe which block your awareness of that love during stressful times. I want to give you a magnifying glass to help you see through the illusion of disconnection and stressful thinking, so you don't have to suffer as much, no matter what struggles you have. In turn, your centered, peaceful, loving presence can be seen and fully experienced, and you can restore a beautiful connection with your child - a connection that was never really lost in the first place. Even if your connection to your child is already strong, I hope this book will help you deepen that connection and manifest more fully your amazing presence, wisdom, and joy, in each moment with your child.

Specifically, I wrote this book for several reasons. The first is to demonstrate that all mothers have similar stressful thoughts, similar challenges and similar struggles when it comes to raising our children. Mothers have so much in common, and can support each other so well. We all have thoughts of doubt, fear, and "unspeakable" things that occur in our homes and in our lives every day. So, first know that you are not alone. I am with you. I am very honest and candid. You will likely be able to recognize your life through reading about mine, even though we may have the appearance of outward differences.

The second reason I wrote this book is to invite you to try and/or regularly practice and/or deepen your practice of this simple, effective self-inquiry process. It is my deepest heart's desire that all mothers have a way to transcend their worries, pain, and sadness, however great or small. The self-inquiry path is a beautiful way out of any depression or anxiety you are feeling about your children, your partner, your ex-partner, or yourself. If practiced with an open mind on a regular basis, self-inquiry can be a way that permanent inner joy can be realized.

Another reason I wanted this book to exist is to let all mothers know that they have every answer to every parenting question right in their own minds and heart. This book shows you exactly how to access those answers. Some of us are afraid to trust ourselves. Many of us have been trained to trust others more than ourselves. There is no blame in what I am saying. There is only understanding to be realized. I am here to let you know that you *can* trust yourself beyond a shadow of a doubt *after* you question the thoughts on your mind that cause all the stress in your life about your children (and your other relatives too, for that matter.)

Finally, I wrote this book because I know from experience that it's one way the world can be a more loving, kind place for our children and our children's children. I love that mothers can experience the transformational power of mothering in the here and now, without worries about the future or guilt over the past. I love that mothers can know about the power of using self-inquiry to raise enlightened children, to know how to do self-inquiry, and to experience its positive effects. I hope for as many children as possible to be able to experience the authentic presence of their mother, in body, mind, and spirit. I love that future generations can be affected by this shift in human consciousness, starting from the start: with the mother-child relationship. When mothers make questioning their stress-inducing thoughts their way of life, peace plants more seeds on our planet; when one more mother has a peaceful mind, that's one more step towards peace everywhere.

How This Book Came Into Existence

Presence is a present moment experience of seeing - it is awareness. Although presence doesn't happen within the apparent illusion of time, this book is organized in a timeline of 40 days. One letter a day is addressed to you, Dear Present Mother. The letters replicate, for the most part, letters I wrote to members of the Present Mothers Community™, a personal and spiritual development community I founded in 2013. Within the community, I offer assistance to mothers wishing to transcend their mothering stress into authentic presence and connection with their children.

On each of 40 consecutive mornings, I emailed a letter to our members with the subject, *Morning Walk with The Present Mothers Community™*. In each letter I shared how presence had manifested in my life after I questioned the stressful thoughts causing disconnection between me and my children. Each letter contained intimate details of my mothering life in order for readers to relate to the experience I shared. Each letter explained how my self-inquiry practice completely transformed my "negative" reactions to my children into presence and a deeper connection with them. Each letter contained an invitation to do self-inquiry, as I had done, to realize the connection and joy of being a present mother.

One of my friends wanted to join our community after I had already written these 40 letters. She asked if she could have copies of all of them. I started putting them all together. I realized as I was putting them together that a book was forming right before my eyes. The result is in your hands right now.

How This Book is Presented

I intentionally write similar ideas in many different ways so that you will have every opportunity to take in the essence of the message. Words are ever only placeholders and pointers for describing what is the indescribable. Words cannot describe presence. They always, in some way, fall short. Presence is an *experience* and so much more. The words merely point in the direction of presence, always directing you inward, to your own innate knowing. I also say similar things in different ways because the mind likes to stay in an "I know" position in order to protect itself from an imagined future full of disastrous scenarios. In reality though, there is ever only this now moment. Every thought of the future, in reality, never exists because there is always and only *right now*.

Some mothers already know this, on an intellectual level. Some already know this from their own experience. Some mothers reading this book may not be open to the information being presented; these mothers may not yet be ready to hear the message. When a mother is identifying strongly with feelings of anxiety, depression, anger, being right, and so on, she could fail to see the value in this book or in doing the exercises presented. So, to benefit the most from this material, I invite you to come to it with an open mind.

The thinking mind turns words that it hears or reads into its own stories and meanings. For this reason, I do not use the word God. There are many definitions, meanings, and stories about God. While I've studied and practiced various religions, including Christianity for more than two decades, my allegiance is to Love, which springs forth in the present moment when the mind is free of all stressful thinking.

I synthesize modern, updated, scientifically proven principles, research, and information into my writing. In this way, I seek to merge timeless spiritual wisdom with today's latest scientific findings about the workings of the mind. I weave in updated information on neuroscience, human development and our biological capacity for evolving our human experience.

Periodically, I put the ~ symbol to indicate a point where I encourage you to stop reading and become aware of what is occurring in your mind and in your body based on what you've just read. I invite you to reflect on what you are noticing within you as you pause for a moment at these special stopping points.

I intend for the pronouns she/her and he/him to be used interchangeably, so you can apply the examples to your own life situation. I recall more times of being triggered by my son's behavior than by my daughter's. For this reason, there are more "he" pronouns in the book. I read to my kids and husband the sections of the book that referenced them. They contributed to their clarity and are happy for me to share these personal examples for the sake of the difference it can make in others' lives.

For clarity, I provide you with an example of a stressful thought to question on the worksheets. By no means do I intend to sway your idea about what stressful thought of yours to question. I only provide it so that you can see the follow-through of the questions being answered. Also, I use a boy name in the example because of my experience investigating so many more stressful thoughts about my son and husband than my daughter.

There is a theme to every letter. You may not necessarily have a stressful thought about the particular theme of each day's letter. That's okay. I invite you to use the daily worksheets to address whatever stressful thoughts are arising for you at that moment. Make it as timely as you can to *your* life. The daily themes are only meant to prompt you to use that or any stressful belief as the doorway to your self-inquiry, and to your freedom. So, please use *your* life as your daily curriculum for growth.

Throughout the book, I use certain words interchangeably to mean the same thing. For instance, the words judgment, concept, belief, statement, assumption, expectation, stressful thought or thought all refer to the same thing: a thought that induces stress in you that I invite you to question in your self-inquiry practice. If the thought doesn't induce any kind of stress, if it creates peace for you, then I don't question it and I'm not suggesting you question it either. The self-inquiry in this book is for you to question just the thoughts that - when we believe them, either consciously or unconsciously - cause a stressful reaction.

I use the term *the* stressful thoughts instead of *my* stressful thoughts. I don't mean to confuse you with this. I say it this way only because of its accuracy. They aren't mine; they're *everyone's*. Therefore, they are not personal in any way. They are merely the collective thought pattern that most of society has believed for centuries…until now.

I use "quotes" around words quite often. The reason for this is that these words with quotes do not have true meaning any more to me. They are not accurate, in reality. They are words we often use in the world when we believe the illusion of disconnection and are therefore not present. They are usually words stemming from a basis of past or future.

There are, of course, many present fathers in the world. There are many fathers in the world who would like to deepen their connection to their children. This book can be useful for fathers as well as mothers. All of the exercises in the book are applicable for mother-child relationships *and* father-child relationships. However, the focus here is on mothers because this book is part memoir, written from my own experience as a mother.

The Power of a Present Mother

Parents, and mothers especially, have the power to change the world because we are *raising* the world. We are responsible for raising the next generation, and as a result, the next, and the next, and the next. That continues on into eternity. Every generation is affected by a mother's thoughts, feelings, words, and actions. The legacy of your love and your life lives on in the hearts and minds of every single human being on the planet, for every single human being on the planet has or had…a mother.

When we change how we see the world, our children and our partners change how they see the world too. We end up raising children who do not inherit our old, fear-based thought patterns, our old debilitating stories, our disconnecting judgments, and our unsupportive beliefs. Since we don't believe them anymore, our children can't believe them. *We don't teach suffering to them anymore.* We don't teach anxiety. We don't teach depression. It just isn't possible to live a life full of suffering anymore when we choose to question our stressful thinking. Motherhood gives us this most special opportunity.

When you experience being present, you are beyond your identity; you are a channel for divine love to live through you, as you.

How to Make the Most of This Book

There's something sacred about the early morning. The mind seems to be very clear and open then. I wrote each of these 40 letters in the early morning on 40 consecutive days while my children were asleep. Because of its power to quickly clear a path for presence to emerge from within you, and to set the tone for the rest of your day, I love the opportunity to replicate that same experience for you.

I invite you to engage with this book as a *presence practice* for 40 consecutive mornings. You certainly don't have to do it that way to get personal benefits from this book. It's perfect however you approach it. We are meeting in the field Rumi calls *beyond right and wrong*. In my experience, you cannot do life, or mothering, or this book, wrong. I love knowing that.

It is a very nurturing ritual to give yourself focused support and listening in order to learn something so important and (possibly) so new about yourself. I invite you to create special quiet time for yourself each morning in order to read and complete the worksheets. Can you do it when the kids are sleeping in the morning? Can someone else help with the kids - your husband, other relative, neighbors? Can they watch a movie while you have some tea and write? Doing self-inquiry every morning in this way can be completely transformational for you and your connection with your child. Questioning your stressful thoughts in the morning makes your whole day go "better." This time you spend with yourself can be some of the most valuable time you'll ever spend in your entire life.

So, each morning, I invite you to do these four things:

1. Read the welcome meditation found on page 16.
2. Read that morning's letter.
3. Make notes on the Presence Practice Notes page that follows each letter. These notes can be anything that comes to your mind as you're reading the letter and preparing to complete the worksheets that follow. They could be questions, current stressful thoughts, inspirations that come to you, or anything you want to record.
4. Answer the questions on the worksheets for that morning.

~

The meditation, letters, and worksheets have no power on their own to help you; all of the power comes from your active participation with them and in your awareness of your inner responses to them. Just like at a gym, you have to decide within yourself to commit to helping your body, structure a routine, work out on the machines and do reps on the weights. That's when you've made the difference in your body. Same here, only we're focusing on the old and new muscles in the brain. You are deepening your connection to yourself when you fully experience the calming meditation, reflect on the heartfelt letters by making some notes, and write down the responses that surface within your open mind as you read the questions on the worksheets. As a result, *all* other connections deepen. Presence is an experience, so I invite you to give yourself the gift of full immersion in the experience by following the four steps above. You are deepening your connection with your child, yourself, and the present moment when you do.

Directions for filling in the worksheets are located on the top of each page. If you find it challenging to complete a worksheet, I invite you to post your question on the private Facebook page for The Present Mothers Community, on The Present Mother website or email me directly at catherine@thepersentmotherscommunity.com. I will be happy to answer your questions.

It doesn't matter how little or how much you know about self-inquiry; you'll get the same benefits. In the beginning, you might spend an hour each morning. After a while exploring how you do with the process, you'll find you can do a quick jotting down of what comes to you on any sheet of paper around, without using the worksheets, and get the same results. Eventually, with consistent practice, you'll be able to do the process in your mind without writing it down and finally it happens even without your effort because you have literally made it your way of life.

The worksheets are exactly the same for every chapter. There are no differences in them even though the theme and letter of each chapter is different. I wanted to standardize the worksheets for you. They are like gravity, unchanging, in order to help ground the – sometimes chaotic - thoughts in the mind. I've included a generic example on them only for clarification of how to answer the questions. The example doesn't change even though the topic of inquiry is different in every chapter. Once you get the hang of filling in the worksheets, you won't even need to look at the example any longer.

Even though there is a theme to every morning's letter, I encourage you to question the stressful thoughts on your mind at the time you come to the worksheet. This may mean that you have no stressful thoughts that relate to that day's letter. That's ok. It's more important that you use your actual life as your guide for which stressful thoughts to question.

If you want extra support in your presence practice, I highly recommend doing the book with a mothering friend. Each of you can act as partner and support for the other. I did self-inquiry with a friend and it had amazing exponential effects. You can provide so much momentum for each other in this way. It's one of the best things you can do to take your presence practice that much deeper.

For the ultimate support in your presence practice, I invite you to join me and other mothers every Saturday morning, except holidays, for our Present Mothers Community group conference calls called *Morning Walks with the Present Mothers Community™*. We start the call with a meditation and then I facilitate the group through self-inquiry. You can remain totally anonymous if you want, while still being able to participate fully with your listening. You'll be with mothers like you, who are committed to being present, questioning their stressful thinking with self-inquiry, and deepening their connections with their children, themselves and the present moment. There will be mothers who are currently working through the book now, as well as mothers who have continued with their presence practice after they've finished the book. There is more information about our community at the end of the book, and we have detailed information about our *Morning Walk* calls at http://www.thepresentmother.com/.

In my experience, over the course of your 40-day presence practice, you will create more and more new thought patterns that will open up your mind and heart to the true soul of your beautiful child, your true self, and the here and now. Your stress will decrease, making a clear path for your wisdom and creativity to emerge. You will have the clarity to address any mothering challenge you encounter.

You will be creating a brand new habit for your mind. The DNA in your body will actually change as a result of this.[3] Your old stressful stories won't have the same power over you that they used to. You won't believe them as much as you once did. You won't get hooked or triggered by them as often. Eventually, you'll stop thinking of them altogether. You'll be a calmer, more loving mother without even trying. You'll start to notice that you get upset less and less often and you are more and more often fully present with your child. You'll have less and less worries about their future and less and less frustrations with them. You won't be pulled out of the precious present moment with your child by thoughts about the past or future. Eventually, your child, your partner (or even ex-partner) won't be able to help but mirror you. I know this to be true from my own experience.

No matter where you are in your mothering journey, your spiritual path, or your path of personal growth, it's possible for you to come to fully trust the awesome power of the present moment. Your mind will begin to notice more and more of the thoughts that could use self-inquiry. Those "negative" feelings in your life will be your stop sign for what thought is next in line to be questioned. Eventually, the beauty of self-inquiry becomes part of who you are. All you are left with is authentic presence. Love springs forth in its myriad of magical ways. Beauty thrives in your life. Love blooms. Your children blossom into their own beautiful, authentic selves, free of your stressful beliefs.

Once you've done your presence practice for these 40 magical days and have incorporated self-inquiry into your everyday life, it could be the last "method" to fall away because you'll

---

[3] https://www.brucelipton.com/books/biology-of-belief

have come home to your true self. You can experience being present, and the peace and joy that follows it, on an ongoing basis while navigating through all the different "chapters" of your life. If you really commit yourself to it, these 40 days can be the most transformational of your entire life.

Are you ready to begin?

~

Morning Meditation

Good morning, beautiful mother.
Together, let's take a morning walk into the mind of beautiful you,
and experience the pure presence at the essence of your being.

Notice your breathing,
notice the in-breath,
notice the out-breath,
be a witness to the breath moving in and moving out,
notice you're *being* breathed.

Notice any thought on your mind,
attach the thought to an imaginary cloud,
and be the watcher of the cloud floating away,
farther,
farther away,
until it's completely gone, and all you see is blue sky.

Notice your breathing,
notice the in-breath,
notice the out-breath,
be a witness to the breath moving in and moving out,
notice you're *being* breathed.

Notice any thought on your mind,
attach the thought to an imaginary cloud,
and be the watcher of the cloud floating away,
farther,

farther away,
until it's completely gone, and all you see is blue sky.

Notice your breathing,
notice the in-breath,
notice the out-breath,
be a witness to the breath moving in and moving out,
notice you're *being* breathed.

Notice any thought on your mind,
attach the thought to an imaginary cloud,
and be the watcher of the cloud floating away,
farther,
farther away,
until it's completely gone, and all you see is blue sky.

Notice your breathing,
notice the in-breath,
notice the out-breath,
be a witness to the breath moving in and moving out,
notice you're *being* breathed.

Notice any thought on your mind,
attach the thought to an imaginary cloud,
and be the watcher of the cloud floating away,
farther,
farther away,
until it's completely gone, and all you see is blue sky.

Notice that you are the awareness that notices the thoughts.
Follow that awareness all the way to its source.
And rest in that.

~

Welcome to the present, dear mother.

Welcome to Morning 1 - *The Power of Presence*

Dear Present Mother,

As I go deeper and deeper into my presence practice, I notice that I eventually experience myself as presence itself. I get to witness two beautiful children - ages 8 and 9 at this time - flowing with them from one perfect moment to the next. I'm present with them; I'm one with them. I find everything I ever wanted in the present.

To truly know the experience, one has to be the one experiencing it. At best, I can only grasp at words to paint a picture of what it's like for me to be present and deeply connected with my children. I will try, knowing that words will never do it justice.

It dawned on me one day that I hadn't gotten upset, frustrated, disappointed, angry, confused, worried, sad, or any other "negative" feeling for about six to nine months. Really. It just sort of occurred to me that that was what was happening - not feeling any suffering. It was kind of like living on another planet, kind of like I was a different person, kind of like there had actually, in reality, always been the absence of any kind of suffering. Each moment just kept perpetuating, from moment to moment, beautiful, peaceful, calm, quietly joyful, content, one moment, then another moment, then another. Yet, within each moment, there was an entire life, an entire universe, nothing lacking, nothing needing fixed, only pure perfection, in all of its glory. The beauty of it makes me cry sometimes; it's so breathtaking and so surreal.

Sometimes, I can't even believe it's me living through all of it. It isn't "me" (the ego) at the same time. There is no "me" (ego) in it, there is only being here, in the presence of three exquisite human beings called "my" children and "my" husband. They happily blossom like the most amazing flowers you've ever seen. One child is programming a computer at the age of 10 and one child is caring for animals and people like Mother Teresa at the age of 9. I cannot believe the beauty. Tears of awe and appreciation run down my cheeks as I write.

I am present, and at the same time, I am out of their business. I also notice I trust them, trust life, feel overwhelmed with gratitude and joy, and I still handle the day-to-day practicalities and functions of mothering. They're not separate from each other - presence (being) and the actions of motherhood. In fact, they are all inseparable. Presence infuses all of what I do. I am present while listening to them, while playing with them, while walking with them, while holding their hands, while folding their shirts, while finding their shoes, while driving them to the yogurt shop, while cooking their meals, while hugging them, and holding them. Each action is a beautiful lifetime, a world unto itself. I'm not worried about anything they say or do anymore. Now I realize that it was and always has been the thoughts *about* them that were worrying me and never them or their behavior.

It did not used to be this way. Sometimes I would feel so worried about my children's safety that I would have debilitating panic attacks. I remember one particularly frightening incident. We had just moved to a town in a higher altitude than I was used to. The kids and I were at home, at dinnertime, alone. They were about 5 and 6 years old at the time. I started getting very dizzy – probably from not drinking enough water. I began to feel so worried that I might faint - or even die - and the kids would be left at home all alone. I started panicking. On top of feeling dizzy, my heart started to race, my palms started to sweat, and my breath quickened. I was so lost in the fear. I called 911, just so someone would be there in *case* I passed out or died.

Sometimes I would have sudden bouts of anger and snap at the kids unexpectedly. Sometimes I would try to control them to either keep them safe or to help me get my needs met in some way. When they would not do what I wanted, I would all-of-a-sudden become upset. As much as I always tried to stay peaceful, that *thing* in me would come out of nowhere as a complete surprise sometimes. I told myself I was an attached parent, an empathic parent, the most loving, kind parent I could possibly be, a parent who would honor my child's path. However, this duality in my behavior - being so kind to them most of the time, and yet every now and then saying or doing something that was so unlike me - gave me such shame and guilt. I felt like I was being ruled by my fears and my feelings. I felt so hopeless. I felt so confused. I started feeling very depressed. I didn't see how I could be the mother I wanted to be.

After I started questioning those thoughts that were causing all of my suffering I realized that the root cause was that I believed (either consciously or unconsciously) those thoughts about the imagined "fearful" future because I believed an unreliable memory about the "negative" past. I believed a story of my past projected into my future. I was living out this story, moment to moment. I was perpetuating all of my suffering by continuing to believe stressful thoughts in that story. I thought I was at the whim of that story, with no say about my happiness. What a huge relief to finally know that I had the power to transcend all of those stressful thoughts, all of those horror movies that kept haunting me my whole life! This feeling of power over my situation was completely liberating. I wanted more. So, I kept asking myself, "Who would I be without these stressful thoughts?" Every time, I saw that my answer was, "I would be present."

~

I invite you now to take a look at the three pages that follow this letter. First you'll find the Presence Practice Notes page. It is there for you to jot down what you're thinking now about what you've read. It's also there for you to write about a current situation that triggers your most stressful reactions with your child. Notice if, when you write, you get caught up in your negative feelings again. Just notice. Then bring yourself back to the present. You're just writing. The event is not happening again in reality. It's only in your memory, and therefore not *real*. The two worksheets that follow will be your doorway out of any of your suffering. *Your answers to the questions on them will be the key to unlocking a deeper connection to your child. They will be the key to unlocking your authentic presence.*

The directions for filling in the two worksheets are found right at the top of each one. Just follow each step, one at a time, exactly how it says to complete it.

To help you get started, let's use the example found right on the worksheets: *Aiden doesn't listen to me.* Think of a time when you truly believed that your child was not listening to you. It could be a recent situation or a long time ago. If your child is an infant, think of a time when you truly believed your spouse or ex-spouse was not listening to you. Remember a *specific* situation. It needs to be as specific as possible. Remember as much as you can about the situation, putting yourself mentally there. Remember, if you can, the location, the time of year, the time of day, the weather, the setting, who else was there, what the conversation was about. Remember your words, your energy, the look on your face, your body language. Remember their words, their behaviors, their energy, the look on their face, their body language. Do you see your situation? *See it as a snapshot in time.*

~

Did you find your situation? If not, let it come to you. Wait for it and be patient for it. When you've found it, follow along on the worksheets after this letter, as I go through them here.

My situation is when my son was riding off on his bike without his helmet and I got worried and reacted very strongly. He was about nine years old at the time. We had just moved to a new neighborhood and I wasn't yet familiar with the traffic there. In retrospect, now I realize there was very little traffic. However, to be safer rather than sorrier, I asked him to put his helmet on, mostly for my comfort and because that's what I had always done. This is not to say that you *should not* set safety limits for your children, and it's not to say that you *should* set safety limits for your children. That's not what this book is about. It's not about me telling you that you should or shouldn't do or say anything. This book simply invites you to question the thoughts that cause all of the suffering you and your family experience so that you can address the root cause of your situation with clarity.

So, back to my situation. I asked him to put the helmet on and he just kept riding without it. So, I'm putting myself mentally back into that situation, seeing it as a snapshot in time, as I answer the questions on the two worksheets. Also, let yourself be as judgmental as you were when you were in that situation. Do *not* try to be wise, spiritual, or psychologically-correct now. This is the time to let those judgments have their life. They're on your mind anyway. Here we see them and catch them in their tracks in order to shine the light of truth on to them, for your peace and happiness.

Worksheet 1, question 1, is, *In this situation, who angers, confuses, saddens, or disappoints you, and why?* "*I am upset with Aiden because he doesn't listen to me.*" Notice how this is a very short, simple statement? Now write your concern about your own loved one. I encourage you to keep your statement simple and short too since the mind can easily get off focus unless it's dealing with just one thought. With a longer statement, we support it in losing its focus. Notice that the mind doesn't like to be pinned down to one statement. It wants to address things on a broader scope, thus perpetuating its confusion. Notice if your mind has difficulty limiting itself to one, simple, short statement. If you see that, just notice it without judgment, and keep focusing on one, simple, short stressful thought.

Worksheet 1, question 2 is, *In this situation, how do you want them to change?* "*I want Aiden to stop what he's doing, look at me, and listen to me.*" I answered this question honestly by putting myself back into my situation with my son, when he would not put on his bike helmet. I wanted him to stop, literally stop pedaling his bike, to look at me, and to listen to me. It's okay to elaborate on this question and on questions 3 - 6 for your situation. I'm shortening it here for the purposes of demonstrating it. The main one you want to keep short and simple is your answer to question 1.

Worksheet 1, question 3 is, *In this situation, what advice would you offer to them?* This question is about what you think the *other person* should be doing. My answer was, "*He should stop what he's doing, come back and put his helmet on. He should follow the safety rules. He should do what I'm asking him to do.*"

Worksheet 1, question 4 is, *In order for you to feel better in this situation, what do you need them to think, say, feel, or do?* This question is about what you think *you need*. In my situation, I thought I needed him to do what I told him to do. I needed him to listen to me. I needed him to be more conscious of his physical safety.

Worksheet 1, question 5 is, *What do you think of them in this situation?* Make a list. Be petty. Write down every judgment you have about them in this situation, exactly as you thought it when the situation occurred. I invite you to let those judgments be *seen*. Expose them. That's the only way we can transcend them, is to become aware of them. My judgment was, "*Aiden is just like his dad - he won't respect me.*"

Worksheet 1, question 6 is, *What is it in or about this situation that you don't ever want to experience again?* What would it be for you? Write that down in the blank space on question 6, exactly the way you see it. For me, it was, "*I don't ever want to be disrespected by Aiden again.*" I didn't really realize I thought this until I filled in my worksheet. I'm so glad I found this thought though. I honestly felt like my son was being so disrespectful to me.

Now, look at what you wrote. Read through each one. Notice what you're aware of within yourself as you read each statement. What do you see in yourself now that you didn't see before? What are you conscious of? Reflect for a moment.

Now, circle the statement you wrote that seems to stand out the most for you. It might be the one that you've thought so many times before. It might be the one that seems to trigger so much stress in you every time it comes up. It might just be one that looks like it's the *one*. After you circle it, rewrite it at the top of worksheet 2, where it says, ***Rewrite the thought you circled on Worksheet 1***. For our purposes, I used my thought, *"Aiden doesn't listen to me."*

~

Worksheet 2 is the second half of our self-inquiry. It's very important to know that Worksheet 2 is a *meditation*. If you've never meditated before, that's okay. You'll still find it works just as well for you. The thing to remember is to ask yourself the question from a place of genuine *curiosity*. Have as open of a mind as you can when you come to this worksheet. Then, close your eyes, be still, be patient, breathe, and *witness* what comes. Do not try to force the answers onto the page. If you first notice an answer in you that creates stress or frustration, witness it without judgment, make a note of it, and do self-inquiry on it later. Then, return to your breath, and return to your curiosity, and wait for an answer that feels peaceful and *completely* true.

~

Worksheet 2, question 1 is, ***In that situation, is it true*** that Aiden doesn't listen to you? This is a yes or no question, and there are no right or wrong answers whatsoever. This is all about you. It's all about what's true for you. If your answer is yes, go to question 2. If your answer is no, move to question 3. My answer, using my situation with my son and his helmet, is *"yes"*

Worksheet 2, question 2 is, ***In this situation, can you absolutely know that it's true,*** that *Aiden doesn't listen to you?* Well, no, I can't absolutely know that it's true. I can't get inside his mind and ears and hear what he hears. My honest answer is *"no."*

Worksheet 2, question 3 is, ***In this situation, how did I react when I believed that thought,*** *Aiden doesn't listen to me?* I ended up shouting at my son. I don't like to shout. I ended up getting very frustrated with him. I remember feeling very confused as to why it looked like he was so mad at me. I searched the past in my memory of why he might be so defiant with me. I remember kind of justifying it in my mind how he would probably be okay without a helmet, but then feeling so responsible for his safety at the same time. I felt very worried about his safety. I saw images of the future of him being hit by a car and very badly injured. I felt like I was doing it (mothering) all wrong. I searched for what I could do differently. I judged myself harshly for not knowing clearly what to do.

Question 4 on Worksheet 2 is, ***In that situation, who would I be without this thought?*** It's helpful to remember some special points and instructions about answering this question:

~ The emphasis of it is on the word *be*. When you ask yourself this, ask it from a place inside of you that is *curious* about *being*.

~ This question is an invitation to close your eyes, and put yourself back into the situation, and live it again *without the thought*. Then, ask yourself, who you would be without it in that same situation.

~ Breathe. Notice your breathing. Go slow. Be patient.

~ Wait for an answer to the question that feels peaceful, has a calming effect on you, and one that surfaces from within you - *not one that is a judgment*.

~ It's not a question to try to change you or make you a better mom. If you find yourself thinking that your answer to this question is, "Well, I would be a hip, confident, enlightened mother but I know I'm not, so I must suck" or something like that, then just make a separate note of this thought and return to it later to question it with another self-inquiry session. For now, know that this thought stems from the ego, and not from who you would *be* without the thought. These types of quick answers and judgments of ourselves happen all the time, without us even realizing it. Self-inquiry brings these subconscious judgments of ourselves to light in order to be questioned. The judgments are simply more stressful thoughts to question later. Keep a list. Especially in the beginning of learning this new process, be a *witness* to them as much as you can. That's why I recommend doing the Morning Meditation on page 16 before you start any worksheet.

~ You've probably never asked yourself this "who you would be" question before in your entire life, so be gentle with yourself.

~ This question is not suggesting you drop the thought.

~ Notice if your first answer is the *opposite* of your answer to the question right before this. If you see that, then it is a *reaction* and not the final, true, authentic answer. For example, if my first answer is, *"I would be fine. I'm sure he wouldn't get hurt. He's just going around the corner,"* then this wouldn't be my final answer. This is just the other side (the "not", the reaction) of the same coin called fear - I'm scared for his safety, I'm *not* scared for his safety.

~ Notice if you come up with answers to this question that are things you *do*. For example, *"I would not let him leave in the first place without a helmet."* This is a *doing*, not a way of *being*. So, if you see *doings* as your first answer, keep waiting. Keep waiting to see states of *being*.

~ Your answer to this question will feel like a warm hug, peaceful, and completely true.

~ If an answer doesn't come to you that feels that way, your answer could simply be, "I don't know." I don't know is a wonderful place to begin.

~

So, Worksheet 2, question 4 in our example is, ***In that situation, who would I be without the thought "Aiden doesn't listen to me?"*** When I waited patiently for my answer to be shown to me, it was, *"I would be discerning. I would discern that sometimes it's not dangerous to go without your bike helmet. I would be calm, realizing that sometimes it is okay - and wonderful - to let the breeze blow through your hair when you ride your bike. I would be happy, watching my son have a great time riding his bike and enjoying the outdoors."*

The next step in the process is to reconstruct the stress-inducing thought by looking at it from at least three new and different points of view. This allows the mind to safely see the situation from many perspectives, to consider a broader picture, to open up the mind to expanded possibilities. With a more open mind I have a more open heart, and I can connect more deeply to my child. One new perspective might be directed toward myself. Another perspective might be to exchange my name with my child's name. Another perspective might be the exact opposite. I will walk you through how to find your new perspectives, step-by-step, below and throughout the rest of the chapters.

With each newly reconstructed thought, I then find at least three genuine, specific examples of how each one is as true or truer than the original stressful one. This gives the mind *proof* that it *believes*. For example, in my situation, if I direct the thought inward, it would be, *"I don't listen to me."* I never really thought about how it is okay to sometimes ride a bike without a helmet, but that actually is what I truly believe; so I wasn't listening to my opinion and that's how I didn't listen to myself. When I believe that he isn't listening to me I'm definitely not listening to myself because I'm in his business and not in mine. Furthermore, "I don't listen to me" is as true as or truer than my original stressful thought in that situation because the *authentic* me (that I always want to listen to) was not heard.

If I reconstruct the thought by exchanging my son's name with mine, the thought becomes, *"I didn't listen to Aiden."* An example of that is that I was the one doing all of the talking and I didn't give him space to say anything. I also didn't ask him his opinion. I was listening to my stressful thought so much that I couldn't hear anything or anyone else.

Finally, if I reconstruct the thought to its exact opposite, the thought becomes, *"Aiden **did** listen to me."* An example of that for me, in that situation, is that he may have heard the words I spoke but just chose to ignore them. Another example for me is that he may have heard me getting upset so he decided to leave the area in fear. A third possibility is that maybe he understood that wearing a helmet is optional because I didn't insist on it before he got on his bike.

~

Are you seeing the process? When you follow it, step by step, it becomes effortless. Just fill in the blank spaces on the two worksheets. If you want any clarification about how to complete the worksheets or about anything else, I invite you to message me directly at catherine@thepresentmotherscommunity.com or on my Facebook page or ask it on the contact page of my website so I can answer it for you as soon as possible.

I love that you would dive right into this beautiful walk with yourself this morning. It's my pleasure to walk with you.

Wishing you, dear one, Presence and Peace today,
Catherine

Presence Practice Notes

The Power of Presence

Self-Inquiry Worksheet 1 of 2

We've been told all of our lives not to judge others. The fact is we do it anyway. This worksheet allows the mind to see itself, to see the reality of its own thoughts, and to truly consider the thoughts by putting them on paper. This is the time to let those judgments have their own life.

DIRECTIONS:

A. Think of a specific person that is triggering stress in you. It could be your child, partner, ex-partner, mom, or dad. (Not yourself) They could be living or not living.

B. Now, recall a specific stressful situation you had with that person. It might have been a face to face interaction, an event, a phone call, or any situation that caused you any feelings of discomfort. Identify the specific stressful situation, and see it as a *single snapshot* in time.

C. Witness that single snapshot. Notice the time, place, words spoken, body language, and energy of each person. Then, 1) Identify and name the primary uncomfortable feeling you were having, 2) identify why you felt that way, and 3) answer the questions below with *short, simple* statements. *Please do not* try to be psychologically correct, spiritual, or wise now. For the purposes of this worksheet, be as judgmental as you were when you were in that situation.

1. In this situation, who angers, confuses, saddens, or disappoints you, and why? *(Example: I'm frustrated with Aiden because he won't listen to me.)*

2. In this situation, how do you want them to change? *(Example: I want Aiden to stop what he's doing, look at me, and listen to me.)*

3. In this situation, what advice would you offer to them? *(Example: Aiden should learn how to listen.)*

4. In order for you to feel better in this situation, what do you need them to think, say, feel, or do? *(Example: I need Aiden to listen.)*

5. What do you think of them in this situation? Make a list. Be petty. *(Example: Aiden is just like his dad - he won't respect me.)*

6. What is it in or about this situation that you don't ever want to experience again? *(Example: I don't ever want to be disrespected by Aiden again.)*

Review what you wrote. Pick one sentence you wrote that feels the most stressful to you right now. Circle it. Rewrite it at the top of Worksheet 2.

Adapted from Byron Katie International, Inc. Rev. 7/2014, with consent.

Self-Inquiry Worksheet 2 of 2

This worksheet is a meditation. When answering the questions, close your eyes, be still, and patiently wait to witness what appears to you. Always give yourself time to let the deeper answers meet the questions.

DIRECTIONS:
A. In the space below, write the thought you circled from Worksheet 1. Then answer questions 1-4.
B. Reconstruct the thought in three new ways. Possibilities are: by directing it inward (number 5 below), exchanging the other person's name with yours (number 6 below), and stating its exact opposite (number 7 below). Examples are provided below. Then, find and record three genuine, specific examples of how each new thought is as true or truer for you in that situation.
C. If you circled the thought from your answer to question 6 on Worksheet 1, you would reconstruct the thought by replacing the words, "I don't ever want to…" with "I am willing to…" and "I look forward to…"

Re-write the thought you circled on Worksheet 1: *(Example: Aiden doesn't listen to me.)*

_____

_____

1. In that situation, is this thought true? *(Yes or no only. There are no right or wrong answers. If no, skip to question 3.)*

2. In that situation, can you absolutely know that it's true? *(Yes or no only)*

3. In that situation, how did you *react* when you believed that thought?

4. In that situation, who would you be if you could not believe that thought?

5. Reconstruct the thought by directing it *inward. (Example: I don't listen to me.)* Find and record three genuine, specific examples in that situation how this new thought is as true or truer than the original thought.

6. Reconstruct the thought by *exchanging* the other person's name with yours. *(Example: I don't listen to Aiden.)* Find and record three genuine, specific examples of how this new thought is as true or truer for you in that situation.

7. Reconstruct the thought by stating the *exact opposite. (Example: Aiden does listen to me.)* Find and record three genuine, specific examples of how this new thought is as true or truer for you in that situation.

Adapted from Byron Katie International, Inc. Rev. 7/2014, with consent.

Welcome to Morning 2 - *Our Children, Our Reflection*

(I invite you to first re-read the Morning Meditation on page 16.)

Dear Present Mother,

Our children are perfect reflections of us. If I am peaceful in my own mind, I see peace outside me. I recognize in others the confusion I once had, before self-inquiry. Then, I have understanding and compassion for them because I had understanding and compassion for myself.

If I think, *"I want you to love me,"* either consciously or unconsciously, then my energy, words, and actions will stem from that. My child will copy my energy, words, and actions and end up thinking it too. There is no way they can think otherwise. Their thinking perfectly matches our thinking. Beliefs are inherited. If they say to you, "I want you to love me," instead of saying to them, "I *do* love you!" it will be more enlightening to question the thought that causes you pain and suffering and stress: "He should *know* I love him."

At one point in my relationship with my son, I desperately wanted him to know I loved him. He seemed so far away -- so lost in his angry, sad world. My guilt felt overwhelming to me. I had unintentionally said and done some things that disconnected me from him in a big way. I felt so confused as to what was going on. He just kept brushing off my attempts to connect with him, to be nice, to hug him, to care for him. I felt sadness like I'd never felt before. Then, I started becoming judgmental of him. I saw him as distant and cold. I felt hurt. My underlying stressful thought was, "He should *know* I love him."

I realized, after questioning that thought, that *I* was the one who should know I love him. I needed to remind myself of my deep, deep love for him, my unconditional love for him, at the core of my being. Then, in perfect reflection, I realized a deep, deep love for myself -- one the reflection of the other. Our relationship was instantly healed.

Another gem I discovered in self-inquiry was "I should know I love me." Complete self-compassion stepped in then. When I said and did the things I thought were "right" at the time, I was doing the best I could. I believed my thoughts, how could I have done otherwise?

I invite you to start noticing in your speech to others that you are saying exactly what you are saying to yourself in your own mind. Just notice, without judgment.

~

A poem bubbled up in me one morning recently. It perfectly describes my understanding of how our children mirror our thinking about ourselves.

Mirror

I know not where I come from.
I know not where you come from,
my precious child.
I know that love,
divine love,
the love that is beyond all understanding,
binds us,
connects us,
at the essence of our being.

We are one.
What I think of myself,
so I think of you.
What I do to myself,
in my own mind,
so I do to you,
with my thoughts,
my words,
my deeds.

All my life is devoted
to understanding, loving, and living
this truth.

Where do you wish your relationship with your child would be instantly healed? Where do you wish your relationship with yourself would be instantly healed? Try remembering one of those situations, and then complete the worksheets that follow.

If you're new to self-inquiry, know that I've been there also. I understand how something so new can seem so foreign to you. I remember feeling a little confused and overwhelmed by the whole thing. Just know that those feelings pass with every new realization you get after doing the process. It is so worth it. I am certain you'll find what you're looking for because what you've been looking for has been there all along, inside of you - only it's been hidden by the thoughts causing all of your suffering. Self-inquiry guides you back to it, back to your beautiful presence.

Wishing you, dear one, Presence and Peace today,
Catherine

Presence Practice Notes

Our Children, Our Reflection

Self-Inquiry Worksheet 1 of 2

We've been told all of our lives not to judge others. The fact is we do it anyway. This worksheet allows the mind to see itself, to see the reality of its own thoughts, and to truly consider the thoughts by putting them on paper. This is the time to let those judgments have their own life.

DIRECTIONS:

A. Think of a specific person that is triggering stress in you. It could be your child, partner, ex-partner, mom, or dad. (Not yourself) They could be living or not living.

B. Now, recall a specific stressful situation you had with that person. It might have been a face to face interaction, an event, a phone call, or any situation that caused you any feelings of discomfort. Identify the specific stressful situation, and see it as a *single snapshot* in time.

C. Witness that single snapshot. Notice the time, place, words spoken, body language, and energy of each person. Then, 1) Identify and name the primary uncomfortable feeling you were having, 2) identify why you felt that way, and 3) answer the questions below with *short, simple* statements. *Please do not* try to be psychologically correct, spiritual, or wise now. For the purposes of this worksheet, be as judgmental as you were when you were in that situation.

1. In this situation, who angers, confuses, saddens, or disappoints you, and why? *(Example: I'm frustrated with Aiden because he won't listen to me.)*

2. In this situation, how do you want them to change? *(Example: I want Aiden to stop what he's doing, look at me, and listen to me.)*

3. In this situation, what advice would you offer to them? *(Example: Aiden should learn how to listen.)*

4. In order for you to feel better in this situation, what do you need them to think, say, feel, or do? *(Example: I need Aiden to listen.)*

5. What do you think of them in this situation? Make a list. Be petty. *(Example: Aiden is just like his dad - he won't respect me.)*

6. What is it in or about this situation that you don't ever want to experience again? *(Example: I don't ever want to be disrespected by Aiden again.)*

Review what you wrote. Pick one sentence you wrote that feels the most stressful to you right now. Circle it. Rewrite it at the top of Worksheet 2.

Adapted from Byron Katie International, Inc. Rev. 7/2014, with consent.

Self-Inquiry Worksheet 2 of 2

This worksheet is a meditation. When answering the questions, close your eyes, be still, and patiently wait to witness what appears to you. Always give yourself time to let the deeper answers meet the questions.

DIRECTIONS:

A. In the space below, write the thought you circled from Worksheet 1. Then answer questions 1-4.

B. Reconstruct the thought in three new ways. Possibilities are: by directing it inward (number 5 below), exchanging the other person's name with yours (number 6 below), and stating its exact opposite (number 7 below). Examples are provided below. Then, find and record three genuine, specific examples of how each new thought is as true or truer for you in that situation.

C. If you circled the thought from your answer to question 6 on Worksheet 1, you would reconstruct the thought by replacing the words, "I don't ever want to…" with "I am willing to…" and "I look forward to…"

Re-write the thought you circled on Worksheet 1: *(Example: Aiden doesn't listen to me.)*

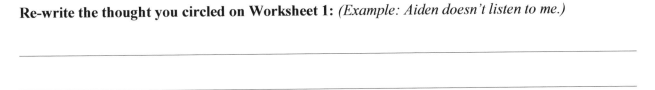

1. In that situation, is this thought true? *(Yes or no only. There are no right or wrong answers. If no, skip to question 3.)*

2. In that situation, can you absolutely know that it's true? *(Yes or no only)*

3. In that situation, how did you *react* when you believed that thought?

4. In that situation, who would you be if you could not believe that thought?

5. Reconstruct the thought by directing it *inward. (Example: I don't listen to me.)* Find and record three genuine, specific examples in that situation how this new thought is as true or truer than the original thought.

6. Reconstruct the thought by *exchanging* the other person's name with yours. *(Example: I don't listen to Aiden.)* Find and record three genuine, specific examples of how this new thought is as true or truer for you in that situation.

7. Reconstruct the thought by stating the *exact opposite. (Example: Aiden does listen to me.)* Find and record three genuine, specific examples of how this new thought is as true or truer for you in that situation.

Adapted from Byron Katie International, Inc. Rev. 7/2014, with consent.

Welcome to Morning 3 - *You Are the Parenting Expert*

(I invite you to first re-read the Morning Meditation on page 16.)

Dear Present Mother,

I used to test out parenting advice a lot. One time I actually said, "I love you" to my son right after he said, "I hate you. I wish you weren't my mother!" Of course, the result was an even larger outburst on his part. My entire family felt so much heartache after this particular outburst. At that point in my parenting, I was so desperate to figure out why it *looked like* my son hated me so much. I was reaching for help, reaching for answers, reaching for anything that I thought could repair our relationship. I felt so desperate, like I was fighting for my life and fighting for my son's life. I grabbed at anything and everything outside of me that I thought could help. I read, researched, and talked to other moms. It didn't occur to me to question the thoughts that were causing all of my suffering.

Finally, after nothing seemed to help, I looked within. I ended up using this incident to get closer to my truth as my own parenting expert to myself.

No other advice could compare to my own when I went through my self-inquiry process. When I questioned the stressful thoughts *causing* my own suffering, I realized that the stressful thoughts were my doorway back to connection with my child. Every time I filled in the worksheets, I would just be still and wait for my answers. I would wait for truth to arise from within. Then a clarity would emerge. If I sat still long enough, and waited long enough, this wise, wise being, would emerge from inside me and show itself. Who would I be without that thought? Let me sit with that question and see what arises this time. After asking myself that so many times, I began to trust. I knew it would be the best advice I would ever find, all the time, no matter what.

Even more clarity emerges when our minds begin to realize that the new thoughts we generate at the end of self-inquiry are truer than our original stressful thought. Every time I would reconstruct a stressful thought into one from a new point of view, I would see my situation from an entirely different, valid perspective. My mind found reasons to believe that this new thought was actually truer than the original stressful one. In scientific terms, new neural pathways were being formed. I was thinking in a whole new way. I was resolving situations that previously seemed impossible to figure out.

It isn't wrong or bad to rely on parenting advice. It's what a lot of us do when we begin our parenting journey. We just want help and we turn to people whom we think are experts. We learned to rely on others for wisdom a long time ago, when we were children. It wasn't wrong or bad then either. Now though, as we begin to be positively moved by our self-inquiry process, we begin to trust ourselves. We start to see a clearer path to solve our parenting dilemmas after self-inquiry. I love that we never know what mothering wisdom might be waiting for us to discover. It's very exciting to me.

Sometimes you might find it kind of unnerving to accept the possibility that you might have the answers you're looking for right inside you. You might think you can't trust yourself. I felt that way in the beginning of my presence practice. To me, I felt like it just couldn't be this simple to get great parenting advice. I thought I had to study and read and research to find out the best thing to do for my children. I felt I had to look "out there" instead of inside me. I read so many parenting books, some contradicting each other, until I finally gave up reading them in complete exasperation. I wanted to just trust my kids and myself to figure it out in our *own* way.

Doing self-inquiry does not mean we don't seek outside help from experts about subjects beyond our understanding, or attend classes, or get help from other professionals. Self-inquiry gives us the clarity to know when and in what direction to look for outside support, advice, counseling or guidance.

My son has not said "I hate you" ever since that day. In fact, now I hear, several times a day, "Mommy, I love you so much."

I'm so lucky.

The thought that I couldn't trust myself cropped up in such a subtle way that sometimes I didn't even notice. I would notice that things just started getting more challenging in the way that I was being with the kids. Then, I would realize that I hadn't done my self-inquiry practice in a while. I wondered if that was why things weren't going so well. Sure enough, right after I would fill in a worksheet, things would take a turn for the better. I hope you are beginning to trust the process also. I love the joy that happens when you do.

Wishing you, dear one, Peace and Presence today,
Catherine

Presence Practice Notes

You Are the Parenting Expert

Self-Inquiry Worksheet 1 of 2

We've been told all of our lives not to judge others. The fact is we do it anyway. This worksheet allows the mind to see itself, to see the reality of its own thoughts, and to truly consider the thoughts by putting them on paper. This is the time to let those judgments have their own life.

DIRECTIONS:

A. Think of a specific person that is triggering stress in you. It could be your child, partner, ex-partner, mom, or dad. (Not yourself) They could be living or not living.

B. Now, recall a specific stressful situation you had with that person. It might have been a face to face interaction, an event, a phone call, or any situation that caused you any feelings of discomfort. Identify the specific stressful situation, and see it as a *single snapshot* in time.

C. Witness that single snapshot. Notice the time, place, words spoken, body language, and energy of each person. Then, 1) Identify and name the primary uncomfortable feeling you were having, 2) identify why you felt that way, and 3) answer the questions below with *short, simple* statements. *Please do not* try to be psychologically correct, spiritual, or wise now. For the purposes of this worksheet, be as judgmental as you were when you were in that situation.

1. In this situation, who angers, confuses, saddens, or disappoints you, and why? *(Example: I'm frustrated with Aiden because he won't listen to me.)*

2. In this situation, how do you want them to change? *(Example: I want Aiden to stop what he's doing, look at me, and listen to me.)*

3. In this situation, what advice would you offer to them? *(Example: Aiden should learn how to listen.)*

4. In order for you to feel better in this situation, what do you need them to think, say, feel, or do? *(Example: I need Aiden to listen.)*

5. What do you think of them in this situation? Make a list. Be petty. *(Example: Aiden is just like his dad - he won't respect me.)*

6. What is it in or about this situation that you don't ever want to experience again? *(Example: I don't ever want to be disrespected by Aiden again.)*

Review what you wrote. Pick one sentence you wrote that feels the most stressful to you right now. Circle it. Rewrite it at the top of Worksheet 2.

Self-Inquiry Worksheet 2 of 2

This worksheet is a meditation. When answering the questions, close your eyes, be still, and patiently wait to witness what appears to you. Always give yourself time to let the deeper answers meet the questions.

DIRECTIONS:

A. In the space below, write the thought you circled from Worksheet 1. Then answer questions 1-4.

B. Reconstruct the thought in three new ways. Possibilities are: by directing it inward (number 5 below), exchanging the other person's name with yours (number 6 below), and stating its exact opposite (number 7 below). Examples are provided below. Then, find and record three genuine, specific examples of how each new thought is as true or truer for you in that situation.

C. If you circled the thought from your answer to question 6 on Worksheet 1, you would reconstruct the thought by replacing the words, "I don't ever want to…" with "I am willing to…" and "I look forward to…"

Re-write the thought you circled on Worksheet 1: *(Example: Aiden doesn't listen to me.)*

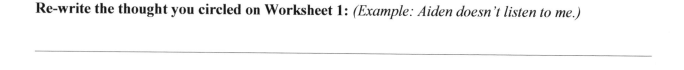

1. In that situation, is this thought true? *(Yes or no only. There are no right or wrong answers. If no, skip to question 3.)*

2. In that situation, can you absolutely know that it's true? *(Yes or no only)*

3. In that situation, how did you *react* when you believed that thought?

4. In that situation, who would you be if you could not believe that thought?

5. Reconstruct the thought by directing it *inward. (Example: I don't listen to me.)* Find and record three genuine, specific examples in that situation how this new thought is as true or truer than the original thought.

6. Reconstruct the thought by *exchanging* the other person's name with yours. *(Example: I don't listen to Aiden.)* Find and record three genuine, specific examples of how this new thought is as true or truer for you in that situation.

7. Reconstruct the thought by stating the *exact opposite. (Example: Aiden does listen to me.)* Find and record three genuine, specific examples of how this new thought is as true or truer for you in that situation.

Adapted from Byron Katie International, Inc. Rev. 7/2014, with consent.

Welcome to Morning 4 - *Being the Teacher of Happiness*

(I invite you to first re-read the Morning Meditation on page 16.)

Dear Present Mother,

At some point, I believe we've all had the wish for our child to be happier. We love our children. We want them to have the most happiness possible. When mine were really young, sometimes they would keep crying so hard, no matter what I did to try to console them. They weren't in any danger; they just weren't happy. I love them with all of my heart. I want them to be happy. However, when they weren't happy during these times, I was so focused on trying to change them, for my own comfort, that I would get completely stressed out. I want them to have a good life, of course. However, when this wanting kept me from being present with them, I felt very disconnected from them and from my true self. The times when their unhappiness would trigger a stressful thought in me were when I had tried everything I could, literally exhausting myself, and they would still keep crying. Then, I would cry in utter exhaustion and frustration because I could not make them happy no matter what I did.

Other times, such as when they were toddler age, they would fall down and scrape their knees. They would cry and cry. I would almost panic because I wanted to stop the crying so fast. I would rush to give them a hug, a kiss, or a band aid. I would feel the rush of hormones in my body. The adrenalin was pumping through my veins. To my kids, I can see how they might think I was acting like it was the end of the world. I don't ever want to give that message to my kids. I want them to feel empowered to be the creator of their own happiness, to weather any storm, no matter what, to be resilient, strong, and empowered. What I really want is to be present with them, helping them in a calm way and having total faith in them that they will be okay, without forcing that to happen any sooner than they exhibit it. I want to trust. I don't want fear to control me.

When were you ever upset because your child wasn't happy? Let's go there this morning. Do you see that situation? See it clearly. Remember the time and place, remember what the conversation was, remember what it was about. Literally, put yourself back into that situation in your mind. When you see the snapshot of the situation, and you are mentally there, I invite you to complete the worksheets for this morning.

~

As I share my self-inquiry here, I invite you to fill in your own answers on the worksheets as I fill in some of mine from years past: *I need my child to be happy.*

Is that true? It's a yes or no question. In my situation, my answer is yes. In that moment, in that situation, when I am remembering how I was, mentally, I believed that I *did* need them to be happy.

Can you absolutely know that it's true, that you need them to be happy? My answer to this is no. Your answer could be yes or no. There are no right or wrong answers.

How do you react when you believe that thought, "I need them to be happy"? I was almost panicking because I wasn't moving quick enough to help them be happier, especially because they were really upset. (I'm not talking about a dangerous situation or ignoring a child who is upset.) I thought, "If my child is crying, then I must not be very good at helping them get their needs met." So I would judge myself and then feel guilty. Whew! It was a downward spiral when I believed this thought!

I notice that the thought, "I need them to be happy" is an old leftover thought pattern from my childhood. "Them" are my mom and my dad. I thought, as a little girl, that I needed them to be happy so that I could be happy. This was my way to cope with any kind of disapproval I assumed they had with me when I did something they didn't like. I wanted them to be happy with me, so I would change myself into the "good" girl, so as not to upset them. I would try to control their happiness, I thought, so I could be happy. Only it turned out that when I tried to be someone I wasn't, I really wasn't happy; especially now that I'm an adult. I want to be myself now - my authentic self. I love knowing this is an old thought pattern that I used to help me cope when I was little. I don't want to pass that thought pattern down to my children.

Who would you be without that thought, "I need them to be happy"? I would be calm, peaceful, and present for them, listening to them, aware of their complete capacity to be happy, and I would patiently wait for the storm to pass. I see clearly now that this would give them great confidence knowing the storm passed because of what *they* did inside their own minds, not because of something I did. That would help them learn that their happiness is in their hands, for the rest of their lives.

Next, I reconstruct the original stressful thought by: 1) directing it *inward*, 2) *exchanging* me with the other person, and 3) stating the *exact opposite*. Then, I find three genuine, specific examples of how each new thought is as true or truer for me in that situation. When finding the examples, I *close my eyes, I am still, and I witness what appears to me.*

Reconstructing the thought so it's directed *inward* would be, "I need *me* to be happy." There we go. That's so true! What are three good reasons that is true? One, that's where it all starts, for me. I have to begin there to have any impact on my child. Two, then I will be more calm and a better role model. Three, that's how I would love to be and, thank goodness that is within my area of control. Wow, what a happy life I can have!

Reconstructing the thought by exchanging the other person's name with yours would be, "They need *me* to be happy." Yes, that is so true, they do, especially when they are upset; if two of us are upset, it just makes it worse. Another reason they need me to be happy? They need the example of loving life and weathering storms no matter what. What a solid, confident mother that can be that role model. Yes, I can be that mother. I am that mother. A third reason they need me to be happy? Well, they will likely feel happier overall if I am in a better mood because I'll be treating them with so much kindness since I'm in such a great state of mind.

Rewriting the thought to the exact opposite would be "I *don't* need them to be happy." Hmmm. That might be a stretch but let me meditate for a minute. What's a valid example of that in my situation? If I needed *them* to fulfill *my* need for happiness, then that makes me totally out of control of my own happiness. I would be giving control over me to a child! That doesn't make much sense now that I look at it that way. My child might feel overly responsible for my well-being. What is another reason I don't need them to be happy? Well, they weren't, so that's reality, and trying to change reality and trying to change them makes me stressed out. What's one more reason I don't need them to be happy? Well, I get to do self-inquiry on it, and realize my own happiness; I stop making my kids responsible for my happiness. I find contentment and joy in my own life and am an example of happiness for them, even when things don't go my way.

~

I hope you are beginning to deeply explore your self-inquiry. I invite you to continue to discover your true happiness this morning by finishing the second worksheet. When you do, your children will be able to find their own true happiness as well. They are our mirror image, remember. It's such a beautiful gift to give to your children: their realization that happiness comes from within. I love that you would be the teacher of authentic happiness.

Whenever I used to feel like self-inquiry was so much work, I just kept remembering the beautiful place I was left in after I completed the process. I liberated my whole life by listening to my true self. It's such an amazing thing when you do; you are dramatically changing your life and your children's lives for the better every time.

Wishing you, dear one, Peace and Presence today,
Catherine

Presence Practice Notes

Being the Teacher of Happiness

Self-Inquiry Worksheet 1 of 2

We've been told all of our lives not to judge others. The fact is we do it anyway. This worksheet allows the mind to see itself, to see the reality of its own thoughts, and to truly consider the thoughts by putting them on paper. This is the time to let those judgments have their own life.

DIRECTIONS:

A. Think of a specific person that is triggering stress in you. It could be your child, partner, ex-partner, mom, or dad. (Not yourself) They could be living or not living.

B. Now, recall a specific stressful situation you had with that person. It might have been a face to face interaction, an event, a phone call, or any situation that caused you any feelings of discomfort. Identify the specific stressful situation, and see it as a *single snapshot* in time.

C. Witness that single snapshot. Notice the time, place, words spoken, body language, and energy of each person. Then, 1) Identify and name the primary uncomfortable feeling you were having, 2) identify why you felt that way, and 3) answer the questions below with *short, simple* statements. *Please do not* try to be psychologically correct, spiritual, or wise now. For the purposes of this worksheet, be as judgmental as you were when you were in that situation.

1. In this situation, who angers, confuses, saddens, or disappoints you, and why? *(Example: I'm frustrated with Aiden because he won't listen to me.)*

2. In this situation, how do you want them to change? *(Example: I want Aiden to stop what he's doing, look at me, and listen to me.)*

3. In this situation, what advice would you offer to them? *(Example: Aiden should learn how to listen.)*

4. In order for you to feel better in this situation, what do you need them to think, say, feel, or do? *(Example: I need Aiden to listen.)*

5. What do you think of them in this situation? Make a list. Be petty. *(Example: Aiden is just like his dad - he won't respect me.)*

6. What is it in or about this situation that you don't ever want to experience again? *(Example: I don't ever want to be disrespected by Aiden again.)*

Review what you wrote. Pick one sentence you wrote that feels the most stressful to you right now. Circle it. Rewrite it at the top of Worksheet 2.

Adapted from Byron Katie International, Inc. Rev. 7/2014, with consent.

Self-Inquiry Worksheet 2 of 2

This worksheet is a meditation. When answering the questions, close your eyes, be still, and patiently wait to witness what appears to you. Always give yourself time to let the deeper answers meet the questions.

DIRECTIONS:

A. In the space below, write the thought you circled from Worksheet 1. Then answer questions 1-4.

B. Reconstruct the thought in three new ways. Possibilities are: by directing it inward (number 5 below), exchanging the other person's name with yours (number 6 below), and stating its exact opposite (number 7 below). Examples are provided below. Then, find and record three genuine, specific examples of how each new thought is as true or truer for you in that situation.

C. If you circled the thought from your answer to question 6 on Worksheet 1, you would reconstruct the thought by replacing the words, "I don't ever want to…" with "I am willing to…" and "I look forward to…"

Re-write the thought you circled on Worksheet 1: *(Example: Aiden doesn't listen to me.)*

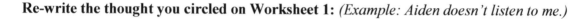

1. In that situation, is this thought true? *(Yes or no only. There are no right or wrong answers. If no, skip to question 3.)*

2. In that situation, can you absolutely know that it's true? *(Yes or no only)*

3. In that situation, how did you *react* when you believed that thought?

4. In that situation, who would you be if you could not believe that thought?

5. Reconstruct the thought by directing it *inward. (Example: I don't listen to me.)* Find and record three genuine, specific examples in that situation how this new thought is as true or truer than the original thought.

6. Reconstruct the thought by *exchanging* the other person's name with yours. *(Example: I don't listen to Aiden.)* Find and record three genuine, specific examples of how this new thought is as true or truer for you in that situation.

7. Reconstruct the thought by stating the *exact opposite. (Example: Aiden does listen to me.)* Find and record three genuine, specific examples of how this new thought is as true or truer for you in that situation.

Adapted from Byron Katie International, Inc. Rev. 7/2014, with consent.

Welcome to Morning 5 - *Presence Is a Whole New Field*

(I invite you to first re-read the Morning Meditation on page 16.)

Dear Present Mother,

I am so in love with being present. It is the love of my life. It's like going on a vacation - I never know, and am always, 100% of the time, so incredibly grateful and overjoyed at what occurs there - or rather *here* - now. So lovely.

The fact is, we are already always present. However, when we believe stressful thoughts, our awareness of that is gone. The process of me becoming more and more identified with presence was so slow and gradual, and yet so all-of-a-sudden sometimes. I had always tried to honor my children's path, to honor their needs and to evolve myself more than to try and make them accommodate my needs. I guess you could say I trusted nature to create human beings that were brilliant and loving when they were born. I trusted that I didn't need to teach them how to become loving and brilliant. I knew that if parents would let them, children could help their parents grow in love, become more of their patient selves, and become more of their kinder selves. I wanted to be a student of that when I became a mother. So, I've always tried to respect their feelings, thoughts, ideas, and wishes. I've always tried to respectfully balance those with mine and my husband's. I have always tried my best to trust them. As a result, they are very expressive, self-directed, creative and articulate, even with adults. They don't fear authority. They feel very comfortable around adults. They look them in the eyes when they're talking with them. They understand that when people get upset about something, and they direct that toward them, those people are really upset about something inside themselves. They know – and sometimes forget - they cannot make someone else upset. My children tend not to take things personally. This preserves their self-confidence. This makes them look to themselves for their own approval. This makes them trust themselves, trust their ideas, trust their capacity to love and to contribute to the world. I love that.

This is a whole new way of treating children: being present with them and yet out of their business. I am totally connected and yet not controlling. That is what has authentically manifested in my relationship with my kids as a result of self-inquiry. I don't treat them this way because I read it or heard about it somewhere and thought it was a great idea. If I had done that, it would not have been authentic for me.

I have a whole new relationship with myself, my children, and with life as a whole. It's the most natural way for me to be. It's the way I would treat anyone else that I loved with all of my heart. When we begin to love all of our stories without unconsciously believing them, and pay attention to them with self-inquiry, and understand them, we begin to do the same with our children. We create a deeper and deeper connection with them every time we do self-inquiry on the beliefs that created the disconnection in the first place. We begin to respect and trust ourselves more deeply. That appears in the world as kind and loving gestures, helpful and warm attitudes, peace and ease with circumstances that used to cause pain and suffering, and the deepest gratitude you can imagine.

Self-inquiry reminds me of neuroscience. Doing self-inquiry is our conscious act of creating new thought patterns every time we question our stressful ones. These new thought patterns (neural pathways) we create in self-inquiry are the ones that are the truth, in reality, in the present. These are the thoughts we're trying to convey to our children, and the ways of being that we'd love for them to exhibit: being aware of others, being kind, being loving, using good judgment, being respectful, being trustworthy, being authentic, going with the flow, having a thankful heart. Doing self-inquiry is a way to *be* these, to *live* these ways of being, more and more often ourselves, so our children see a living example of how to do it.

I've come to love that I ever was *not* present with my children. It was always the ticket to my freedom and, in that, my children's. Each time I noticed that I said or did something I wanted to change, I just pulled out my self-inquiry worksheets. After a while, it just became a habit to write down these stressful thoughts and question them. Then, as I would go about my day, when I had a few minutes to myself, I would ask myself, "Is it true?" (the first question). Then, I would continue on, in my mind, asking myself the rest of the questions as I went about my day and had little breaks here and there. "Could I absolutely know that it's true?" (the second question).

"How do I react when I think that thought?" (the third question). This question was being answered as I would find a shoe, or drink water, or kiss my child. "Who would I be without that thought?" (the fourth question). I loved sitting for a while with these questions, in and out of responding to the kids, myself, the house, my husband, et cetera. It was like a walking meditation for me. I was walking through my day, moment by moment, one step at a time, waiting for the wisdom to appear, as the questions were answered without me even trying.

Then, the world would shift. I began to see how true it is that when I created those new neural pathways, my whole world shifted... son, daughter, husband, mother, and father shifted too. What an amazing miracle. My cares just seemed to fall away, and what remained was even better than I could have imagined.

I love that you're here with me, as we experience self-inquiry together. It's such a beautiful walk to share with someone. How are you doing with completing the worksheets? Are you clear about how to complete them? What questions do you have about completing them? If you'd like some help in completing them, I invite you to go to http://www.thepresentmother.com/ or email me personally to learn more. Are you making the time to complete the worksheets? It may take a little more time in the beginning than it will take as you begin to make it a habit. I encourage you to be so patient with yourself. It took me a while to get the hang of it. You can make a huge impact on your life, no matter where you are in your practice.

Wishing you, dear one, Peace and Presence today,
Catherine

Presence Practice Notes

Presence Is a Whole New Field

Self-Inquiry Worksheet 1 of 2

We've been told all of our lives not to judge others. The fact is we do it anyway. This worksheet allows the mind to see itself, to see the reality of its own thoughts, and to truly consider the thoughts by putting them on paper. This is the time to let those judgments have their own life.

DIRECTIONS:

A. Think of a specific person that is triggering stress in you. It could be your child, partner, ex-partner, mom, or dad. (Not yourself) They could be living or not living.

B. Now, recall a specific stressful situation you had with that person. It might have been a face to face interaction, an event, a phone call, or any situation that caused you any feelings of discomfort. Identify the specific stressful situation, and see it as a *single snapshot* in time.

C. Witness that single snapshot. Notice the time, place, words spoken, body language, and energy of each person. Then, 1) Identify and name the primary uncomfortable feeling you were having, 2) identify why you felt that way, and 3) answer the questions below with *short, simple* statements. *Please do not* try to be psychologically correct, spiritual, or wise now. For the purposes of this worksheet, be as judgmental as you were when you were in that situation.

1. In this situation, who angers, confuses, saddens, or disappoints you, and why? *(Example: I'm frustrated with Aiden because he won't listen to me.)*

2. In this situation, how do you want them to change? *(Example: I want Aiden to stop what he's doing, look at me, and listen to me.)*

3. In this situation, what advice would you offer to them? *(Example: Aiden should learn how to listen.)*

4. In order for you to feel better in this situation, what do you need them to think, say, feel, or do? *(Example: I need Aiden to listen.)*

5. What do you think of them in this situation? Make a list. Be petty. *(Example: Aiden is just like his dad - he won't respect me.)*

6. What is it in or about this situation that you don't ever want to experience again? *(Example: I don't ever want to be disrespected by Aiden again.)*

Review what you wrote. Pick one sentence you wrote that feels the most stressful to you right now. Circle it. Rewrite it at the top of Worksheet 2.

Adapted from Byron Katie International, Inc. Rev. 7/2014, with consent.

Self-Inquiry Worksheet 2 of 2

This worksheet is a meditation. When answering the questions, close your eyes, be still, and patiently wait to witness what appears to you. Always give yourself time to let the deeper answers meet the questions.

DIRECTIONS:

A. In the space below, write the thought you circled from Worksheet 1. Then answer questions 1-4.

B. Reconstruct the thought in three new ways. Possibilities are: by directing it inward (number 5 below), exchanging the other person's name with yours (number 6 below), and stating its exact opposite (number 7 below). Examples are provided below. Then, find and record three genuine, specific examples of how each new thought is as true or truer for you in that situation.

C. If you circled the thought from your answer to question 6 on Worksheet 1, you would reconstruct the thought by replacing the words, "I don't ever want to…" with "I am willing to…" and "I look forward to…"

Re-write the thought you circled on Worksheet 1: *(Example: Aiden doesn't listen to me.)*

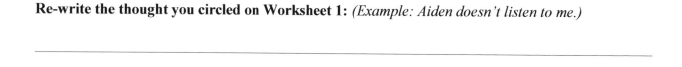

1. In that situation, is this thought true? *(Yes or no only. There are no right or wrong answers. If no, skip to question 3.)*

2. In that situation, can you absolutely know that it's true? *(Yes or no only)*

3. In that situation, how did you *react* when you believed that thought?

4. In that situation, who would you be if you could not believe that thought?

5. Reconstruct the thought by directing it *inward. (Example: I don't listen to me.)* Find and record three genuine, specific examples in that situation how this new thought is as true or truer than the original thought.

6. Reconstruct the thought by *exchanging* the other person's name with yours. *(Example: I don't listen to Aiden.)* Find and record three genuine, specific examples of how this new thought is as true or truer for you in that situation.

7. Reconstruct the thought by stating the *exact opposite. (Example: Aiden does listen to me.)* Find and record three genuine, specific examples of how this new thought is as true or truer for you in that situation.

Adapted from Byron Katie International, Inc. Rev. 7/2014, with consent.

Welcome to Morning 6 - *Cleaning the House in Your Mind*

(I invite you to first re-read the Morning Meditation on page 16.)

Dear Present Mother,

When something "out there" is the least bit irritating to us, we start to see, by doing self-inquiry, that our self-inquiry practice is not complete. Our home, inside our mind, is not clean yet. If anything is bothering us, and we believe it is caused by another person or thing, we can know for sure that it's really - in reality - the thought on our mind *about* it that's bothering us. In that, our cleaning job is defined for us. Thoughts that still bother us are like dust still in the corner of the room.

I grew up believing that it's very important to have a clean, organized, and beautiful home. For years, I watched my mother make our home so beautiful, and then I did the same thing. I subscribed to all kinds of home decorating magazines, took interior design classes, invested money in a lot of externally beautiful things.

As a mother of young children, there was no way I could keep up with the house being clean, much less organized and beautiful. My love for and desire to give attention to my infant and toddler children would pull me into the present moment like nothing else. Yet, at the same time, thoughts like, *"The house is a wreck!"* and *"This place is disgusting!"* would enter my mind and pull me out of the present. I felt this constant pull in two seemingly opposite directions, like a tug of war in my mind, between my wanting to pay attention to my children and my worries about the house.

I love that now I am the interior designer of my own mind. Questioning the thoughts that cause my suffering cleans, organizes and beautifies me and my house and my entire world from the inside-out. After doing self-inquiry for seven years or so, a poem surfaced from within me. It describes my vision for the real home I forever wish to create for my children and my family.

The Present Mother

Let me be spacious,
let me be empty,
let me be the home,
for this blessed creature,
sent to me to love.

Let me be free
of beliefs and concepts,
of thoughts and judgments,
of fears and guilt,
so that I may be present,
in the here and now,
with this blessed creature,
sent to me to love.

Let me not blindly copy,
nor react,
to what others have done,
to what my parents have done,
to what clergy have done,
to what teachers have done,
to what society has done,
so that I may be present,
in the here and now,
with this blessed creature,
sent to me to love.

~

What stressful thought would keep you from being present with the blessed creature sent to you to love? I invite you to stop that thought right in its tracks by writing it down and doing self-inquiry on it this morning. Whether it's, *"They should clean their room"* (when they don't), or *"My husband should wash the dishes"* (when he doesn't), or even, *"I can't live in a messy house"* (when it *is* messy and I *do* live there), these thoughts and those like them are your door to freedom every time that you question them. Your power to be authentically present lies in your responses to the questions on those worksheets.

What would stop you from actually filling in the worksheets and doing self-inquiry today? I invite you to share those thoughts with yourself today too, by writing them down. I love that the mind gives us these thoughts. They are the door to our freedom 100% of the time. I invite you to treat *all* of your stressful thoughts like your beloved children: listen to them, consider them, stop them (the mind) by putting them on paper, look at them, and then find the truth with self-inquiry.

When I first started focusing on doing self-inquiry, I remember my house was getting messier and messier. I even did self-inquiry on my judgments about my house: *it shouldn't be so hard to keep clean, I need more help, the kids should pick up their mess*, and on and on about the house. I loved questioning these thoughts. It freed me up so much to be present for the kids, to be present with myself, to not be so worried about how the house looked, and to happily clean the house as just one of the many things I did during the day while being present. Trying to control the way my house looked turned out to be how I was managing my thoughts; I was trying to control them, keep the "ugly" ones at bay, and only focus on the "pretty" ones. I love now that I love all of my thoughts and all of the "mess" in my house. My home looks lived in and exciting; many creations are all happening at the same time. Fun is being experienced and, miraculously, there are even clean dishes in the dishwasher!

Your house should be cleaner, is it true? What's the reality of it? What is the reality of why it should *not* be cleaner? Do you work outside the home in order to make ends meet? Do you home school? Do you spend time listening to your children? Do you not like doing the dishes? I wonder what realizations you'll get when you question your stressful thoughts about your home. I remember that I had more peace about it, *and* I had a cleaner house, without even thinking it was work. You can have a messy house and love it or hate it. You can have a clean house and love it or hate it. I prefer to love it however it is, which is just a reflection of a mind that loves its thoughts, however they are.

I am with you as you fill in your answers on the worksheets. I love that you would be the one cleaning the house in your own mind and making the same kind of beautiful home for your children.

Wishing you, dear one, Peace and Presence today,
Catherine

Presence Practice Notes

Cleaning the House in Your Mind

Self-Inquiry Worksheet 1 of 2

We've been told all of our lives not to judge others. The fact is we do it anyway. This worksheet allows the mind to see itself, to see the reality of its own thoughts, and to truly consider the thoughts by putting them on paper. This is the time to let those judgments have their own life.

DIRECTIONS:

A. Think of a specific person that is triggering stress in you. It could be your child, partner, ex-partner, mom, or dad. (Not yourself) They could be living or not living.

B. Now, recall a specific stressful situation you had with that person. It might have been a face to face interaction, an event, a phone call, or any situation that caused you any feelings of discomfort. Identify the specific stressful situation, and see it as a *single snapshot* in time.

C. Witness that single snapshot. Notice the time, place, words spoken, body language, and energy of each person. Then, 1) Identify and name the primary uncomfortable feeling you were having, 2) identify why you felt that way, and 3) answer the questions below with *short, simple* statements. *Please do not* try to be psychologically correct, spiritual, or wise now. For the purposes of this worksheet, be as judgmental as you were when you were in that situation.

1. In this situation, who angers, confuses, saddens, or disappoints you, and why? *(Example: I'm frustrated with Aiden because he won't listen to me.)*

2. In this situation, how do you want them to change? *(Example: I want Aiden to stop what he's doing, look at me, and listen to me.)*

3. In this situation, what advice would you offer to them? *(Example: Aiden should learn how to listen.)*

4. In order for you to feel better in this situation, what do you need them to think, say, feel, or do? *(Example: I need Aiden to listen.)*

5. What do you think of them in this situation? Make a list. Be petty. *(Example: Aiden is just like his dad - he won't respect me.)*

6. What is it in or about this situation that you don't ever want to experience again? *(Example: I don't ever want to be disrespected by Aiden again.)*

Review what you wrote. Pick one sentence you wrote that feels the most stressful to you right now. Circle it. Rewrite it at the top of Worksheet 2.

Adapted from Byron Katie International, Inc. Rev. 7/2014, with consent.

Self-Inquiry Worksheet 2 of 2

This worksheet is a meditation. When answering the questions, close your eyes, be still, and patiently wait to witness what appears to you. Always give yourself time to let the deeper answers meet the questions.

DIRECTIONS:

A. In the space below, write the thought you circled from Worksheet 1. Then answer questions 1-4.

B. Reconstruct the thought in three new ways. Possibilities are: by directing it inward (number 5 below), exchanging the other person's name with yours (number 6 below), and stating its exact opposite (number 7 below). Examples are provided below. Then, find and record three genuine, specific examples of how each new thought is as true or truer for you in that situation.

C. If you circled the thought from your answer to question 6 on Worksheet 1, you would reconstruct the thought by replacing the words, "I don't ever want to…" with "I am willing to…" and "I look forward to…"

Re-write the thought you circled on Worksheet 1: *(Example: Aiden doesn't listen to me.)*

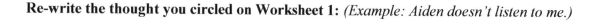

1. In that situation, is this thought true? *(Yes or no only. There are no right or wrong answers. If no, skip to question 3.)*

2. In that situation, can you absolutely know that it's true? *(Yes or no only)*

3. In that situation, how did you *react* when you believed that thought?

4. In that situation, who would you be if you could not believe that thought?

5. Reconstruct the thought by directing it *inward. (Example: I don't listen to me.)* Find and record three genuine, specific examples in that situation how this new thought is as true or truer than the original thought.

6. Reconstruct the thought by *exchanging* the other person's name with yours. *(Example: I don't listen to Aiden.)* Find and record three genuine, specific examples of how this new thought is as true or truer for you in that situation.

7. Reconstruct the thought by stating the *exact opposite. (Example: Aiden does listen to me.)* Find and record three genuine, specific examples of how this new thought is as true or truer for you in that situation.

Adapted from Byron Katie International, Inc. Rev. 7/2014, with consent.

Welcome to Morning 7 - *Your Approval of Yourself*

(I invite you to first re-read the Morning Meditation on page 16.)

Dear Present Mother,

Have you ever wished for your child to be more thankful to you, or to think better of you as a parent, or to be more approving of you? I know I have. When you notice this and then question your stressful thoughts about it, it will help you transform your connection to your child and improve all of your relationships.

I invite you to do a powerful exercise with me this morning and for our next time; there will be two parts. As you're doing this exercise, I encourage you to be gentle and compassionate with yourself. When you do notice wishing for your child's approval, just welcome yourself to being a mother - a human - in our society. Everyone is innocent in the way they are with their children. Most all of us mothers unconsciously believe our stressful thoughts, until we question them. We are all doing the best we can. We're not "wrong" to wish for our child's approval. We just unconsciously do that. We even think it's "right" to want our children to approve of us and that they *should* be grateful to us for what we've done for them. I'm not saying either way is right or wrong. Remember, we're here together in the field beyond wrongdoing and rightdoing, as Rumi says. Now that I've done self-inquiry for so long, I know for sure we can't do anything "wrong." There are only opportunities for loving more of ourselves, and in turn, more of our children. We're just looking at a situation and practicing presence. I can't be present if I'm in my child's emotional business.

~

To begin the process of self-inquiry, we first need to revisit the past to identify the thought *behind* your stress of wishing for your child to be more grateful toward you or wishing they would be more approving of you when they were not. This stressful thought - remembered in the

57

present - has to be undone before presence can be realized now or in the future. Self-inquiry stops the stressful stories from being repeated.

I invite you to remember a time in your past when you wanted your child to be more *loving* toward you, or to be more *approving* of you or to be more *appreciative* of you, and they weren't. Maybe you thought you deserved some appreciation from them because you went out of your way to do something for them, and they weren't thankful in any way. Maybe they kept brushing off your attempts to express your love to them and you just wanted them to receive your love or return that loving kindness to you. Maybe it was when your child was telling you that you were so mean to them and you just wished they didn't feel that way

~

Did you find your situation? If not, give yourself more time, even throughout the day, to notice the situations where you think the thought, *"She/he should be more approving/appreciative/loving toward me."* My situation is when my children used to *beg* for more screen time (using the computer, playing video games, or watching TV) when they were only allowed a certain amount. I wanted them to stop begging, and instead to start *accepting* the limits we had agreed on, and to be *appreciative* of the amount of time they did have to use screens. I wanted them to be less mad at me for wanting them to stick to the limits. There was a lot of heartache, struggle, arguing, and crying about screen time in our home. Many, many hours were spent going back and forth - complaining, arguing, negotiating, et cetera - about how much screen time, when to use the screen time, and for what purposes. As a result, I felt *so* disconnected from my children.

Once you have your stressful situation in your mind, take in the whole scene. See the pictures in the scene, see where you were. Look at you: your body language, your energy, your face, the words you said. Look at your child: their face, their body movements, their words if you can remember. See it all. Put yourself mentally there. Revisit this stressful situation as if you were reliving it.

Now, I invite you to identify a feeling you were having at the time. Was it embarrassment? Was it pride? Regret? Guilt? Fear? Whatever it was, identify it. Make it simple. Then, identify *why* you felt that way.

Once you've identified how you felt and why you felt that way, in that situation, I invite you to fill in the first line on Worksheet 1 for this morning. As you're filling in the worksheets, really mentally *be* in the situation. Put the words on the paper that you actually thought and felt at the time. Make them as true as they were then, do not censor them, and write them down exactly as you experienced them. Make the words petty, mean, and arrogant, whatever they were. For instance, one time, early in my self-inquiry practice, I thought, and actually said in anger, *"You both are so ungrateful! You're spoiled rotten!"* I couldn't even believe that popped out of my mouth, but it did. Luckily I stopped myself before saying anything else I might regret, and quickly did self-inquiry on my stressful thoughts. I apologized to the kids later, and felt so much better.

I tell you this to invite you to let it all hang out when filling out the first worksheet. Your transformation will be that much more powerful when you do because you're getting those thoughts that are on your mind *anyway* out of your mind and on to the paper and stopping them to look at them. When you do this, they're "caught" and can't grab you with such strength any more in the future. Feel free to continue on to Worksheet 2 after that. In your next letter, I'll walk us through a detailed example of wanting your child's approval using Worksheet 2.

Your own approval of yourself is the reward in all of this. Once you get this approval of yourself, it frees you up like never before. You will be so secure in yourself, so confident, that you will never ever think - consciously or unconsciously - that you need anyone else's approval, praise, encouragement, thanks, or even love. Really. You will never need any of that from other people again. You will never burden them with pumping up your ego. You will never be let down by your expectations of other people. You will be so approving of yourself that you'll know in your cells that you can never do anything "wrong" or "bad" or "terrible." You'll never feel needy of others' approval of you ever again. Then you'll be able to also see that in your child. You will have set your child free from worrying about your or anyone else's approval. They will be guided by whether or not they have their own approval of themselves. They can now pay attention to it and hear it, because they won't be so worried about getting it from you. Wow! What a free, self-confident, powerful force your child will be in the world. That *is* actually possible. It's all starting with you.

Wishing you, dear one, Peace and Presence today,
Catherine

Presence Practice Notes

Your Approval of Yourself

Self-Inquiry Worksheet 1 of 2

We've been told all of our lives not to judge others. The fact is we do it anyway. This worksheet allows the mind to see itself, to see the reality of its own thoughts, and to truly consider the thoughts by putting them on paper. This is the time to let those judgments have their own life.

DIRECTIONS:

A. Think of a specific person that is triggering stress in you. It could be your child, partner, ex-partner, mom, or dad. (Not yourself) They could be living or not living.

B. Now, recall a specific stressful situation you had with that person. It might have been a face to face interaction, an event, a phone call, or any situation that caused you any feelings of discomfort. Identify the specific stressful situation, and see it as a *single snapshot* in time.

C. Witness that single snapshot. Notice the time, place, words spoken, body language, and energy of each person. Then, 1) Identify and name the primary uncomfortable feeling you were having, 2) identify why you felt that way, and 3) answer the questions below with *short, simple* statements. *Please do not* try to be psychologically correct, spiritual, or wise now. For the purposes of this worksheet, be as judgmental as you were when you were in that situation.

1. In this situation, who angers, confuses, saddens, or disappoints you, and why? *(Example: I'm frustrated with Aiden because he won't listen to me.)*

2. In this situation, how do you want them to change? *(Example: I want Aiden to stop what he's doing, look at me, and listen to me.)*

3. In this situation, what advice would you offer to them? *(Example: Aiden should learn how to listen.)*

4. In order for you to feel better in this situation, what do you need them to think, say, feel, or do? *(Example: I need Aiden to listen.)*

5. What do you think of them in this situation? Make a list. Be petty. *(Example: Aiden is just like his dad - he won't respect me.)*

6. What is it in or about this situation that you don't ever want to experience again? *(Example: I don't ever want to be disrespected by Aiden again.)*

Review what you wrote. Pick one sentence you wrote that feels the most stressful to you right now. Circle it. Rewrite it at the top of Worksheet 2.

Adapted from Byron Katie International, Inc. Rev. 7/2014, with consent.

Self-Inquiry Worksheet 2 of 2

This worksheet is a meditation. When answering the questions, close your eyes, be still, and patiently wait to witness what appears to you. Always give yourself time to let the deeper answers meet the questions.

DIRECTIONS:

A. In the space below, write the thought you circled from Worksheet 1. Then answer questions 1-4.

B. Reconstruct the thought in three new ways. Possibilities are: by directing it inward (number 5 below), exchanging the other person's name with yours (number 6 below), and stating its exact opposite (number 7 below). Examples are provided below. Then, find and record three genuine, specific examples of how each new thought is as true or truer for you in that situation.

C. If you circled the thought from your answer to question 6 on Worksheet 1, you would reconstruct the thought by replacing the words, "I don't ever want to…" with "I am willing to…" and "I look forward to…"

Re-write the thought you circled on Worksheet 1: *(Example: Aiden doesn't listen to me.)*

_____

_____

1. In that situation, is this thought true? *(Yes or no only. There are no right or wrong answers. If no, skip to question 3.)*

2. In that situation, can you absolutely know that it's true? *(Yes or no only)*

3. In that situation, how did you *react* when you believed that thought?

4. In that situation, who would you be if you could not believe that thought?

5. Reconstruct the thought by directing it *inward. (Example: I don't listen to me.)* Find and record three genuine, specific examples in that situation how this new thought is as true or truer than the original thought.

6. Reconstruct the thought by *exchanging* the other person's name with yours. *(Example: I don't listen to Aiden.)* Find and record three genuine, specific examples of how this new thought is as true or truer for you in that situation.

7. Reconstruct the thought by stating the *exact opposite. (Example: Aiden does listen to me.)* Find and record three genuine, specific examples of how this new thought is as true or truer for you in that situation.

Adapted from Byron Katie International, Inc. Rev. 7/2014, with consent.

Welcome to Morning 8 - *Deepening Your Approval of Yourself*

(I invite you to first re-read the Morning Meditation on page 16.)

Dear Present Mother,

Today, I'm walking us through Worksheet 2 on seeking our *child's* approval. If you already completed Worksheet 2 from Morning 7, I invite you to continue completing worksheets on any stressful situation where you see that you are trying to get your child's love, appreciation, or approval. My situation was where I just wanted my children to accept the limits we had agreed on for their screen time and to be appreciative of the amount I was agreeing to. I was so tired of going back and forth about it, I just wanted everyone to accept it and move on.

Have you noticed a situation where you wanted your child's love, approval, or appreciation and you weren't getting it? If not, that's okay. Now that you're aware of how it can happen, you might notice it in some subtle way as we go through the self-inquiry process here. As you read my answers to the inquiry questions, I invite you to look for how this new awareness can apply to your life. Here we go.

Is it true that I need my child's approval? Yes (For me, this was a yes then. For you, answer truthfully about your situation.) *Can I absolutely know that it's true, that I need my child's approval?* No.

How do you react when you believe that thought? I negotiate with them. I listen to them because I think I *should* listen to them, not because I *want* to listen to them. I panic that they'll get too mad and hurt someone or themselves in the future. I treat them like they can't handle the word "no." I give them more time even though I think it's too much for them, so I say yes when I really want to say no. I want to say no and really mean it and stick to it. I am out of my integrity. I let them control me! I feel muddy and unclear in my own wisdom. I see images of when I was a child and I desperately wanted my parents' approval. I would say "yes" to them for certain things that I really wanted to say "no" to. I see so many images of me doing that with them in the past.

Who would you be without that thought? I would be present to what's true for me, what my own integrity is, what's truly clear for me about the situation. I would be authentically me. I would be trustworthy. I would trust myself. There would be no way to get upset with my child, or with another human being for that matter, because I wouldn't be depending so much on their opinion of me. I would be unaffected by their criticism of me, or their upset feelings, if they had any. Wow. I would be free from thinking that I needed anyone else's approval of me. I would be genuinely self-confident. Oh, my goodness! I would love that!

~

Now, here are the newly reconstructed thoughts which are 1) directed inward, 2) exchanging the other person's name with mine, and 3) the exact opposite, with examples of each.

1. *"I need my approval."* Examples of that are a) Yes! I need only my approval. That is so freeing. b) Ultimately, that's all that matters. That is the final word for me. It's clear and trustworthy. I can rely on that (my approval). It's solid, unmoving, like gravity. c) I only need my own approval because that's who I am always with and always have been with and always will be with. I stay in my own business that way. I take care of myself. I don't make others dependent on my approval by trying to get *their* approval. I am a great role model for my children to rely on their own approval instead of their friends' or mine or my husband's or anyone else's in society. I teach them that they can trust themselves.

2. *"My child needs my approval."* Examples of that are a) I teach them to need my approval by always telling or showing them if I approve or don't approve of what they're doing. b) This makes them hostages to mine and other people's opinions about them. c) It teaches them to look outside themselves to know whether they are okay or not. That is not what I want to teach my children. d) It supports me to know this so I can be aware of it and stop myself from judging them in the future.

3. *"I don't need my child's approval."* Examples of that are a) I am the adult, the parent, and they are the children, my children. b) I can trust my internal wisdom. I can trust the wisdom that arises in me when I am present. c) I trust that my happiness truly comes from inside, not from my child's approval. d) I can never really know if I have their approval anyway. In fact, the smile on their face has nothing to do with me; it's only there because they believed they "needed" the screen time and they got what they thought they "needed," so it's temporary.

~

I loved doing self-inquiry on my stressful thoughts on this situation. I must have questioned 20 thoughts about it. It freed up my entire family to be present, present to ourselves, present with each other, with more kindness, and more love. I stopped living in fear and my kids stopped feeling like they had to make me happy. To top it all off, my daughter learned to read and write by playing a computer game and my son taught himself the basics of astrophysics by doing the same. Now, they either do or don't use the computer or watch TV. I notice there are no stressful thoughts arising in me anymore about "screen time." The screen monster has flown away from my mind and therefore from our house. I see now that we do lots of things in our lives besides look at a screen. There is a lot more harmony flowing between us all. It's amazing. When I think back on the time we "lost" arguing about it for so long, I see now that it was perfect the way it all played out. It was good. We all learned so much in the process. We gained a new understanding of each other. We returned back to our love and commitment to authenticity, presence and grace.

~

It's important to note that your self-inquiry around "screen time" may lead you to a very different solution than mine. Honor your perspective and your personal process. Notice if a thought comes across your mind that compares and/or judges me and how I currently address this very common, hot-button topic. Notice how you react. Just notice. Don't judge yourself. Then come back to your own inquiry process. Doing self-inquiry yourself doesn't mean you'll come to the same solution on screen use as someone else. It's also important to note that my way of handling "screen time" – or any other topic - may surely shift based on my self-inquiry on any additional stressful thoughts that may arise in my mind in the apparent future.

~

If doing self-inquiry on the statement *I need my child's approval* did not come easy for you, I completely understand. Most people never get to see how they can be so controlled by this thought. It's so subconscious to most of us to think we need the approval of someone else. Yet we go around thinking about what others think of us all the time. We either get upset when we think others are judging us or we don't share all of ourselves for fear we *might* be judged. It's such a human condition. With self-inquiry, however, we can end all of that for good.

You're doing so great so far. You've been at this for a week. What realizations have you experienced? Just keep reminding yourself of those and it will be even easier to continue. I used to sometimes doubt myself in my process of self-inquiry, especially when I was new at it. If you do too, don't feel discouraged. If you ever feel blocked in your ability to do your self-inquiry, just write down those thoughts about why you feel blocked and do self-inquiry on those first. You'll be so glad you did.

Another way to make it easier is to go back to doing self-inquiry on thoughts you have about your child instead of your thoughts about you. For instance, instead of using yourself as the subject like *I need my child's approval* you would say *She should thank me*, or *He should be more understanding of me*, or *She should trust me*. Especially in the beginning of our presence practice the mind clears much faster when we do self-inquiry on our thoughts about *others* compared to when we do self-inquiry on our thoughts about ourselves. The reason this happens is because of that sweet little, cute little, sticky so called ego/illusion/pain body/duality (fill in your word) that wants to protect itself because it fears its own demise, because it has to be *right* to survive. Its job is to find evidence to make it feel *right*, and biologically-speaking, it protected our bodies - thankfully - from tigers attacking us centuries ago. If we do self-inquiry on our thoughts about others first, then it calms the ego. The ego doesn't fear so much because we're looking at another person instead of ourselves. The mind can be more open because it doesn't feel so much like it has to protect us. It doesn't feel as threatened. I introduce this here, at the end of our first week, so you can see and realize the difference between questioning thoughts about others and questioning thoughts about ourselves.

Either way, we're doing self-inquiry on *ourselves*; every thought you write on those worksheets are *your* thoughts, coming out of *your* mind. There's no way you can ever talk about another person; you (we, everyone) are talking about yourself since the thoughts are coming out of *your* own mind (*your* lens). "Your" mind looks at everyone else as you. Spiritually-speaking, that's the truth. In self-inquiry, especially in the beginning of our learning it, we just help the mind help us, by looking at another first, then turning those thoughts inward to find our own freedom.

Just in case you didn't know, underneath all of your stressful thinking, you've had your own approval of yourself all along. You may have just lost your awareness of it because you unconsciously believed your stressful thoughts that said that you needed to get it from other people. You are innocent in that. You learned that a long time ago when you were a child. When you were born, you were a totally confident being, totally self-approving, without even knowing it. You trusted yourself. Look at or remember your children when they were toddlers: weren't they so approving of themselves? Toddlers don't seem to ever doubt themselves. Then we unintentionally, and innocently, take that away from them by teaching them, like our parents taught us, that they *need* our approval. We "learned" not to trust ourselves when we were young. Just like you started relying on your parents' and others' approval when you were little, now your children come to rely on you for your approval of them. Unintentionally we make our kids addicted to our approval of them. Then they grow up to be adults who depend on people outside themselves for approval. They lose their self-confidence.

They don't have to anymore though, with your self-inquiry. Now, you have a new way. You can actually transform human evolution by doing self-inquiry about wanting other people's approval. It's beautiful how it all works out for the good.

So let your courage shine, and allow your determination to be present to become your guiding light. Your unshakeable approval of yourself is waiting for you at the end of your self-inquiry. I love that you would be the only one from whom you ever need approval. What an amazing power you will have.

Wishing you, dear one, Peace and Presence today,
Catherine

Presence Practice Notes

Deepening Your Approval of Yourself

Self-Inquiry Worksheet 1 of 2

We've been told all of our lives not to judge others. The fact is we do it anyway. This worksheet allows the mind to see itself, to see the reality of its own thoughts, and to truly consider the thoughts by putting them on paper. This is the time to let those judgments have their own life.

DIRECTIONS:

A. Think of a specific person that is triggering stress in you. It could be your child, partner, ex-partner, mom, or dad. (Not yourself) They could be living or not living.

B. Now, recall a specific stressful situation you had with that person. It might have been a face to face interaction, an event, a phone call, or any situation that caused you any feelings of discomfort. Identify the specific stressful situation, and see it as a *single snapshot* in time.

C. Witness that single snapshot. Notice the time, place, words spoken, body language, and energy of each person. Then, 1) Identify and name the primary uncomfortable feeling you were having, 2) identify why you felt that way, and 3) answer the questions below with *short, simple* statements. *Please do not* try to be psychologically correct, spiritual, or wise now. For the purposes of this worksheet, be as judgmental as you were when you were in that situation.

1. In this situation, who angers, confuses, saddens, or disappoints you, and why? *(Example: I'm frustrated with Aiden because he won't listen to me.)*

2. In this situation, how do you want them to change? *(Example: I want Aiden to stop what he's doing, look at me, and listen to me.)*

3. In this situation, what advice would you offer to them? *(Example: Aiden should learn how to listen.)*

4. In order for you to feel better in this situation, what do you need them to think, say, feel, or do? *(Example: I need Aiden to listen.)*

5. What do you think of them in this situation? Make a list. Be petty. *(Example: Aiden is just like his dad - he won't respect me.)*

6. What is it in or about this situation that you don't ever want to experience again? *(Example: I don't ever want to be disrespected by Aiden again.)*

Review what you wrote. Pick one sentence you wrote that feels the most stressful to you right now. Circle it. Rewrite it at the top of Worksheet 2.

Adapted from Byron Katie International, Inc. Rev. 7/2014, with consent.

Self-Inquiry Worksheet 2 of 2

This worksheet is a meditation. When answering the questions, close your eyes, be still, and patiently wait to witness what appears to you. Always give yourself time to let the deeper answers meet the questions.

DIRECTIONS:
A. In the space below, write the thought you circled from Worksheet 1. Then answer questions 1-4.
B. Reconstruct the thought in three new ways. Possibilities are: by directing it inward (number 5 below), exchanging the other person's name with yours (number 6 below), and stating its exact opposite (number 7 below). Examples are provided below. Then, find and record three genuine, specific examples of how each new thought is as true or truer for you in that situation.
C. If you circled the thought from your answer to question 6 on Worksheet 1, you would reconstruct the thought by replacing the words, "I don't ever want to…" with "I am willing to…" and "I look forward to…"

Re-write the thought you circled on Worksheet 1: *(Example: Aiden doesn't listen to me.)*

_____

_____

1. In that situation, is this thought true? *(Yes or no only. There are no right or wrong answers. If no, skip to question 3.)*

2. In that situation, can you absolutely know that it's true? *(Yes or no only)*

3. In that situation, how did you *react* when you believed that thought?

4. In that situation, who would you be if you could not believe that thought?

5. Reconstruct the thought by directing it *inward. (Example: I don't listen to me.)* Find and record three genuine, specific examples in that situation how this new thought is as true or truer than the original thought.

6. Reconstruct the thought by *exchanging* the other person's name with yours. *(Example: I don't listen to Aiden.)* Find and record three genuine, specific examples of how this new thought is as true or truer for you in that situation.

7. Reconstruct the thought by stating the *exact opposite. (Example: Aiden does listen to me.)* Find and record three genuine, specific examples of how this new thought is as true or truer for you in that situation.

Adapted from Byron Katie International, Inc. Rev. 7/2014, with consent.

Welcome to Morning 9 - *Momentum with a Partner*

(I invite you to first re-read the Morning Meditation on page 16.)

Dear Present Mother,

Before I started practicing self-inquiry in 2007 my life was what I would call a wild rollercoaster. I was in my early forties, had just given birth to two children, was entering menopause, was practicing Attachment Parenting, and hadn't yet learned to *balance* everyone else's needs with my own. Also, my husband and I were arguing so much about how to raise our children that I thought we would end up divorced, just like my parents had. I woke up each morning fearing I would not have the capacity to make it happily through my day. I dreaded getting up to face the day. I felt like I had a constant case of the most intense PMS I had ever had. "Could marriage and family life really be like this?" I thought. The idea even occurred to me that death had to be better than this life. That thought triggered so much fear in me that it woke me up. There was no way that was going to happen. I knew there was a way out of this pain. Doing self-inquiry then was a matter of life and death for me.

I am so grateful that I started seeing glimpses of light when I filled out those worksheets. I started noticing my stressful thoughts, my story, about my reality. I started noticing *how many* stressful thoughts I experienced. I thought, *"Wow, there are so many stressful thoughts. I'll never be able to do self-inquiry on all of these."* I wanted to tackle each one like I had tackled a chapter of my homework when I was in school. *I wanted to get it over with as quickly as possible.* It seemed like so much work! *Life was hard enough,* I thought, why would I add *more* work to my already overwhelming life?

But I kept noticing, every time I questioned my stressful thoughts, more and more glimpses of light would come into my life. More and more peace would enter into situations that were previously stressful for me. I loved this new way of being. I remember thinking, "What is happening?" and *"How* could this be happening?" It was so subtle, so much like I wasn't trying to do anything better. It was just getting better, way better, all on its own, after I did self-inquiry.

A momentum, a flow, a beautiful way of being started to build at that point. I attribute it to one primary factor: I found a friend and partner to do self-inquiry with on a regular basis. She was a mom too. We both wanted to raise our children in a way that felt true to us, a way that I can only describe as being present, in our way of being with our children. We were both so committed to changing all of the unproductive thought patterns we saw in our lives. We both already knew of the power of self-inquiry. We both had already been applying it to our mothering lives on a regular basis, unraveling age-old thought patterns that were no longer serving us and no longer true. We met about once a week, sometimes more often, at a coffee shop, in our cars, on a hiking trail, sometimes on the phone - anywhere we could. We traded facilitating each other through self-inquiry. One by one, we met our stressful thoughts with understanding, with non-judgment, in the field beyond right and wrong. We helped each other question the thoughts that caused disconnection with our children, our husbands, and our parents. We both found our freedom, together. We were amazed every time. We celebrated every time.

I remember one especially moving experience I had after questioning a stressful thought with my friend. The thought was *divorce is devastating.* I was considering the idea of divorcing my husband. This thought was planted in my brain as a child, when my parents got divorced. I kept fearing the re-creation of my past. I remember feeling scared of divorce because of my belief that *divorce is devastating.* However, I could not believe how open my mind was when I considered the opposite thought: *divorce is liberating.* Now I saw all the ways that divorce was liberating for some people and how it could be liberating for me. I saw this as it related to my present life. Then, I saw it as it related to my life when I was a child. My mind found all the reasons why my parents' divorce was liberating to me as a child. I experienced such peace about that possibility after we questioned that thought. Oddly enough, I found the idea of continuing to question my stressful thoughts about my husband more appealing than divorcing him. I'm so glad I did.

My friend and I became so close by facilitating self-inquiry for each other. We are cemented together by our experiences, our common understanding of one another, and our commitment to be the most present mothers we can possibly be for ourselves and our children. I am forever grateful.

Imagine if mothers all over the world could come to support each other in this way. I thought, "Wow, the power of two mothers doing self-inquiry together is absolutely incredible. What if there were more of us? Imagine what sustainable positive change could take place in our lives, in our families, in our communities, in our world." I kept looking for mother's groups like that. So far I haven't found one. So that's when the thought came to me - *start one.* So, I started The Present Mothers Community, a personal and spiritual development community for mothers. You can find more information about it on our website at http://www.thepresentmother.com/.

As you continue your self-inquiry remember that I am with you in spirit. I remember doing the same thing you are doing and I have so much compassion for you. If you are doing our weekly group coaching calls, I hope you are enjoying our time together. I do. I also hope you get to work with a partner sometime very soon. Even though you're completing the worksheets for each day on your own, a partner can facilitate you on the same or related thoughts and you can get even deeper realizations. For now, if you don't yet have a partner, know that you are getting exactly what you need. It's beautiful to do, with or without a partner. I love that you and I are the mothers in this world who can realize that.

Wishing you, dear one, Peace and Presence today,
Catherine

Presence Practice Notes

Momentum with a Partner

Self-Inquiry Worksheet 1 of 2

We've been told all of our lives not to judge others. The fact is we do it anyway. This worksheet allows the mind to see itself, to see the reality of its own thoughts, and to truly consider the thoughts by putting them on paper. This is the time to let those judgments have their own life.

DIRECTIONS:

A. Think of a specific person that is triggering stress in you. It could be your child, partner, ex-partner, mom, or dad. (Not yourself) They could be living or not living.

B. Now, recall a specific stressful situation you had with that person. It might have been a face to face interaction, an event, a phone call, or any situation that caused you any feelings of discomfort. Identify the specific stressful situation, and see it as a *single snapshot* in time.

C. Witness that single snapshot. Notice the time, place, words spoken, body language, and energy of each person. Then, 1) Identify and name the primary uncomfortable feeling you were having, 2) identify why you felt that way, and 3) answer the questions below with *short, simple* statements. *Please do not try to be psychologically correct, spiritual, or wise now.* For the purposes of this worksheet, be as judgmental as you were when you were in that situation.

1. In this situation, who angers, confuses, saddens, or disappoints you, and why? *(Example: I'm frustrated with Aiden because he won't listen to me.)*

2. In this situation, how do you want them to change? *(Example: I want Aiden to stop what he's doing, look at me, and listen to me.)*

3. In this situation, what advice would you offer to them? *(Example: Aiden should learn how to listen.)*

4. In order for you to feel better in this situation, what do you need them to think, say, feel, or do? *(Example: I need Aiden to listen.)*

5. What do you think of them in this situation? Make a list. Be petty. *(Example: Aiden is just like his dad - he won't respect me.)*

6. What is it in or about this situation that you don't ever want to experience again? *(Example: I don't ever want to be disrespected by Aiden again.)*

Review what you wrote. Pick one sentence you wrote that feels the most stressful to you right now. Circle it. Rewrite it at the top of Worksheet 2.

Adapted from Byron Katie International, Inc. Rev. 7/2014, with consent.

Self-Inquiry Worksheet 2 of 2

This worksheet is a meditation. When answering the questions, close your eyes, be still, and patiently wait to witness what appears to you. Always give yourself time to let the deeper answers meet the questions.

DIRECTIONS:
A. In the space below, write the thought you circled from Worksheet 1. Then answer questions 1-4.
B. Reconstruct the thought in three new ways. Possibilities are: by directing it inward (number 5 below), exchanging the other person's name with yours (number 6 below), and stating its exact opposite (number 7 below). Examples are provided below. Then, find and record three genuine, specific examples of how each new thought is as true or truer for you in that situation.
C. If you circled the thought from your answer to question 6 on Worksheet 1, you would reconstruct the thought by replacing the words, "I don't ever want to…" with "I am willing to…" and "I look forward to…"

Re-write the thought you circled on Worksheet 1: *(Example: Aiden doesn't listen to me.)*

_____

_____

1. In that situation, is this thought true? *(Yes or no only. There are no right or wrong answers. If no, skip to question 3.)*

2. In that situation, can you absolutely know that it's true? *(Yes or no only)*

3. In that situation, how did you *react* when you believed that thought?

4. In that situation, who would you be if you could not believe that thought?

5. Reconstruct the thought by directing it *inward. (Example: I don't listen to me.)* Find and record three genuine, specific examples in that situation how this new thought is as true or truer than the original thought.

6. Reconstruct the thought by *exchanging* the other person's name with yours. *(Example: I don't listen to Aiden.)* Find and record three genuine, specific examples of how this new thought is as true or truer for you in that situation.

7. Reconstruct the thought by stating the *exact opposite. (Example: Aiden does listen to me.)* Find and record three genuine, specific examples of how this new thought is as true or truer for you in that situation.

Adapted from Byron Katie International, Inc. Rev. 7/2014, with consent.

Welcome to Morning 10 - *Your Belief Systems*

(I invite you to first re-read the Morning Meditation on page 16.)

Dear Present Mother,

I honestly believed my parents were responsible for my belief system and my problems for almost 20 years. I blamed them for me feeling so horrible about how they raised me. When I became a mother, I discovered that a lot of other mothers believe the same thing or variations of this belief like, *"They really screwed me up,"* or *"They deeply wounded me in the way they raised me,"* or *"They did a terrible job,"* or *"They made me so scared,"* or *"They taught me to..."* *(Fill in your word for something "negative,")* or *"They never taught me to...."* *(Fill in your word for something "positive.")*

I wanted my relationship with my parents to be unaffected by this thought I believed but I could never seem to figure out *how*. There were many times that I dreaded conversations with them. It seemed we had nothing really to talk about. I just couldn't be myself with them. It felt so uncomfortable. I pretended not to feel this way, too, which felt rotten. After a while I started just accepting the distance between us, the way that I felt when I was around them, and the stilted conversations. I always felt such relief at the end of each conversation. Does that sound familiar? Some people spend a lifetime doing this with their parents.

After observing, researching, and reading for a while, I realized that I was making my negative thought patterns about them stronger. I was reinforcing stressful, unproductive neural pathways about my parents. Once I saw this, I completely stopped blaming them. But then, I thought, *"How will I heal?"* I thought that getting my feelings "out" of me would help. I spent a *decade* writing volumes and volumes of journals. I spent *hundreds* of hours sharing my feelings with others about how I felt about the way my parents raised me. I paid *thousands* of dollars to personal coaches and therapists. Does this sound the least bit familiar to you?

At first, it felt good to acknowledge my feelings, sharing them with myself on paper and talking about them with others. I believed, as many do, that I needed to get those feelings out of my body, purge them, so that they would release. But you know what? Nothing ever *shifted* in me. In fact, my anger and disappointment toward my parents got even *worse*. The more I reminded myself of those negative feelings by writing about them and telling the stories over and over, the more they grew! My parents and I grew more and more disconnected, in perfect reflection of me becoming more and more disconnected from my love for them.

Amazingly, when I discovered self-inquiry, I realized that I didn't even *need* to heal! I only needed to *question my thinking* about how my parents raised me. I had added meaning on top of events that I remembered. We *all* do this unconsciously. The meaning I gave those events was meaning *I* (the ego) created. What I believed about my parents was *my story* and not even *reality!* Yes, they may have done what they did but my thoughts about them were *mine*. Can you imagine spending all those years believing I had to purge those feelings in order to "heal"? Most people believe this is what we have to do to feel okay, and I was no exception. I spent all those years believing my parents were the reason I was not where I wanted to be emotionally.

After that realization I found so much freedom because I learned to question my stressful thoughts about my parents whenever they arose. I was the one who made up the meaning of what I remembered them doing, so I knew that I was the one who could change all that. I was the one who could realize the actual truth by questioning my stressful thoughts about them.

Doing self-inquiry helps us get to truth. I love the truth. Truth really does set us free. We don't even know our parents, in reality. All we know is our story about them, until we question it, and discover the truth.

I am so in love with my parents now. They are so precious to me. I love all aspects of them. I love the way they are and the way they are with me. In perfect reflection of my thoughts about them, I see how they love me so much too.

~

Today, I invite you to do self-inquiry on the thought, *"My parents are responsible for my belief systems and my problems"* or a version of your own. Find a place where you blame your parents for something they did or didn't do in your childhood and go from there. It's okay if they're not even living; we still carry around our stressful thoughts about them even when we aren't with them. So, here we go. Start by writing that stressful thought at the top of Worksheet 2.

"My parents are responsible for my belief systems and my problems" (or your version).

Question number one is, Is *it true?* (Yes or no, only. There are no right or wrong answers.).

The second question is *Can you absolutely know that it's true?* (Again, yes or no only).

The third question is *How do you react when you believe that thought?* Subsets of this question are: How do you treat your children when you believe that thought? How do you think about yourself when you believe that thought? What behaviors do you do with your parents when you believe that thought? Is it a stressful thought or a peaceful one? What memories surface, of the past, when you believe this thought? What movies do you project into the future when you believe this thought?

The fourth question is *Who would you be without that thought,* "My parents are responsible for my belief systems and my problems"? Is it hard to answer this question? Maybe you don't know how you would be. That's okay. Not knowing is a great place to start from. Would you be free to control your own life? Would you be at peace? Would you be present with your child… now?

Now, reconstruct the thought into new thoughts that are as true as or truer than "My parents are responsible for my belief systems and my problems." Reconstruct it from three new perspectives: 1) directed inward, 2) exchanging the other person's name with yours, and 3) the exact opposite.

The new thought directed *inward* would be: *"I am responsible for my belief systems and my problems."* Here's where the freedom lies. What are three specific, genuine examples of how *you* are responsible for your belief systems and your problems? The examples have to be ones that you authentically believe are true.

When you *exchange* the other person's name (or names) with yours, the new thought would be: *"I am responsible for my parents' belief systems and their problems."* Do you see any genuine, specific examples of how this statement could be as true or truer than the original one? If not, that's okay. This thought might not fit in your situation. This thought might not feel freeing for you and if it isn't, I wouldn't use it. These new thoughts we're creating are supposed to have an eye-opening and calming effect on us, not one that's equally or more stressful. So, in this case, this new thought wouldn't apply.

The *exact opposite* thought would be, *"My parents are **not** responsible for my belief systems and my problems."* How could that statement be as true as or truer than that they *are* responsible? What is an example of that, that your mind would believe? Can you find at least three examples?

I invite you to patiently wait for these examples to surface today and get a taste of true freedom: freedom to raise your children in the present moment, in a way that's true to your heart, without reaction to, or unconsciously copying, your past stressful story. I invite you to be the present mother you wish to be by continuing to do your self-inquiry on your stressful thoughts about your parents. When you do, your own children will have no way of blaming you for *their* belief systems and their problems. You won't be the teacher of that any more. There will be no way for you to believe it, so there will be no way for your children to believe it either. Amazing. How beautiful for them to know that they are the author of their own life. I love that you would be the mother who knows for sure that she is the author of her own life. Wow.

You are a courageous, committed soul. By bravely completing the worksheets, you are changing the course of your life. You're actually doing it!

Wishing you, dear one, Peace and Presence today,
Catherine

Presence Practice Notes

Your Belief Systems

Self-Inquiry Worksheet 1 of 2

We've been told all of our lives not to judge others. The fact is we do it anyway. This worksheet allows the mind to see itself, to see the reality of its own thoughts, and to truly consider the thoughts by putting them on paper. This is the time to let those judgments have their own life.

DIRECTIONS:

A. Think of a specific person that is triggering stress in you. It could be your child, partner, ex-partner, mom, or dad. (Not yourself) They could be living or not living.

B. Now, recall a specific stressful situation you had with that person. It might have been a face to face interaction, an event, a phone call, or any situation that caused you any feelings of discomfort. Identify the specific stressful situation, and see it as a *single snapshot* in time.

C. Witness that single snapshot. Notice the time, place, words spoken, body language, and energy of each person. Then, 1) Identify and name the primary uncomfortable feeling you were having, 2) identify why you felt that way, and 3) answer the questions below with *short, simple* statements. *Please do not* try to be psychologically correct, spiritual, or wise now. For the purposes of this worksheet, be as judgmental as you were when you were in that situation.

1. In this situation, who angers, confuses, saddens, or disappoints you, and why? *(Example: I'm frustrated with Aiden because he won't listen to me.)*

2. In this situation, how do you want them to change? *(Example: I want Aiden to stop what he's doing, look at me, and listen to me.)*

3. In this situation, what advice would you offer to them? *(Example: Aiden should learn how to listen.)*

4. In order for you to feel better in this situation, what do you need them to think, say, feel, or do? *(Example: I need Aiden to listen.)*

5. What do you think of them in this situation? Make a list. Be petty. *(Example: Aiden is just like his dad - he won't respect me.)*

6. What is it in or about this situation that you don't ever want to experience again? *(Example: I don't ever want to be disrespected by Aiden again.)*

Review what you wrote. Pick one sentence you wrote that feels the most stressful to you right now. Circle it. Rewrite it at the top of Worksheet 2.

Adapted from Byron Katie International, Inc. Rev. 7/2014, with consent.

Self-Inquiry Worksheet 2 of 2

This worksheet is a meditation. When answering the questions, close your eyes, be still, and patiently wait to witness what appears to you. Always give yourself time to let the deeper answers meet the questions.

DIRECTIONS:

A. In the space below, write the thought you circled from Worksheet 1. Then answer questions 1-4.

B. Reconstruct the thought in three new ways. Possibilities are: by directing it inward (number 5 below), exchanging the other person's name with yours (number 6 below), and stating its exact opposite (number 7 below). Examples are provided below. Then, find and record three genuine, specific examples of how each new thought is as true or truer for you in that situation.

C. If you circled the thought from your answer to question 6 on Worksheet 1, you would reconstruct the thought by replacing the words, "I don't ever want to…" with "I am willing to…" and "I look forward to…"

Re-write the thought you circled on Worksheet 1: *(Example: Aiden doesn't listen to me.)*

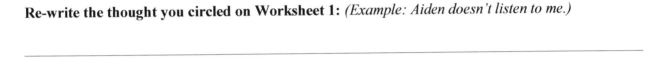

1. In that situation, is this thought true? *(Yes or no only. There are no right or wrong answers. If no, skip to question 3.)*

2. In that situation, can you absolutely know that it's true? *(Yes or no only)*

3. In that situation, how did you *react* when you believed that thought?

4. In that situation, who would you be if you could not believe that thought?

5. Reconstruct the thought by directing it *inward. (Example: I don't listen to me.)* Find and record three genuine, specific examples in that situation how this new thought is as true or truer than the original thought.

6. Reconstruct the thought by *exchanging* the other person's name with yours. *(Example: I don't listen to Aiden.)* Find and record three genuine, specific examples of how this new thought is as true or truer for you in that situation.

7. Reconstruct the thought by stating the *exact opposite. (Example: Aiden does listen to me.)* Find and record three genuine, specific examples of how this new thought is as true or truer for you in that situation.

Adapted from Byron Katie International, Inc. Rev. 7/2014, with consent.

Welcome to Morning 11 - *On Teaching Children*

(I invite you to first re-read the Morning Meditation on page 16.)

Dear Present Mother,

Your truest lesson to your children is in how you live your life. By becoming a student of your own mind, you question its stressful thinking and remove yourself from the role of teacher, in the most common definition of the word. It's a change in perspective. Now you stop teaching your children by telling them what to do and instead begin teaching them by modeling how you're *being.* You start walking your talk. You start realizing how much you don't know yet. You start realizing how much you can learn. Your lesson plan for yourself becomes welcoming all of your stressful thoughts like you welcome your beloved children - with open arms. You become the student of your own judgments about your children. You become the student of your stressful thoughts, and in that, the teacher of love.

I really love nature. I love being outdoors. Part of that love is my reaction to always having to stay indoors for school and homework when I was young. As a result, I used to push my children really hard to spend time outside. I was definitely not peaceful about them being inside during their free time. Before self-inquiry, our conversations would go something like this:

We're inside and my child is very engrossed in playing a video game.

Mom (tapping child on shoulder gently): "Sweetie, I'm noticing it's a beautiful time of year outside, and I'm also noticing that we've been indoors a lot lately. How would you like to do a nature camp next week? I found one that sounds like so much fun for you. I think you would feel great getting more fresh air than you've been getting. It isn't healthy to stay inside so much. You need your natural Vitamin D. So, how long will it take you to finish up your game so we can talk about this?"

Child: (doesn't say anything, keeps playing video game.)

Mom: "Sweetie, please listen to me when I'm talking to you. You need to get outside more. This nature camp would be so good for you. I think your body really needs it."

Child: (still doesn't say anything, still focused on game.)

Mom: (starting to get frustrated and sounding a little angry) "Honey, I'm going to turn that off if you don't listen to me. I'm starting to feel frustrated because you're not paying attention to what I'm saying."

Child: "Okay, okay. What?" (still looking at and playing game)

Mom: "I think we need to start video game restrictions again because you seem so disconnected from the rest of the world, buddy."

At that point, things might go one of several ways, depending on where *I* was with my self-inquiry practice:

1. Before self-inquiry, it would escalate and we would get more and more upset, angry and disconnected or I would just walk away, completely frustrated.

2. Later, when I first started doing self-inquiry, I would just leave him to his game and stop talking because I didn't want to get into an argument or say anything I would regret later.

3. During my immersion into self-inquiry, I would say to him, "Well, I think I'll just go question my stressful thought about it," and he would say, "Yes, mom, that sounds like a great idea."

4. When self-inquiry was very active for me and *visible* to the rest of my family, he would say, "Mom, do you want to question your stressful thought now?"

5. About three to four years into doing self-inquiry, I would not go and interrupt him in the first place. Instead, I would go out back and try to enjoy the beautiful day, while I questioned the stressful thoughts on my mind.

6. About five to seven years into doing self-inquiry, I would never interrupt him in the first place because the thought to interrupt him did not occur to me. I didn't have a thought that I knew what was best for him. I didn't have a thought that I wanted him to do anything other than stay connected to his own present moment.

7. Today, I might go and be interested in his game, sitting next to him, just because I love being with him, without talking to him or interrupting him in any way. Then he might say, "Hi Mom. I love you. Want to play with me?" I might say yes or no, depending on what I wanted. I might pat his back or rub his hair lightly or kiss his head. I might go outside and enjoy the sunshine, knowing he was happy and so was I. He might join me out there, or not. Either way, he's free to choose. He's free to listen to his own internal compass. He's free to be with me or not be with me, outside or inside. He's free to follow his voice inside his head that says, "Go to the nature camp," without it being a way to escape from my overbearing control. He can freely go without it being a way to just do what I say because he would feel devastated without my approval. He could freely choose without it being a disconnection from me or himself because what he really wants to do at that moment is play the video game. I love that the authenticity in my child has been preserved. I love that he doesn't do something that isn't true to himself.

~

"He should do the nature camp I want him to do." The reconstructed thought directed inward would be *I should do the nature camp I want him to do.* Ahhhhhhh. Therein lies my own freedom. Therein lies my son's freedom. How can I do my own nature camp? When I answered this for myself and then did it, I *lived* congruent with the new thoughts I created. I went outside and enjoyed nature. Life flowed. Joy flowed again. I love it.

In that example, *I* am the one who wants nature in my life. The mind is pretty smart, it just confuses other people with itself, which is really not even confusing when you remember that we are all one entity: love, to our core. The moment I leave my business and I try to control my child's mind, is the moment I've stepped out of the here and now. I've stepped out of this blissful, beautiful present moment.

If I had felt any stress about him playing the video game and said - with this hint of anxiety in my voice - something like, "I know you want to do the video game. I'm still going to turn it off now," do you see how that energy and those words go against what was currently happening then? He was playing a video game. I was interrupting him. I was the one stressed, not him, as I projected. Do you see how my thought that goes against reality takes me out of the present moment, with myself, and with my son? Do you see how that would have taken him out of his own present moment, and made him doubt himself and feel like he's not supposed to be in his flow, timeless, enjoying life, connected to his own present moment? My imagination about how unhealthy he was being was a pointer to myself about how my imagination was making our relationship unhealthy. It was making me disconnected from him and from the precious present moment. Was there really any danger to him playing a video game then? Notice how the mind extrapolates words it hears and sees. Notice how it puts its own horror movie on to reality. Just notice.

So, how do you do what you'd like to do, or how do you get your child to do what you'd like them to do and still stay connected in the present moment? Ah, the big question. My answer would be: you practice self-inquiry on the thoughts that stress you out about your child. That's it. Authentic presence, creative solutions, and love spring forth *as a result* of self-inquiry.

I truly believe motherhood is the quickest and steepest path to enlightenment, if we voluntarily put ourselves on a self-directed learning path using self-inquiry. Motherhood begins to become for the sake of ourselves. Then, in that, it becomes for our children, again. Doing that in a community of mothers, all committed to this growth, makes the growth exponential. Our being-ness starts to exist on a whole different plane - the present moment. In reality though, we already are that which we aspire to be; we already are present. Our stressful thoughts are there to be used for us to practice presence. When we realize this, the thoughts we used to call stressful begin to be called love.

Are you beginning to see that this is true? Appreciating the stressful thoughts doesn't bring more of them; it gives you food for your spiritual awakening. After you've questioned these stressful thoughts for a while, you'll notice that they occur to you less and less often, and you meet each one that comes with understanding. Soon you're understanding your child even more, you're connecting to them even more, you're deepening your connection to yourself, and therefore to your child. Isn't it so lovely how it works?

Of course if my son or another child were in any immediate, real, physical danger, I would naturally move swiftly to do whatever I needed to do to remove him or the other child from the situation. Self-inquiry is not about letting your children run off into some obviously dangerous situation. If you have that thought now, it is simply the ego doing the thing it does; it seeks to protect - a wonderful thing to have when you're a parent, right? But in this situation, does it apply? Neither self-inquiry nor this book is about any kind of situation. It's about the stressful thoughts you have *about* any kind of situation. When we're free of stressful thinking, we naturally move to protect the ones we love if they are in immediate physical danger. That's just how love flows. We don't make it stressful though. We just swiftly yet calmly move the child's body out of danger, without struggle or fighting the reality of the oncoming car, for example.

Remember, if you're having any stressful thoughts about actually doing self-inquiry, filling in the worksheets, or about your ability or time required, I encourage you to do self-inquiry on *those* stressful thoughts about the process. If you notice a judgment about *self-inquiry* that it is about letting your child do whatever they want, then that is another thought taking you out of the present moment and one to question. It can prohibit or limit your personal and spiritual growth *when you believe the thought* that self-inquiry is anything other than questioning your stressful thoughts that take you out of the present moment. It can be challenging to add one more thing to your plate *when you believe the thought* that you don't have time. It can be upsetting sometimes to see all the ways we've not been present in the past *when we believe the thought* that we should have been present. I understand that. I've been there. In my experience, when I just dropped self-inquiry because I was mad at "it," scared of what I was seeing, worried about the future of it, or didn't have time for it, I always delayed myself from developing an even deeper connection and understanding of myself, my child, and the present moment. You'll be so glad you made the time and that you filled out the worksheets regularly, and so will your precious child. I love that you would be the one to teach yourself about yourself. I love that your child would get to experience you, a present mother. What a breathtaking thing.

Wishing you, dear one, Peace and Presence today,
Catherine

Presence Practice Notes

On Teaching Children

Self-Inquiry Worksheet 1 of 2

We've been told all of our lives not to judge others. The fact is we do it anyway. This worksheet allows the mind to see itself, to see the reality of its own thoughts, and to truly consider the thoughts by putting them on paper. This is the time to let those judgments have their own life.

DIRECTIONS:

A. Think of a specific person that is triggering stress in you. It could be your child, partner, ex-partner, mom, or dad. (Not yourself) They could be living or not living.

B. Now, recall a specific stressful situation you had with that person. It might have been a face to face interaction, an event, a phone call, or any situation that caused you any feelings of discomfort. Identify the specific stressful situation, and see it as a *single snapshot* in time.

C. Witness that single snapshot. Notice the time, place, words spoken, body language, and energy of each person. Then, 1) Identify and name the primary uncomfortable feeling you were having, 2) identify why you felt that way, and 3) answer the questions below with *short, simple* statements. *Please do not* try to be psychologically correct, spiritual, or wise now. For the purposes of this worksheet, be as judgmental as you were when you were in that situation.

1. In this situation, who angers, confuses, saddens, or disappoints you, and why? *(Example: I'm frustrated with Aiden because he won't listen to me.)*

2. In this situation, how do you want them to change? *(Example: I want Aiden to stop what he's doing, look at me, and listen to me.)*

3. In this situation, what advice would you offer to them? *(Example: Aiden should learn how to listen.)*

4. In order for you to feel better in this situation, what do you need them to think, say, feel, or do? *(Example: I need Aiden to listen.)*

5. What do you think of them in this situation? Make a list. Be petty. *(Example: Aiden is just like his dad - he won't respect me.)*

6. What is it in or about this situation that you don't ever want to experience again? *(Example: I don't ever want to be disrespected by Aiden again.)*

Review what you wrote. Pick one sentence you wrote that feels the most stressful to you right now. Circle it. Rewrite it at the top of Worksheet 2.

Adapted from Byron Katie International, Inc. Rev. 7/2014, with consent.

Self-Inquiry Worksheet 2 of 2

This worksheet is a meditation. When answering the questions, close your eyes, be still, and patiently wait to witness what appears to you. Always give yourself time to let the deeper answers meet the questions.

DIRECTIONS:

A. In the space below, write the thought you circled from Worksheet 1. Then answer questions 1-4.

B. Reconstruct the thought in three new ways. Possibilities are: by directing it inward (number 5 below), exchanging the other person's name with yours (number 6 below), and stating its exact opposite (number 7 below). Examples are provided below. Then, find and record three genuine, specific examples of how each new thought is as true or truer for you in that situation.

C. If you circled the thought from your answer to question 6 on Worksheet 1, you would reconstruct the thought by replacing the words, "I don't ever want to…" with "I am willing to…" and "I look forward to…"

Re-write the thought you circled on Worksheet 1: *(Example: Aiden doesn't listen to me.)*

_____

_____

1. In that situation, is this thought true? *(Yes or no only. There are no right or wrong answers. If no, skip to question 3.)*

2. In that situation, can you absolutely know that it's true? *(Yes or no only)*

3. In that situation, how did you *react* when you believed that thought?

4. In that situation, who would you be if you could not believe that thought?

5. Reconstruct the thought by directing it *inward. (Example: I don't listen to me.)* Find and record three genuine, specific examples in that situation how this new thought is as true or truer than the original thought.

6. Reconstruct the thought by *exchanging* the other person's name with yours. *(Example: I don't listen to Aiden.)* Find and record three genuine, specific examples of how this new thought is as true or truer for you in that situation.

7. Reconstruct the thought by stating the *exact opposite. (Example: Aiden does listen to me.)* Find and record three genuine, specific examples of how this new thought is as true or truer for you in that situation.

Adapted from Byron Katie International, Inc. Rev. 7/2014, with consent.

Welcome to Morning 12 - *Your Truth*

(I invite you to first re-read the Morning Meditation on page 16.)

Dear Present Mother,

I love the clarity that comes with truth -- *my* truth. How do I know what *my* truth is? I do self-inquiry on any thought that would come into my mind that would cause the least bit of disconnection with my child.

After doing self-inquiry for about seven years, I had the most intense sensation of falling into Love. It was kind of like falling backwards onto a trampoline. I had just done self-inquiry on the two or three thoughts that had triggered so much fear of me totally trusting Love. These thoughts originated, from the best of my remembering, when I was seven years old. My thoughts were *"I can't trust love"* and *"I can't trust myself."* The dam completely broke when I found valid reasons to believe the reconstructed thoughts, "I *can* trust love," and "I *can* trust myself." There aren't any words to fully describe my experience after that. It was like a river of Love was flowing in me and I *was* the river. It was so strange compared to how I had "normally" lived. It was and is so wonderful. It's the real thing.

My family followed the river with me. They started to trust themselves more and more, a perfect reflection of my trust in me. My children were speaking their minds more, in ways that were non-threatening to others. They were very clear when they spoke and very articulate. For example, they started saying to me, "Mom, I don't like it when you talk like that to me. Will you take a deep breath and then try again?" Wow. They were also flexible when it came to what we were all going to do. I saw more teamwork in both kids' interactions with one another. They flowed with each other as I was flowing with them, not fighting them and not defending myself, and not arguing with what they were doing or saying. They started playing happily together more often. I had been telling my children to do the things that I couldn't yet do for myself - trust your instincts, listen to your gut, trust yourself. Until I trusted myself, they couldn't do it. They didn't have an example. Now, they do.

So, is there anything today that would stop you from doing self-inquiry? Is there anything that would stop you from making it a priority? For me, it could be *"I don't have enough time"* or *"I need more help around the house"* or *"I just don't have the energy"* or *"I need a babysitter."* So, if these are my thoughts, I question them. Once I do, a solution to my "problem" presents itself somehow, seemingly out of nowhere (now-here). Then the "problem" is solved. It doesn't even get solved with the thinking mind; it gets solved by Love, once I am open enough to it. I can't be open to receive it if I'm focused – consciously or unconsciously - on any stressful thought that blocks it.

If you decide not to do self-inquiry this morning, it's okay. Either way, my experience is that you can't do it wrong. I love that. It's perfect.

Wishing you, dear one, Peace and Presence today,
Catherine

Presence Practice Notes

Your Truth

Self-Inquiry Worksheet 1 of 2

We've been told all of our lives not to judge others. The fact is we do it anyway. This worksheet allows the mind to see itself, to see the reality of its own thoughts, and to truly consider the thoughts by putting them on paper. This is the time to let those judgments have their own life.

DIRECTIONS:

A. Think of a specific person that is triggering stress in you. It could be your child, partner, ex-partner, mom, or dad. (Not yourself) They could be living or not living.

B. Now, recall a specific stressful situation you had with that person. It might have been a face to face interaction, an event, a phone call, or any situation that caused you any feelings of discomfort. Identify the specific stressful situation, and see it as a *single snapshot* in time.

C. Witness that single snapshot. Notice the time, place, words spoken, body language, and energy of each person. Then, 1) Identify and name the primary uncomfortable feeling you were having, 2) identify why you felt that way, and 3) answer the questions below with *short, simple* statements. *Please do not* try to be psychologically correct, spiritual, or wise now. For the purposes of this worksheet, be as judgmental as you were when you were in that situation.

1. In this situation, who angers, confuses, saddens, or disappoints you, and why? *(Example: I'm frustrated with Aiden because he won't listen to me.)*

2. In this situation, how do you want them to change? *(Example: I want Aiden to stop what he's doing, look at me, and listen to me.)*

3. In this situation, what advice would you offer to them? *(Example: Aiden should learn how to listen.)*

4. In order for you to feel better in this situation, what do you need them to think, say, feel, or do? *(Example: I need Aiden to listen.)*

5. What do you think of them in this situation? Make a list. Be petty. *(Example: Aiden is just like his dad - he won't respect me.)*

6. What is it in or about this situation that you don't ever want to experience again? *(Example: I don't ever want to be disrespected by Aiden again.)*

Review what you wrote. Pick one sentence you wrote that feels the most stressful to you right now. Circle it. Rewrite it at the top of Worksheet 2.

Adapted from Byron Katie International, Inc. Rev. 7/2014, with consent.

Self-Inquiry Worksheet 2 of 2

This worksheet is a meditation. When answering the questions, close your eyes, be still, and patiently wait to witness what appears to you. Always give yourself time to let the deeper answers meet the questions.

DIRECTIONS:
A. In the space below, write the thought you circled from Worksheet 1. Then answer questions 1-4.
B. Reconstruct the thought in three new ways. Possibilities are: by directing it inward (number 5 below), exchanging the other person's name with yours (number 6 below), and stating its exact opposite (number 7 below). Examples are provided below. Then, find and record three genuine, specific examples of how each new thought is as true or truer for you in that situation.
C. If you circled the thought from your answer to question 6 on Worksheet 1, you would reconstruct the thought by replacing the words, "I don't ever want to…" with "I am willing to…" and "I look forward to…"

Re-write the thought you circled on Worksheet 1: *(Example: Aiden doesn't listen to me.)*

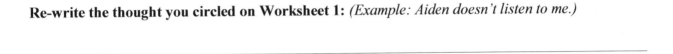

1. In that situation, is this thought true? *(Yes or no only. There are no right or wrong answers. If no, skip to question 3.)*

2. In that situation, can you absolutely know that it's true? *(Yes or no only)*

3. In that situation, how did you *react* when you believed that thought?

4. In that situation, who would you be if you could not believe that thought?

5. Reconstruct the thought by directing it *inward. (Example: I don't listen to me.)* Find and record three genuine, specific examples in that situation how this new thought is as true or truer than the original thought.

6. Reconstruct the thought by *exchanging* the other person's name with yours. *(Example: I don't listen to Aiden.)* Find and record three genuine, specific examples of how this new thought is as true or truer for you in that situation.

7. Reconstruct the thought by stating the *exact opposite. (Example: Aiden does listen to me.)* Find and record three genuine, specific examples of how this new thought is as true or truer for you in that situation.

Adapted from Byron Katie International, Inc. Rev. 7/2014, with consent.

Welcome to Morning 13 - *Our Children, Our Teachers*

(I invite you to first re-read the Morning Meditation on page 16.)

Dear Present Mother,

Today my son suggested I question a thought that was somewhat stressful to me. What a brilliant boy. I did. Now I don't even remember what the thought was. It feels like that conversation was a million years ago.

I love that my family has this way of working together. When I was a new mother, I didn't know about self-inquiry. When I would get upset with one of my children, I would try so hard to stay calm, even when I just wanted to burst. Sometimes I did stay calm. Sometimes I would just burst, and the volume of my voice would go up, almost uncontrollably. Then, I would feel guilty and swear I would never do that again. I was in a loop. The more I tried not to do it again, the more I did, and the guiltier I felt. When I was so confused there was so much suffering. What a gift that was though. It's what propelled me to find a better way. Now I have this new way of being, and it's wonderful.

To me, there are so few things in life that are more important than our relationships with the people we love most in the world. Our relationships with our parents, the first relationship we ever have, are of significance partly because that's where all of our beliefs about ourselves began to be formed. We know our brains are programmed, similar to computers, by our thought patterns when we are young. Neuroscience tells us that we can always form new thought patterns, even into very old age.[4] This is very good news. I love working with the mind. Every time I question my mind, I fall more and more in love with all of its thoughts. I fall more and more in love with each person on the planet. I can't help it. It's all a projection of my mind, as is yours.

---

[4] *The Brain That Changes Itself: Stories of Personal Triumph from the Frontiers of Brain Science*, December 18, 2007, Norman Doidge M.D. , Penguin, 2007.

Like my son asking me if I'd like to go and do some self-inquiry, our children can be our best teachers, when we let them, and when we question the stressful thoughts we have about them. Your life with them will give you all the material you need to be present. If they're young, you can see how deeply connected they are to the present moment. You can mimic them, meeting them right there every time. When they're older, we have more opportunities to practice presence, rather than blaming them. I love the possibility that all mothers can be present, in mind as well as body, with their kids. I love that you would be that mother.

What questions do you have about doing your self-inquiry? I invite you to bring them to http://www.thepresentmother.com/. You may find your answer there. If not, I would love for you to email me directly or ask it on our weekly calls so I can answer it. It is my honor to support you. Wherever you are with your self-inquiry practice, know that it is the perfect place. In my experience, it took dedication and courage for me to stay with it. My reward was my connection with my kids.

I invite you to use your worksheets this morning to address *any* situation that seems to cause stress for you and your kids right now. It might be in the area of a judgment you hold about your child or anything else. Every stressful thought you have about anyone or anything is fair game for your self-inquiry if it interferes with your connection with your child.

Wishing you, dear one, Peace and Presence today,
Catherine

Presence Practice Notes

Our Children, Our Teachers

Self-Inquiry Worksheet 1 of 2

We've been told all of our lives not to judge others. The fact is we do it anyway. This worksheet allows the mind to see itself, to see the reality of its own thoughts, and to truly consider the thoughts by putting them on paper. This is the time to let those judgments have their own life.

DIRECTIONS:

A. Think of a specific person that is triggering stress in you. It could be your child, partner, ex-partner, mom, or dad. (Not yourself) They could be living or not living.

B. Now, recall a specific stressful situation you had with that person. It might have been a face to face interaction, an event, a phone call, or any situation that caused you any feelings of discomfort. Identify the specific stressful situation, and see it as a *single snapshot* in time.

C. Witness that single snapshot. Notice the time, place, words spoken, body language, and energy of each person. Then, 1) Identify and name the primary uncomfortable feeling you were having, 2) identify why you felt that way, and 3) answer the questions below with *short, simple* statements. *Please do not* try to be psychologically correct, spiritual, or wise now. For the purposes of this worksheet, be as judgmental as you were when you were in that situation.

1. In this situation, who angers, confuses, saddens, or disappoints you, and why? *(Example: I'm frustrated with Aiden because he won't listen to me.)*

2. In this situation, how do you want them to change? *(Example: I want Aiden to stop what he's doing, look at me, and listen to me.)*

3. In this situation, what advice would you offer to them? *(Example: Aiden should learn how to listen.)*

4. In order for you to feel better in this situation, what do you need them to think, say, feel, or do? *(Example: I need Aiden to listen.)*

5. What do you think of them in this situation? Make a list. Be petty. *(Example: Aiden is just like his dad - he won't respect me.)*

6. What is it in or about this situation that you don't ever want to experience again? *(Example: I don't ever want to be disrespected by Aiden again.)*

Review what you wrote. Pick one sentence you wrote that feels the most stressful to you right now. Circle it. Rewrite it at the top of Worksheet 2.

Adapted from Byron Katie International, Inc. Rev. 7/2014, with consent.

Self-Inquiry Worksheet 2 of 2

This worksheet is a meditation. When answering the questions, close your eyes, be still, and patiently wait to witness what appears to you. Always give yourself time to let the deeper answers meet the questions.

DIRECTIONS:

A. In the space below, write the thought you circled from Worksheet 1. Then answer questions 1-4.

B. Reconstruct the thought in three new ways. Possibilities are: by directing it inward (number 5 below), exchanging the other person's name with yours (number 6 below), and stating its exact opposite (number 7 below). Examples are provided below. Then, find and record three genuine, specific examples of how each new thought is as true or truer for you in that situation.

C. If you circled the thought from your answer to question 6 on Worksheet 1, you would reconstruct the thought by replacing the words, "I don't ever want to…" with "I am willing to…" and "I look forward to…"

Re-write the thought you circled on Worksheet 1: *(Example: Aiden doesn't listen to me.)*

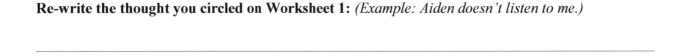

1. In that situation, is this thought true? *(Yes or no only. There are no right or wrong answers. If no, skip to question 3.)*

2. In that situation, can you absolutely know that it's true? *(Yes or no only)*

3. In that situation, how did you *react* when you believed that thought?

4. In that situation, who would you be if you could not believe that thought?

5. Reconstruct the thought by directing it *inward. (Example: I don't listen to me.)* Find and record three genuine, specific examples in that situation how this new thought is as true or truer than the original thought.

6. Reconstruct the thought by *exchanging* the other person's name with yours. *(Example: I don't listen to Aiden.)* Find and record three genuine, specific examples of how this new thought is as true or truer for you in that situation.

7. Reconstruct the thought by stating the *exact opposite. (Example: Aiden does listen to me.)* Find and record three genuine, specific examples of how this new thought is as true or truer for you in that situation.

Adapted from Byron Katie International, Inc. Rev. 7/2014, with consent.

Welcome to Morning 14 - *Children Find Their Own Happiness*

(I invite you to first re-read the Morning Meditation on page 16.)

Dear Present Mother,

Where does it show up in your life that you are unhappy because of something your child is doing or not doing? Do you see how that's making them responsible for your happiness?

I can think of one area that was a huge learning curve for me: the area of *sleep*. I wanted so badly for my kids to go to sleep some nights that I would find myself totally upset because they weren't and because I felt physically exhausted. I tried all the different ways I could think of to control them. They tried everything they could to avoid my control. I did self-inquiry on many of these thoughts around bedtime and sleep. Today, we all go to sleep when we're tired and we wake up when we're rested. On days when they have a friend coming over early in the morning, or if they have an appointment or something fun we've planned to do in the early morning, they ask me to wake them earlier than they would normally get up. At night, if I'm sleepy before they are, I just go to sleep since my husband stays up late anyway. They follow their own internal compass, they're in touch with their own rhythms, and they stay connected to the present moment. Each day is a little different, and it always works out where we all get plenty of rest. My husband and I get "alone" time in the mornings sometimes, sometimes when both kids are at friends' houses, or when we plan a date with a sitter. Somehow, some way, we all get what we need.

For me, I couldn't be present, especially in the area of sleep, just by reading what someone else had to say about sleep solutions or presence. I needed to actually fill in the self-inquiry worksheets myself and experience the presence that came with that. If I tried a solution I found in a parenting book or heard from a friend, or tried to control things in any way, it just seemed to backfire. If I only read things about being present, yes, sure, I was aware of the concepts and thoughts about it, but I never *experienced* it. Reading about peace never helped me experience peace in the area of sleep, that's for sure. If I read about it, it was only knowledge, coming to me from the outside-in. On the other hand, self-inquiry creates an *experience* of presence in you that gets deeper and deeper, and purer and purer, as "time" goes by. It's an *inside-out* experience, meaning that you realize a "knowing" that starts from the inside. Without the experience, the things I read only lasted until the next upset I had with the kids about bedtime. The least bit of impatience I had with them might have triggered a reaction in me that I did not want to have. I would never make any lasting, sustainable changes until I actually experienced my realizations for myself by completing the worksheets or having a friend facilitate me through the questions.

Once you get on the ride called self-inquiry, it's a wonderful, beautiful experience. This process, this method, creates three magical things…

~ It solidifies who I already am - pure Love.
~ It dissolves all illusions and all of the stressful thoughts I used to believe.
~ It helps me *consciously create* new thoughts that are grounded in this new awareness.

When illusions are gone, only Love remains. I don't even have to *do* anything else to "let go" of the stressful thinking. The stressful thinking lets go of me *all by itself!* Then you are left with a natural way of responding to your child with authentic, loving speech and actions that *work with* all of the reality of the present moment. And you are left with overwhelming gratitude.

This is not about letting your child remain in, what you perceive is, a harmful situation. If your mind is coming up with that thought, it's just the ego trying to protect you again from imagined fear, when there is no danger in reality. This *is* about being present with your child *and* experiencing the release of your attachment to controlling their happiness.

After doing self-inquiry, you start to realize for yourself that you can't control their happiness. You can never know if they are truly happy or not anyway. You only used to believe the illusion that you could control their happiness. After self-inquiry, that illusion has let go of you. Then all that remains are your experiences of pure presence, pure Love: The Love you were born as, the Love that's always there, like our warm sun, nourishing and life-sustaining. You are that Love - pure, perfect, beautiful. Then, Love moves through you to meet your child in the present moment, with complete faith that solutions to the "unhappiness" will present themselves through you and your child's clear minds.

Each mother has her own unique path and is in her own perfect place in her process of becoming more aware and present. No two mothers are in the same place. No matter where you are on your path, know that it is the best place for you to be. If you find yourself ever comparing yourself to me, or to any other mother, and believing it causes you to disconnect from the present, it's just another thought to do self-inquiry on. For example, *"She knows more than I do."* Can you absolutely know that it's true? *"She's enlightened and I'm not."* Can you absolutely know that that's true? *"I should be more enlightened than I am now, given everything I've done."* And so on. I love that you would love yourself, no matter where you are in your practice. In the practice of presence, there is no better than or worse than, no higher or lower, no closer or further away. When you do self-inquiry on any of the thoughts that would have you react by feeling "less than" someone else, or even "better than" someone else, you realize we are all the same, and we are all love.

What situation do you believe is stressful today for you? I invite you to mentally put yourself back into that situation during that single snapshot in time. Remember the time, place, words, et cetera and complete the worksheets. At some point in your practice, you may find it useful to do your inquiry on the person or situation that you believe is your biggest and deepest block to your own happiness. Is there someone whom you just can't seem to forgive? Is there a situation that you believe is just absolutely wrong that happened or is happening? In my experience, when I went for what I believed was the deepest darkest place inside me, I found the most light and Love. *Your* own deepest happiness and joy is waiting on the other side of your inquiry on anything that has been the complete opposite experience to you before now. I love that self-inquiry gives us this great gift. And, I love it for you and your child.

Wishing you, dear one, Presence and Peace today,
Catherine

Presence Practice Notes

Children Find Their Own Happiness

Self-Inquiry Worksheet 1 of 2

We've been told all of our lives not to judge others. The fact is we do it anyway. This worksheet allows the mind to see itself, to see the reality of its own thoughts, and to truly consider the thoughts by putting them on paper. This is the time to let those judgments have their own life.

DIRECTIONS:

A. Think of a specific person that is triggering stress in you. It could be your child, partner, ex-partner, mom, or dad. (Not yourself) They could be living or not living.

B. Now, recall a specific stressful situation you had with that person. It might have been a face to face interaction, an event, a phone call, or any situation that caused you any feelings of discomfort. Identify the specific stressful situation, and see it as a *single snapshot* in time.

C. Witness that single snapshot. Notice the time, place, words spoken, body language, and energy of each person. Then, 1) Identify and name the primary uncomfortable feeling you were having, 2) identify why you felt that way, and 3) answer the questions below with *short, simple* statements. *Please do not* try to be psychologically correct, spiritual, or wise now. For the purposes of this worksheet, be as judgmental as you were when you were in that situation.

1. In this situation, who angers, confuses, saddens, or disappoints you, and why? *(Example: I'm frustrated with Aiden because he won't listen to me.)*

2. In this situation, how do you want them to change? *(Example: I want Aiden to stop what he's doing, look at me, and listen to me.)*

3. In this situation, what advice would you offer to them? *(Example: Aiden should learn how to listen.)*

4. In order for you to feel better in this situation, what do you need them to think, say, feel, or do? *(Example: I need Aiden to listen.)*

5. What do you think of them in this situation? Make a list. Be petty. *(Example: Aiden is just like his dad - he won't respect me.)*

6. What is it in or about this situation that you don't ever want to experience again? *(Example: I don't ever want to be disrespected by Aiden again.)*

Review what you wrote. Pick one sentence you wrote that feels the most stressful to you right now. Circle it. Rewrite it at the top of Worksheet 2.

Adapted from Byron Katie International, Inc. Rev. 7/2014, with consent.

Self-Inquiry Worksheet 2 of 2

This worksheet is a meditation. When answering the questions, close your eyes, be still, and patiently wait to witness what appears to you. Always give yourself time to let the deeper answers meet the questions.

DIRECTIONS:

A. In the space below, write the thought you circled from Worksheet 1. Then answer questions 1-4.

B. Reconstruct the thought in three new ways. Possibilities are: by directing it inward (number 5 below), exchanging the other person's name with yours (number 6 below), and stating its exact opposite (number 7 below). Examples are provided below. Then, find and record three genuine, specific examples of how each new thought is as true or truer for you in that situation.

C. If you circled the thought from your answer to question 6 on Worksheet 1, you would reconstruct the thought by replacing the words, "I don't ever want to…" with "I am willing to…" and "I look forward to…"

Re-write the thought you circled on Worksheet 1: *(Example: Aiden doesn't listen to me.)*

1. In that situation, is this thought true? *(Yes or no only. There are no right or wrong answers. If no, skip to question 3.)*

2. In that situation, can you absolutely know that it's true? *(Yes or no only)*

3. In that situation, how did you *react* when you believed that thought?

4. In that situation, who would you be if you could not believe that thought?

5. Reconstruct the thought by directing it *inward. (Example: I don't listen to me.)* Find and record three genuine, specific examples in that situation how this new thought is as true or truer than the original thought.

6. Reconstruct the thought by *exchanging* the other person's name with yours. *(Example: I don't listen to Aiden.)* Find and record three genuine, specific examples of how this new thought is as true or truer for you in that situation.

7. Reconstruct the thought by stating the *exact opposite. (Example: Aiden does listen to me.)* Find and record three genuine, specific examples of how this new thought is as true or truer for you in that situation.

Welcome to Morning 15 - *Wants*

(I invite you to first re-read the Morning Meditation on page 16.)

Dear Present Mother,

I should give him what he wants. Is it true? This thought came into my mind today when my son kept asking me for something he really wanted. I didn't want to give it to him. Luckily, I wasn't hooked by the judgment of myself for more than two seconds. I decided to still question the thought anyway just to see what came up with it. I'll share it with you.

Before I start, I invite you to recall a time in your own life, with your child, where you thought you should give him/her what he/she wanted and you really didn't want to. As you're reading my answers, I invite you to apply your situation to the process. That way, as your own answers meet the questions, you get to do your own self-inquiry too. This opportunity is there for you every time you hear or read someone else questioning *their* stress-inducing thoughts.

~

Is it true, *I should give him what he wants*? No.

How do I react, what happens, when I believe this thought, I should give him what he wants? I get flashbacks to childhood of doing things because my parents said to, when I really didn't want to do them. I play a movie about the past that has me saying "ok" but really wanting to say "no." So, I see me not being true to my integrity. I feel like a little girl with no say, voiceless, following along because I was told to. I feel so pressured when I believe this thought. It feels like a mild form of panic. I go into fight or flight mode: I start to try to control my son. I get irritated and a little angry. I want to try and stop him from asking. I try to convince him not to ask me, and not to keep asking me.

Alternatively, sometimes I say yes, giving in to everything he asks for when I really don't want to. Then, I regret doing that, and I react by saying "no" sometimes to his requests without even thinking them through. I don't give myself enough time to consider his request and let my true answer surface. I feel like I have to come up with an answer right away.

What is my payoff for continuing to believe this thought that "I should give him what he wants"? (This question is a subset of the "how do I react" question on Worksheet 2.) Well, when I do say yes, I get to be "liked" by him, I get to be seen by him as a wonderful mom. This reinforces my insecure ego's need for outside validation that I'm a good mom. I see the flaw in that illusion even when my ego takes over and I continue to crave this type of reinforcement. Believing this thought gets me the reinforcement I "think" I need.

What am I not able to do when I believe the thought that "I should give him what he wants"? (This question is also a subset of the "how do I react" question.) Since I'm in fight or flight mode, either saying "yes" when I really would like to say "no" or I'm saying "no" when I would really like to say "yes," I'm not able to come up with workable solutions for us, ones that are in line with my integrity. I'm not able to connect with him. I'm not able to be present.

Who would I be without this thought that, "I should give him what he wants"? I would be wise, responsible, mature, creative, kind, present, and clear.

Reconstruct the stressful thought to a thought that is as true as or truer than "I should give him what he wants":

A. I should give *me* what I want. Examples of that, in this particular situation would be 1) Because I stay in my own business that way, 2) I take care of my own happiness that way; I don't make him responsible for my happiness, 3) It feels good to be empowered and to know I can give me what I want; I am responsible for me. I am able to take care of myself and be the one who gets to control my own happiness, 4) It's in my integrity to say yes to me when I want to say yes to me, and to say no when I want to say no, to me or to him, 5) I get clearer and clearer, and I feel stronger and stronger, more rooted in myself, more authentic, every time I am the one to give me what I want and to not require anyone else to do so.

B. I should *not* give him what he wants. Examples of that, in this particular situation, would be: 1) I didn't, 2) I didn't want to 3) It was in my integrity to say no and I prefer to stay in my integrity; I prefer to live in a way that is true for me.

C. I look *forward* to thinking the thought, *I should give him what he wants.* (This is the *opposite* thought from my answer to question six on Worksheet 1.) Examples of that in this particular situation would be: 1) I get to practice being clearer and clearer about what is a true yes for me and what is a true no for me, and in that I am extremely grateful to my son for being so persistent. 2) It might be what actually occurs in the future, so it would be *reality* if it did, and I want to live *in* reality, in the present moment. 3) This thought might occur to me again if he continues to ask me for what he wants. I love knowing his mind and knowing what he wants because I get to be included in his thought-life that way. 4) Because I would be loving that he feels comfortable enough with me to let me know his wants and desires; he trusts me with his inner wishes.

~

My experience in doing this exercise is that I got clearer and clearer and more and more trusting of myself in my mothering and more and more connected to him. I especially loved my new thought in "C" above - it really connected me to him. I can relate to my child because sometimes I have desires that are not fulfilled. I find power inside myself when I fulfill them on my own. Now they do too. I'm relying on the wisdom that lives - always - inside of me. Every time I do self-inquiry I reinforce that realization. When I find my own joy, especially after I don't get what I want, I teach him to do the same. Life is always good, no matter what the circumstances.

~

Now, I invite you to find a situation with your child when they wanted something so bad and you didn't want to give it to them and you started to get irritated or even all-out angry with your child for continuing to ask, or you tried to control them by threatening them with some kind of punishment if they didn't stop asking. Go there now, in your mind. Remember that situation. Remember the words, your body language, the location, the time. How were you feeling? Why were you feeling that way? When you see those two things, grab a pen and start filling in Worksheet 1 for this morning.

When you get to Worksheet 2, and start reconstructing the stressful thoughts into new thoughts that are as true or truer, you will find your own peace, even when your child keeps asking for something you don't want to give them. Peace will happen without you trying to change your child. Sooner or later they won't be able to help but model after you. You'll be fine with them, exactly how they are, and they will model you and be fine with you exactly how you are. You'll both be free to be.

Wishing you, dear one, Presence and Peace today,
Catherine

Presence Practice Notes

Wants

Self-Inquiry Worksheet 1 of 2

We've been told all of our lives not to judge others. The fact is we do it anyway. This worksheet allows the mind to see itself, to see the reality of its own thoughts, and to truly consider the thoughts by putting them on paper. This is the time to let those judgments have their own life.

DIRECTIONS:
A. Think of a specific person that is triggering stress in you. It could be your child, partner, ex-partner, mom, or dad. (Not yourself) They could be living or not living.
B. Now, recall a specific stressful situation you had with that person. It might have been a face to face interaction, an event, a phone call, or any situation that caused you any feelings of discomfort. Identify the specific stressful situation, and see it as a *single snapshot* in time.
C. Witness that single snapshot. Notice the time, place, words spoken, body language, and energy of each person. Then, 1) Identify and name the primary uncomfortable feeling you were having, 2) identify why you felt that way, and 3) answer the questions below with *short, simple* statements. *Please do not* try to be psychologically correct, spiritual, or wise now. For the purposes of this worksheet, be as judgmental as you were when you were in that situation.

1. In this situation, who angers, confuses, saddens, or disappoints you, and why? *(Example: I'm frustrated with Aiden because he won't listen to me.)*

2. In this situation, how do you want them to change? *(Example: I want Aiden to stop what he's doing, look at me, and listen to me.)*

3. In this situation, what advice would you offer to them? *(Example: Aiden should learn how to listen.)*

4. In order for you to feel better in this situation, what do you need them to think, say, feel, or do? *(Example: I need Aiden to listen.)*

5. What do you think of them in this situation? Make a list. Be petty. *(Example: Aiden is just like his dad - he won't respect me.)*

6. What is it in or about this situation that you don't ever want to experience again? *(Example: I don't ever want to be disrespected by Aiden again.)*

Review what you wrote. Pick one sentence you wrote that feels the most stressful to you right now. Circle it. Rewrite it at the top of Worksheet 2.

Adapted from Byron Katie International, Inc. Rev. 7/2014, with consent.

Self-Inquiry Worksheet 2 of 2

This worksheet is a meditation. When answering the questions, close your eyes, be still, and patiently wait to witness what appears to you. Always give yourself time to let the deeper answers meet the questions.

DIRECTIONS:

A. In the space below, write the thought you circled from Worksheet 1. Then answer questions 1-4.

B. Reconstruct the thought in three new ways. Possibilities are: by directing it inward (number 5 below), exchanging the other person's name with yours (number 6 below), and stating its exact opposite (number 7 below). Examples are provided below. Then, find and record three genuine, specific examples of how each new thought is as true or truer for you in that situation.

C. If you circled the thought from your answer to question 6 on Worksheet 1, you would reconstruct the thought by replacing the words, "I don't ever want to…" with "I am willing to…" and "I look forward to…"

Re-write the thought you circled on Worksheet 1: *(Example: Aiden doesn't listen to me.)*

_____

_____

1. In that situation, is this thought true? *(Yes or no only. There are no right or wrong answers. If no, skip to question 3.)*

2. In that situation, can you absolutely know that it's true? *(Yes or no only)*

3. In that situation, how did you *react* when you believed that thought?

4. In that situation, who would you be if you could not believe that thought?

5. Reconstruct the thought by directing it *inward. (Example: I don't listen to me.)* Find and record three genuine, specific examples in that situation how this new thought is as true or truer than the original thought.

6. Reconstruct the thought by *exchanging* the other person's name with yours. *(Example: I don't listen to Aiden.)* Find and record three genuine, specific examples of how this new thought is as true or truer for you in that situation.

7. Reconstruct the thought by stating the *exact opposite. (Example: Aiden does listen to me.)* Find and record three genuine, specific examples of how this new thought is as true or truer for you in that situation.

Adapted from Byron Katie International, Inc. Rev. 7/2014, with consent.

Welcome to Morning 16 - *Ending the Cycle of Violence*

(I invite you to first re-read the Morning Meditation on page 16.)

Dear Present Mother,

If you do or say anything to your child that you feel guilt or shame about, you are actually perpetuating the cycle of violence; you are being violent with yourself after you do it. You can't stop the cycle of violence, ever, with your child, whether it's physical or verbal, if you don't stop the violence toward yourself first. I know this from experience.

Together, let's end all forms of violence toward ourselves and our children, forever. Let's end your own suffering about it forever. Doing so will give your child a pain-free vaccination from any kind of violence coming from you or themselves ever again. It *is* possible. I know what it's like to feel that kind of pain. I know what it's like to end the violence, through self-inquiry. I've experienced it first-hand. When the violence you direct toward yourself is transcended, through self-inquiry, into compassion, understanding and presence, then all forms of violence toward your child will stop all on its own, without you doing anything but questioning the stressful thoughts on your mind.

~

I invite you to remember a time when you did or said something to your child that you feel guilt or shame about. Remember it to transcend it with self-inquiry. Remember the time, the location, what you said, what you did, your energy, the volume of your voice, the tone of your voice. Take it all in. Mentally revisit it.

If you're feeling worried that remembering it will make you do it again, know that I've been there. I remember feeling that intense fear. Please know that doing self-inquiry on the thoughts you have about it will do the exact opposite: It will increase and deepen the love and kindness you were *born with*. It will help you turn the corner on this and set you on a trajectory toward the

111

most compassion you may have ever experienced. Please know that when you remember it this time, it will be to turn it into presence and love.

If it feels terrifying to you to go further, I invite you to write down the thoughts that create the fear in you, and do self-inquiry on them first. Go slow. Question one simple, short thought at a time, with as open of a mind as you can. There is so much love and light at the end of what you might see as a "dark tunnel." I've realized that the "dark tunnel" was all in my imagination. When I believed it was real, I kept myself in it. When I questioned it, I was completely liberated.

~

I invite you to hold my hand and close your eyes. Breathe. Be breathed. Notice the in-breath. Notice the out-breath. Remember, you are only doing self-inquiry. You are just asking yourself questions and giving yourself answers. If you notice yourself feeling overcome by your feelings, you have left self-inquiry. That's okay. Just notice and gently guide yourself back. We're inquiring into our thoughts to notice and witness.

~

Remembering that specific situation with your child, in that location, at that time, how do you treat yourself when you believe the thought, *"I shouldn't have said/done that to my child."*? Be the witness of yourself, in that situation. Witness the feelings that come after you think you shouldn't have said or done what you did, without letting yourself get pulled into those feelings. Just notice what feelings they are. Notice, without getting hooked, the judgments you have of yourself. See how you condemn yourself. If you notice feeling guiltier for judging yourself, notice that too, without getting carried away by it. Just notice. You're doing great.

Now, name those feelings and those judgments. It helps to write them down as you see them. That way the ego cannot get carried away with its story. Capture the thoughts and judgments on paper. It's like pinning them down so they can't move you with them anymore. Now, just notice the thoughts written on the paper. Notice that they are just words, appearing now, in the present moment, on paper.

I invite you to close your eyes again and meditate on the fourth question on Worksheet 2, "Who would you be, without the thought, *I shouldn't have done/said that to my child?*" This is not about saying you should be violent to your child. Not at all. The mind would have us think that if we don't keep the thought, then we will be violent toward our child again. Believing those thoughts kept me from a solid connection with my child for *four* years. So, please, don't believe your mind if it tells you that. You don't have to suffer that long. It is 100% within your control to end the suffering completely, right now, in this moment while doing self-inquiry. It is a miracle. That miracle is possible for you.

Notice any fear you experience, when you ask yourself this question, "Who would you be without the thought, *I shouldn't have done/said that to my child?*" If you see fear first, it is only the illusory ego wanting to hold on so tight to an illusion of control. Be with that fear as you always wish to be with your child when she feels scared. Welcome that fear, notice it, and pay attention to it. Just in the witnessing, it will lose some of its power. Write the fears down and do self-inquiry on them later.

I invite you to meditate on question four until a peaceful answer arises from within you. "Who would you be without the thought, *I shouldn't have done/said that to my child*"?

When I patiently waited for the peaceful answer to bubble up in me, I saw that I would have so much compassion for myself. I would realize I don't know how to do this mothering thing sometimes. I would realize that I believed my stressful thought, "*He has to get into his car seat or we'll be mugged.*" Since I would realize that, I would realize that I was doing the best that I could when I slapped his leg to get his attention to quickly strap him into his car seat. How could I have done otherwise when I believed this stressful thought? I would be aware of a deep understanding of my situation. I would see that I was totally petrified right before I slapped his leg. I would be aware that the complete terror I felt right before I slapped him was an old fearful thought pattern that I first believed a very long time ago, when I was a young girl. I would realize that when I was young, I thought I *had* to protect myself from a frightening situation where I thought I would be attacked. I had no other choice because I believed my stressful thoughts then too.

In realizing all of this, I found my innocence. This thought pattern got created to protect myself from what I thought was going to be a dangerous situation a long, long time ago. I saw how it had repeated itself over and over again in my life, while I still believed it. Self-love entered at that point, and so did total understanding for myself, and so did total compassion and love for myself, for my life, and for my situation. This was a new kind of love for me, one I had not experienced before. It felt so new, so kind, and so eternal.

~

On your own, I invite you to reconstruct the thought, "*I shouldn't have done/said that to him/her,*" to a thought directed inward and a thought that's the exact opposite. When reconstructing the thought by exchanging your child's name with yours, do it a little differently this time. Use your "thoughts" instead of your child's name. So, it would read, "*My thoughts shouldn't have done/said that to me.*" If it fits for you, an example of why that might be true would be: because when they do, and I forget to question them, I feel so much guilt, and that contributes to me perpetuating the violence in me that I'm trying to stop. Continue to find at least three specific, genuine examples of why the reconstructed thoughts are true for you in your specific situation.

When doing your own self-inquiry, pay special attention to what you notice in yourself as you answer the first two questions on Worksheet 2: *Is it true, and can you absolutely know that it's true?* It's very important to know that these are not *moral* questions. Is it true that I shouldn't have hit my child? Morally, my answer was "yes!" *Never* should I hit my child. Yet, that, in reality is what happened. Herein lies the core of the self-judgment - and the pain. When I did self-inquiry on this one, I judged that self-inquiry wanted me to say "no" to this question so I could open my mind. This scared me. I judged falsely that self-inquiry would validate that it was okay to hit my child. Then, I got into an argument in my mind *with* self-inquiry itself. I said to myself, "I can't answer 'no' because that would mean it's okay to hit your child." To me, it was never okay to do that. Since I *had* done that - unintentionally, as a reaction to intense fear - I condemned myself. Do you see where my conundrum was?

So I condemned myself, condemned self-inquiry and left self-inquiry for those *four* years. But really, I left me and I left my child for those four years, lost in my depression about my behavior. I was so hard on myself. My sadness and guilt over what I had done sent me spiraling down, into a dark, dark place. I only came "out" when I summoned my courage and trust to go to the next step in my self-inquiry. I realized that the dark, dark place was - in reality - an illusion that kept me from myself and my child. In reality, I was projecting my judgments about myself and about violence toward children on to self-inquiry.

So, please know that the first two questions of self-inquiry are not in any way related to judgments about you *at all*. The beauty of love springs forth where there is a *lack* of judgment, in the field beyond all rightdoing and all wrongdoing, as Rumi calls it. If you're judging self-inquiry (which is really your projection of your judgment of *yourself*) when you are answering those questions, write the judgments down on another piece of paper and continue with the next question in your self-inquiry. You can do self-inquiry on those other judgments at another time.

~

The next thought I questioned was, *"He has to get into his car seat or we'll be mugged."* First, I questioned, *"He has to get into his car seat."* Then, I questioned, *"We'll be mugged."* I did this in two separate self-inquiry processes so that the mind could handle it. It has to work with thoughts that are very simple and very short in order to keep it focused.

You may discover an underlying stressful thought about your child or your situation after you complete your self-inquiry process on, *"I shouldn't have done that."* When you do see your underlying stressful thought about your child, take that thought all the way through Worksheet 2. The wonderful turning point with me was when I answered the question, "How do I react when I think that thought, *He has to get into his car seat?*" I went right into my feeling of wanting to control and of feeling all-powerful exerting that control, in order to avoid the terror of another thought, *"We'll be mugged."* (Do you see the progressive layers of formerly unconscious stressful thoughts?) I started shaking at that point, feeling dizzy, and even feeling like I wasn't on the ground. I realized that these physical sensations experienced during self-inquiry were my body's way of releasing so much of the fear I carried around for so long!

~

Next, I questioned the thought, *"We'll be mugged."* Through self-inquiry, I saw how false this was. I saw so clearly how believing a thought that wasn't true is what started the entire situation. The message I want you to get is to go deep, keep uncovering the stressful root thought behind any "violent" - by your definition - reactions toward your child. You will release everything when you do.

Each time we do self-inquiry on our stressful thoughts, a new layer of understanding emerges. Also, new stressful thoughts emerge that were unconscious previously. It is literally like peeling away the old, dead skin of an onion each time we inquire, revealing truth. Finally, you create so many new neural pathways in your mind that are completely congruent with the *truth*, that you magically are "more" present.

I love that I trusted the process enough to completely end any form of violence toward my children and toward myself. I love that I get to share that experience with you now. I love that you and I can end violence in ourselves and with our children, forever, with self-inquiry. The divine in me acknowledges and honors the divine in you.

Wishing you, dear one, Peace and Presence today,
Catherine

Presence Practice Notes

Ending the Cycle of Violence

Self-Inquiry Worksheet 1 of 2

We've been told all of our lives not to judge others. The fact is we do it anyway. This worksheet allows the mind to see itself, to see the reality of its own thoughts, and to truly consider the thoughts by putting them on paper. This is the time to let those judgments have their own life.

DIRECTIONS:

A. Think of a specific person that is triggering stress in you. It could be your child, partner, ex-partner, mom, or dad. (Not yourself) They could be living or not living.

B. Now, recall a specific stressful situation you had with that person. It might have been a face to face interaction, an event, a phone call, or any situation that caused you any feelings of discomfort. Identify the specific stressful situation, and see it as a *single snapshot* in time.

C. Witness that single snapshot. Notice the time, place, words spoken, body language, and energy of each person. Then, 1) Identify and name the primary uncomfortable feeling you were having, 2) identify why you felt that way, and 3) answer the questions below with *short, simple* statements. *Please do not* try to be psychologically correct, spiritual, or wise now. For the purposes of this worksheet, be as judgmental as you were when you were in that situation.

1. In this situation, who angers, confuses, saddens, or disappoints you, and why? *(Example: I'm frustrated with Aiden because he won't listen to me.)*

2. In this situation, how do you want them to change? *(Example: I want Aiden to stop what he's doing, look at me, and listen to me.)*

3. In this situation, what advice would you offer to them? *(Example: Aiden should learn how to listen.)*

4. In order for you to feel better in this situation, what do you need them to think, say, feel, or do? *(Example: I need Aiden to listen.)*

5. What do you think of them in this situation? Make a list. Be petty. *(Example: Aiden is just like his dad - he won't respect me.)*

6. What is it in or about this situation that you don't ever want to experience again? *(Example: I don't ever want to be disrespected by Aiden again.)*

Review what you wrote. Pick one sentence you wrote that feels the most stressful to you right now. Circle it. Rewrite it at the top of Worksheet 2.

Adapted from Byron Katie International, Inc. Rev. 7/2014, with consent.

Self-Inquiry Worksheet 2 of 2

This worksheet is a meditation. When answering the questions, close your eyes, be still, and patiently wait to witness what appears to you. Always give yourself time to let the deeper answers meet the questions.

DIRECTIONS:

A. In the space below, write the thought you circled from Worksheet 1. Then answer questions 1-4.

B. Reconstruct the thought in three new ways. Possibilities are: by directing it inward (number 5 below), exchanging the other person's name with yours (number 6 below), and stating its exact opposite (number 7 below). Examples are provided below. Then, find and record three genuine, specific examples of how each new thought is as true or truer for you in that situation.

C. If you circled the thought from your answer to question 6 on Worksheet 1, you would reconstruct the thought by replacing the words, "I don't ever want to..." with "I am willing to..." and "I look forward to..."

Re-write the thought you circled on Worksheet 1: *(Example: Aiden doesn't listen to me.)*

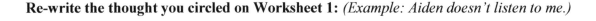

1. In that situation, is this thought true? *(Yes or no only. There are no right or wrong answers. If no, skip to question 3.)*

2. In that situation, can you absolutely know that it's true? *(Yes or no only)*

3. In that situation, how did you *react* when you believed that thought?

4. In that situation, who would you be if you could not believe that thought?

5. Reconstruct the thought by directing it *inward. (Example: I don't listen to me.)* Find and record three genuine, specific examples in that situation how this new thought is as true or truer than the original thought.

6. Reconstruct the thought by *exchanging* the other person's name with yours. *(Example: I don't listen to Aiden.)* Find and record three genuine, specific examples of how this new thought is as true or truer for you in that situation.

7. Reconstruct the thought by stating the *exact opposite. (Example: Aiden does listen to me.)* Find and record three genuine, specific examples of how this new thought is as true or truer for you in that situation.

Adapted from Byron Katie International, Inc. Rev. 7/2014, with consent.

Welcome to Morning 17 - *Peace Requires Only One Person*

(I invite you to first re-read the Morning Meditation on page 16.)

Dear Present Mother,

From experience, I know that peace between my child and I only requires peace within me, not both of us. I find that so comforting. When I question thoughts that appear in my mind that are not peaceful, I end up with peace in my mind. That peace gets projected out into my mothering life with my every thought, word, and deed. After self-inquiry, there is just no way that I or my children ever have to suffer again. It is 100% optional when we practice self-inquiry. There is always the possibility of peace and presence because we always have the option to question our stressful thoughts with self-inquiry.

Now that self-inquiry is my way of life, I can transcend any "negative" emotion into presence very quickly and easily. With practice it's possible for you too. Since your children are your mirrors, they transcend their "negative" emotions after you do. They are quicker learners than we are! As soon as I recognize a stressful thought, or start to defend myself, and I experience any feelings I have that are forms of defensiveness, sadness, depression, impatience, frustration, overwhelm, anxiety, or any state that I would call not peaceful, then that is my reminder to walk through the inquiry door. That door leads to peace and love and presence 100% of the time.

I love knowing that peace does not require two people. I used to think it did, which was great since it gave me a *lot* of thoughts to question. All of my strategies to try to create peace inevitably created thoughts like, *"My kids should make an agreement with me"* (reconstructed to "I should make an agreement with me.") *"My husband should want to work this out with me,"* (reconstructed to, "I should want to work this out with me.") *"If he would just listen to me we could work this out"* (reconstructed to "If I would just listen to me, we could work this out") etc., etc. I love that self-inquiry taught me that this was material to find peace within myself.

If I am peaceful and present, it can't help but be projected out "there." I hope you get to experience that too, as you continue your practice of filling in the worksheets and becoming aware of the positive changes in your life.

When I practice self-inquiry, my husband and I don't argue or raise our voices with each other. There is harmony and peace in our home, not because he changes, but because I do self-inquiry and then my thoughts *about* him change. I am still as committed as ever to my values, how I live my life, what I hold dear; I just don't force those on to him. I notice that he copies more of my values now than he used to whenever I would get mad at him for *not* valuing what I did. I notice that because I also see *me* copying what I say is valuable. In other words, I see me being true to myself, without expecting him to agree with me or do what I say or do. I love how peace only requires one person.

~

The results of self-inquiry will manifest itself in a way that is true for *you*. Your daily conversations and interactions with your child and your partner will look different than mine. What you will have in common with me is that you will begin to witness more kindness and love in your home when you do self-inquiry. So I invite you to notice if you see yourself comparing your mothering to mine or to anyone's or trying to reduce your fear of diving into self-inquiry by seeing what I or others have done. Notice how thoughts like this take you out of the present moment with your child, and how they disconnect you from yourself. Notice how peace is gone when you believe these thoughts. Remember, when you notice this happening, you can always create peace within yourself again by picking up a pen, filling in the worksheets, and doing self-inquiry on those thoughts. I invite you to love yourself right where you are in your mothering journey, and, in that, you are modeling peace and love for your precious child, right where they are.

If you find it hard to love yourself right where you are, I invite you to identify a situation where you found it hard to love yourself, write down your stressful thoughts about it and question it. There is always a place to start with self-inquiry: it's where you feel something other than peace. That's your doorway. I love that you would be the one to walk through the peace door and be the change you wish to see in the world.

Wishing you, dear one, Peace and Presence today,
Catherine

Presence Practice Notes

Peace Requires Only One Person

Self-Inquiry Worksheet 1 of 2

We've been told all of our lives not to judge others. The fact is we do it anyway. This worksheet allows the mind to see itself, to see the reality of its own thoughts, and to truly consider the thoughts by putting them on paper. This is the time to let those judgments have their own life.

DIRECTIONS:

A. Think of a specific person that is triggering stress in you. It could be your child, partner, ex-partner, mom, or dad. (Not yourself) They could be living or not living.

B. Now, recall a specific stressful situation you had with that person. It might have been a face to face interaction, an event, a phone call, or any situation that caused you any feelings of discomfort. Identify the specific stressful situation, and see it as a *single snapshot* in time.

C. Witness that single snapshot. Notice the time, place, words spoken, body language, and energy of each person. Then, 1) Identify and name the primary uncomfortable feeling you were having, 2) identify why you felt that way, and 3) answer the questions below with *short, simple* statements. *Please do not* try to be psychologically correct, spiritual, or wise now. For the purposes of this worksheet, be as judgmental as you were when you were in that situation.

1. In this situation, who angers, confuses, saddens, or disappoints you, and why? *(Example: I'm frustrated with Aiden because he won't listen to me.)*

2. In this situation, how do you want them to change? *(Example: I want Aiden to stop what he's doing, look at me, and listen to me.)*

3. In this situation, what advice would you offer to them? *(Example: Aiden should learn how to listen.)*

4. In order for you to feel better in this situation, what do you need them to think, say, feel, or do? *(Example: I need Aiden to listen.)*

5. What do you think of them in this situation? Make a list. Be petty. *(Example: Aiden is just like his dad - he won't respect me.)*

6. What is it in or about this situation that you don't ever want to experience again? *(Example: I don't ever want to be disrespected by Aiden again.)*

Review what you wrote. Pick one sentence you wrote that feels the most stressful to you right now. Circle it. Rewrite it at the top of Worksheet 2.

Adapted from Byron Katie International, Inc. Rev. 7/2014, with consent.

Self-Inquiry Worksheet 2 of 2

This worksheet is a meditation. When answering the questions, close your eyes, be still, and patiently wait to witness what appears to you. Always give yourself time to let the deeper answers meet the questions.

DIRECTIONS:

A. In the space below, write the thought you circled from Worksheet 1. Then answer questions 1-4.

B. Reconstruct the thought in three new ways. Possibilities are: by directing it inward (number 5 below), exchanging the other person's name with yours (number 6 below), and stating its exact opposite (number 7 below). Examples are provided below. Then, find and record three genuine, specific examples of how each new thought is as true or truer for you in that situation.

C. If you circled the thought from your answer to question 6 on Worksheet 1, you would reconstruct the thought by replacing the words, "I don't ever want to…" with "I am willing to…" and "I look forward to…"

Re-write the thought you circled on Worksheet 1: *(Example: Aiden doesn't listen to me.)*

_____

_____

1. In that situation, is this thought true? *(Yes or no only. There are no right or wrong answers. If no, skip to question 3.)*

2. In that situation, can you absolutely know that it's true? *(Yes or no only)*

3. In that situation, how did you *react* when you believed that thought?

4. In that situation, who would you be if you could not believe that thought?

5. Reconstruct the thought by directing it *inward. (Example: I don't listen to me.)* Find and record three genuine, specific examples in that situation how this new thought is as true or truer than the original thought.

6. Reconstruct the thought by *exchanging* the other person's name with yours. *(Example: I don't listen to Aiden.)* Find and record three genuine, specific examples of how this new thought is as true or truer for you in that situation.

7. Reconstruct the thought by stating the *exact opposite. (Example: Aiden does listen to me.)* Find and record three genuine, specific examples of how this new thought is as true or truer for you in that situation.

Adapted from Byron Katie International, Inc. Rev. 7/2014, with consent.

Welcome to Morning 18 - *Projecting Our Needs*

(I invite you to first re-read the Morning Meditation on page 16.)

Dear Present Mother,

Before self-inquiry was in my life, I didn't know how to love my family without conditions. I thought I did. I proudly believed I did. In reality, however, I didn't actually know how to love unconditionally when I was triggered by the behavior of one of my children or my husband. I didn't want my children to see me being triggered. I did not want to pass on unhealthy ways of reacting. I wanted the best for them. I wanted a mommy for them that was calm and peaceful, loving and warmly responsive. I didn't want to get triggered any more. I wanted a way to peacefully transcend all those stressful thoughts, quickly, if I ever did get triggered again. I found that in self-inquiry.

Yesterday, I experienced a depth of awareness that I've never experienced before. I experienced directly that my family is a projected image of my thinking. They are my story of them; nothing else is possible. Before yesterday, I had known that as a piece of information, not as an experience. Here's what happened.

I was doing self-inquiry on the thought "*He needs to calm down.*" What I clearly and deeply experienced, for the very first time, was that there is no possible way that I can ever know for sure what my son or daughter needs. Ever. I can only know what *I* need because I am always only looking through the lens of my *own* mind. I think I do know what they need sometimes, and when they agree with me, then it's the truth. When they don't agree with me, it's not my reality, and therefore isn't the truth. I realized that sometimes I don't even know what *I* need. When I think I need him to calm down, and he doesn't, then I obviously don't need it because it isn't my reality at that time. If I honestly believe that I don't need him to calm down even when he's very upset, then because I'm a very calm mother for him I can respond to him with love. If I honestly believe I do need him to calm down when he's not, then I'm confused and not a very happy person and I treat him with conditional love unintentionally. This isn't about not responding to your child if

124

he's upset, nor is it about causing a huge disruption in public; on the contrary, this is about responding to your child with unconditional love, without a thought that he should be any other way than the way he's being at that moment. I notice that when I'm calm, he seems to calm down much faster than when I'm not. I can't "do" calm parenting though. I have to question the thought in my mind that causes stress in me: *"He needs to calm down."*

I cannot get into my child's mind. I can't help but project the thoughts in my own mind on to my child. There is just no other way. When I saw that, so clearly and so deeply.... I began to laugh hysterically! I had made a huge discovery and seen right through the magic trick: the illusion of the ego. It was so funny to me!

A new neural pathway, based in conscious awareness, had formed in my brain. I was aware of awareness itself. That stressful thought I'd had now transcended itself into my own realization of my own awareness. I was pure awareness. I was pure presence, aware of the awareness itself.

Then, I completely saw how my children are the beloved in disguise. Our children are there to help us evolve into kinder, gentler human beings. There is no separation or disconnection, ever, between us. The disconnection is all an illusion. When I (you) see through that illusion, we are unconditional love itself, so free, and so happy, like I was. (See how I projected my own experience on to you!)

I am eternally grateful to my children, for being in my life and for showing me where I am not done with my self-inquiry yet. I love that they assist me with my goal of loving all of me and all of them, unconditionally. I am eternally grateful for self-inquiry being so alive in my life. I am eternally grateful for me being willing and committed to practicing it, every day. You, friend, are a blessing to me in my life. I cherish your presence every morning as I write this letter to you.

If you're completing your self-inquiry worksheets on your stressful thoughts every morning, I just love that for you. If you're not completing them, I love that for you too. Either way, you're doing what's perfect for you. Keep noticing any thought that would keep you from your own freedom. Keep questioning it. You'll be so glad you did.

Wishing you, dear one, Peace and Presence today,
Catherine

Presence Practice Notes

Projecting Our Needs

Self-Inquiry Worksheet 1 of 2

We've been told all of our lives not to judge others. The fact is we do it anyway. This worksheet allows the mind to see itself, to see the reality of its own thoughts, and to truly consider the thoughts by putting them on paper. This is the time to let those judgments have their own life.

DIRECTIONS:

A. Think of a specific person that is triggering stress in you. It could be your child, partner, ex-partner, mom, or dad. (Not yourself) They could be living or not living.

B. Now, recall a specific stressful situation you had with that person. It might have been a face to face interaction, an event, a phone call, or any situation that caused you any feelings of discomfort. Identify the specific stressful situation, and see it as a *single snapshot* in time.

C. Witness that single snapshot. Notice the time, place, words spoken, body language, and energy of each person. Then, 1) Identify and name the primary uncomfortable feeling you were having, 2) identify why you felt that way, and 3) answer the questions below with *short, simple* statements. *Please do not* try to be psychologically correct, spiritual, or wise now. For the purposes of this worksheet, be as judgmental as you were when you were in that situation.

1. In this situation, who angers, confuses, saddens, or disappoints you, and why? *(Example: I'm frustrated with Aiden because he won't listen to me.)*

2. In this situation, how do you want them to change? *(Example: I want Aiden to stop what he's doing, look at me, and listen to me.)*

3. In this situation, what advice would you offer to them? *(Example: Aiden should learn how to listen.)*

4. In order for you to feel better in this situation, what do you need them to think, say, feel, or do? *(Example: I need Aiden to listen.)*

5. What do you think of them in this situation? Make a list. Be petty. *(Example: Aiden is just like his dad - he won't respect me.)*

6. What is it in or about this situation that you don't ever want to experience again? *(Example: I don't ever want to be disrespected by Aiden again.)*

Review what you wrote. Pick one sentence you wrote that feels the most stressful to you right now. Circle it. Rewrite it at the top of Worksheet 2.

Adapted from Byron Katie International, Inc. Rev. 7/2014, with consent.

Self-Inquiry Worksheet 2 of 2

This worksheet is a meditation. When answering the questions, close your eyes, be still, and patiently wait to witness what appears to you. Always give yourself time to let the deeper answers meet the questions.

DIRECTIONS:
A. In the space below, write the thought you circled from Worksheet 1. Then answer questions 1-4.
B. Reconstruct the thought in three new ways. Possibilities are: by directing it inward (number 5 below), exchanging the other person's name with yours (number 6 below), and stating its exact opposite (number 7 below). Examples are provided below. Then, find and record three genuine, specific examples of how each new thought is as true or truer for you in that situation.
C. If you circled the thought from your answer to question 6 on Worksheet 1, you would reconstruct the thought by replacing the words, "I don't ever want to…" with "I am willing to…" and "I look forward to…"

Re-write the thought you circled on Worksheet 1: *(Example: Aiden doesn't listen to me.)*

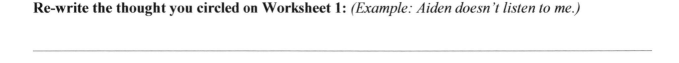

1. In that situation, is this thought true? *(Yes or no only. There are no right or wrong answers. If no, skip to question 3.)*

2. In that situation, can you absolutely know that it's true? *(Yes or no only)*

3. In that situation, how did you *react* when you believed that thought?

4. In that situation, who would you be if you could not believe that thought?

5. Reconstruct the thought by directing it *inward. (Example: I don't listen to me.)* Find and record three genuine, specific examples in that situation how this new thought is as true or truer than the original thought.

6. Reconstruct the thought by *exchanging* the other person's name with yours. *(Example: I don't listen to Aiden.)* Find and record three genuine, specific examples of how this new thought is as true or truer for you in that situation.

7. Reconstruct the thought by stating the *exact opposite. (Example: Aiden does listen to me.)* Find and record three genuine, specific examples of how this new thought is as true or truer for you in that situation.

Adapted from Byron Katie International, Inc. Rev. 7/2014, with consent.

Welcome to Morning 19 - *Our Mothers*

(I invite you to first re-read the Morning Meditation on page 16.)

Dear Present Mother,

I'm so in love with my mother. Her birthday is next week. As a tribute to her and to all mothers, whether yours is living or deceased, I'm inspired to write and inquire about our thoughts about our own mothers today.

Questioning my stress-inducing thoughts about my children was always so freeing. When I started questioning thoughts about my mother though, oh my goodness, there was so much peace and connection to be found in so many areas of my life! It was amazing. I have a *lot* of experiences doing self-inquiry on stressful thoughts about my mother. They all got reconstructed and turned into truer thoughts in the process. She didn't change; my thoughts about her did. That's why I'm so in love with her now. Remember, it's all your story. *No matter* what things you think your mother has done that you would call "horrible" - even if it was what you would call "physical abuse" - or what love you think she has not given you, with your self-inquiry practice you have the opportunity to find your own freedom from believing stressful thoughts about her and unintentionally continuing to recreate your own suffering. You have your own ticket to being present with your beautiful mother and your beautiful child. As long as you have leftover anger toward your mother, or anyone for that matter, you will unconsciously project that anger onto your child and everyone in your life. Now you have another way though. You can use inquiry to question the stressful thoughts you notice about your mother. I invite you to join me today as we transcend our stressful thoughts and memories about our mothers, even if they're deceased, and find the mother we've always been looking for, within ourselves.

Before self-inquiry, I spent almost *two decades* complaining - to myself and others - about my mother and the way she raised me to anyone that would listen. I spent countless hours writing my feelings in countless journals about how angry I was with her that she had treated me the way she did and lived her life the way she had. I had gotten in many arguments with her in my mind and in real life. I thought that was just the way it had to be. I just had to deal with it, try to ignore what I didn't like, and try to love her the best that I could. I did love her, I just didn't like her as a mother, or so I thought. In reality, what I learned was that I didn't like my *thoughts* about her.

For example, one of my biggest stressful thoughts about my mother was, *"She should support me."* (For you, maybe the thought, "She *should have supported* me" has more of a hold on you.) The support *I* am referring to is for her to treat my children the same way that I always try to treat them. I wanted her to care for them with respect and trust. I didn't want her to be condescending or patronizing to them. I wanted her to be with them without using old parenting ideas about how to talk to children and treat children. When I believed these thoughts, and she would not support me, I treated her the exact way that I didn't want her to treat the kids… patronizingly, condescendingly – a mirror image of my thinking.

Who I was without this thought was *respectful and trusting of her* - sound familiar? When I reconstructed the thought to *She should **not** support me, **I** should support her,* and *I should support me,* I found examples of how those thoughts were so much truer, in reality. They were also thoughts that gave me my power back. Suddenly, I found compassion for her, and love for her. I started to support myself by having her visit the kids only - or mostly - when I was around, and trusting that the kids would decide how much time they wanted to spend with her after that, and not forcing them to be alone together for a long time while I was gone. I was staying in my own business and supporting myself. I had solved my own "problem" and didn't try and force anyone to do anything they didn't want to do. I stayed connected to myself, my mom, and the kids the whole time. Lovely.

My self-inquiry process on thoughts about my mother lasted for about six months. Like the example above, I would experience glimpses of love and connection after doing self-inquiry, then another stressful thought about her would come to my awareness again. As I began to regularly do self-inquiry on those thoughts about my mother, all of my stories about her slowly began to unravel, slight shifts would take place, she would say or do things and I slowly stopped getting triggered by things that used to upset me. I couldn't believe I had found my way out of years of wishing she had done things differently, years of wishing she would change, years of anguish. My reality then was total happiness when I would talk with her, total freedom, freedom from the thoughts that had caused all of my past suffering. I was free - free to love my mother. In that, I was free to love myself and my children.

Today, I invite you to taste what it's like to be your own nurturing, supportive mother to yourself. Now that you have self-inquiry in your life, and you know you don't have to suffer any more, what is a stressful thought you have about your mother right now? If she is deceased, we still carry around stressful thoughts about her. We're really dealing with thoughts *about* our mother and not our actual mother anyway. You can start with anything. *She shouldn't be so crabby. I need her and she isn't here. She doesn't understand. She shouldn't have divorced dad. She is so judgmental. She should be kinder to the kids.* Whatever it is, I invite you to write it down. How do you treat her when you believe this thought? Who would you be, in the presence of your mother, if you didn't believe this thought? What are the newly reconstructed thoughts that are as true or truer, and three examples of each? I love inviting you to question those stressful thoughts on your mind about your mother. I love that you have the possibility of stepping into the fullness of your mothering power.

If questioning thoughts about your deceased mother brings up very strong memories and emotions, I invite you to do self-inquiry with a partner, or to be the volunteer who is facilitated on our weekly call, or to seek professional help. There is always someone to support you. All you have to do is ask.

~

How are you doing with your presence practice? I want to make sure you are supported as much as you would like. I remember starting out in my practice. My mind used to come up with all sorts of stressful thoughts about why I didn't need to do self-inquiry. Sometimes I just felt so exhausted looking at all the judgments and beliefs that caused stress, exhausted doing the process, and I just didn't want to be the one to have to do it anymore. It was almost like making myself go and exercise. I knew it was great for my health, yet my mind would come up with all sorts of reasons not to go. After I questioned those thoughts, exercising, or doing self-inquiry, seemed like just another activity I did in my day. I hope you are able to peacefully do your self-inquiry. I hope you are able to realize more and more your deep connection with yourself, and in perfect reflection, your child. I love that we have a way to give ourselves our own mothering now. What a complete joy.

Wishing you, dear one, Peace and Presence today,
Catherine

Presence Practice Notes

Our Mothers

Self-Inquiry Worksheet 1 of 2

We've been told all of our lives not to judge others. The fact is we do it anyway. This worksheet allows the mind to see itself, to see the reality of its own thoughts, and to truly consider the thoughts by putting them on paper. This is the time to let those judgments have their own life.

DIRECTIONS:

A. Think of a specific person that is triggering stress in you. It could be your child, partner, ex-partner, mom, or dad. (Not yourself) They could be living or not living.

B. Now, recall a specific stressful situation you had with that person. It might have been a face to face interaction, an event, a phone call, or any situation that caused you any feelings of discomfort. Identify the specific stressful situation, and see it as a *single snapshot* in time.

C. Witness that single snapshot. Notice the time, place, words spoken, body language, and energy of each person. Then, 1) Identify and name the primary uncomfortable feeling you were having, 2) identify why you felt that way, and 3) answer the questions below with *short, simple* statements. *Please do not* try to be psychologically correct, spiritual, or wise now. For the purposes of this worksheet, be as judgmental as you were when you were in that situation.

1. In this situation, who angers, confuses, saddens, or disappoints you, and why? *(Example: I'm frustrated with Aiden because he won't listen to me.)*

2. In this situation, how do you want them to change? *(Example: I want Aiden to stop what he's doing, look at me, and listen to me.)*

3. In this situation, what advice would you offer to them? *(Example: Aiden should learn how to listen.)*

4. In order for you to feel better in this situation, what do you need them to think, say, feel, or do? *(Example: I need Aiden to listen.)*

5. What do you think of them in this situation? Make a list. Be petty. *(Example: Aiden is just like his dad - he won't respect me.)*

6. What is it in or about this situation that you don't ever want to experience again? *(Example: I don't ever want to be disrespected by Aiden again.)*

Review what you wrote. Pick one sentence you wrote that feels the most stressful to you right now. Circle it. Rewrite it at the top of Worksheet 2.

Adapted from Byron Katie International, Inc. Rev. 7/2014, with consent.

Self-Inquiry Worksheet 2 of 2

This worksheet is a meditation. When answering the questions, close your eyes, be still, and patiently wait to witness what appears to you. Always give yourself time to let the deeper answers meet the questions.

DIRECTIONS:

A. In the space below, write the thought you circled from Worksheet 1. Then answer questions 1-4.

B. Reconstruct the thought in three new ways. Possibilities are: by directing it inward (number 5 below), exchanging the other person's name with yours (number 6 below), and stating its exact opposite (number 7 below). Examples are provided below. Then, find and record three genuine, specific examples of how each new thought is as true or truer for you in that situation.

C. If you circled the thought from your answer to question 6 on Worksheet 1, you would reconstruct the thought by replacing the words, "I don't ever want to…" with "I am willing to…" and "I look forward to…"

Re-write the thought you circled on Worksheet 1: *(Example: Aiden doesn't listen to me.)*

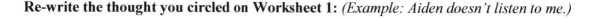

1. In that situation, is this thought true? *(Yes or no only. There are no right or wrong answers. If no, skip to question 3.)*

2. In that situation, can you absolutely know that it's true? *(Yes or no only)*

3. In that situation, how did you *react* when you believed that thought?

4. In that situation, who would you be if you could not believe that thought?

5. Reconstruct the thought by directing it *inward. (Example: I don't listen to me.)* Find and record three genuine, specific examples in that situation how this new thought is as true or truer than the original thought.

6. Reconstruct the thought by *exchanging* the other person's name with yours. *(Example: I don't listen to Aiden.)* Find and record three genuine, specific examples of how this new thought is as true or truer for you in that situation.

7. Reconstruct the thought by stating the *exact opposite. (Example: Aiden does listen to me.)* Find and record three genuine, specific examples of how this new thought is as true or truer for you in that situation.

Adapted from Byron Katie International, Inc. Rev. 7/2014, with consent.

Welcome to Morning 20 - *Self-Love*

(I invite you to first re-read the Morning Meditation on page 16.)

Dear Present Mother,

After practicing self-inquiry regularly for a while, I started to love that I would get triggered by thoughts about my mother. In that, I was starting to love all of me. I was realizing that everything about me was love, including the stressful thoughts. Love was who I was. Love is who I am. Love is who you are too. Love is who your child is. Love is who your mother is. There is really no such thing as self-love because love is the very *essence* of who you are. It's more like: *be* love. Be your true self.

One of the new thoughts you can create in self-inquiry, using the opposite perspective is, "I look forward to................" and fill in the stressful thought about your mother. So, for example, if there was a specific situation with my mother where I thought "*My mother should let me know how much she loves me,*" it got reconstructed to, "I look *forward* to thinking that my mother should let me know how much she loves me." Then I'd find three specific, genuine examples of how this new thought was true for me. Every time, I would say, "because I get to do self-inquiry on it and become more and more clear, loving, connected and present."

If the thought was, "*My mom shouldn't have done that to me,*" it got reconstructed to, "I shouldn't have done that to me." Then, I would find three specific, genuine examples of how I shouldn't have done something to me, in that situation. One of my examples was usually, "I shouldn't have replayed the old movie over and over and over again about how she shouldn't have done that to me." That wasn't helpful for me to do to myself. Then, I would see my own humanity right along with it. We can't stop the old movies unless we realize for ourselves that they are there and then do self-inquiry on the thought that causes the old movies. Right when I would see that, and do self-inquiry, they stopped, all on their own. There was no other possibility for them to live in me again after I saw them and questioned them. Awareness was born again. Not living in the past was born again. Living in the present was born again.

Every time we unravel our knotted-up thought patterns in self-inquiry, we release the brain's connection between thoughts of past or future and the present moment. We begin to see that thoughts of past or future live in our minds most all of the time unless we catch them and question them. Right when we see that they are there and we question them, the present moment is born again in us. It's like a curtain to a stage opens up and we see the beautiful, shining present moment, and we see our child, exactly as they are, without stories about past or future. Our minds are no longer clouded by our unawareness that we are attaching to stressful thoughts about the past projected into the future. Then, our feelings, speech, and behavior are no longer clouded by that either. When we put those thoughts on paper and do self-inquiry, they can no longer provoke a reaction in us because they've been *discovered*. In the seeing of them, they disappear all on their own. You've rewired your brain in the process. New neural connections are created. I find it absolutely amazing.

I love how the brain works. What an incredible machine. My son is very into science and computer programming. He reads and does all sorts of things that have exposed me more and more to this amazing organism called our brain. As I mentioned earlier, it is capable, scientists have recently learned, of rewiring itself all the way up until we die. We can, on our own, do self-inquiry on any belief that we see as unhelpful to us now. When we do, that belief can be *used* to completely transform us into the present moment, grounded in complete Love. Self-awareness, just in the noticing, has the power to transform stressful beliefs we've identified with since we were babies. We can no longer pass on these stressful thoughts to our kids. How freeing for us! How freeing for them!

I love that our children have the possibility to experience life with a mother who is aware of her stressful thoughts. I love that their mother has a quick, simple, effective tool to transcend them into her presence, and deepen her connection to them. How wonderful.

As of today, you are halfway through the 40-day presence practice. You are doing an amazing thing, questioning your stressful thoughts about your mother, deepening your connection to yourself, the present moment, and your child. It is no small task. It is a *life's* work. I invite you to remind yourself how far you've come, and how much more aware you are at this moment than before you picked up this book. Even though you're remembering the "past" when you do this, it helps to reinforce these realizations in the present moment, and helps you create a "future" full of more of that. I honor you and your commitment to being present, and your commitment to deepening your connection with your child.

Wishing you, dear one, Peace and Presence today,
Catherine

Presence Practice Notes

Self-Love

Self-Inquiry Worksheet 1 of 2

We've been told all of our lives not to judge others. The fact is we do it anyway. This worksheet allows the mind to see itself, to see the reality of its own thoughts, and to truly consider the thoughts by putting them on paper. This is the time to let those judgments have their own life.

DIRECTIONS:
A. Think of a specific person that is triggering stress in you. It could be your child, partner, ex-partner, mom, or dad. (Not yourself) They could be living or not living.
B. Now, recall a specific stressful situation you had with that person. It might have been a face to face interaction, an event, a phone call, or any situation that caused you any feelings of discomfort. Identify the specific stressful situation, and see it as a *single snapshot* in time.
C. Witness that single snapshot. Notice the time, place, words spoken, body language, and energy of each person. Then, 1) Identify and name the primary uncomfortable feeling you were having, 2) identify why you felt that way, and 3) answer the questions below with *short, simple* statements. *Please do not* try to be psychologically correct, spiritual, or wise now. For the purposes of this worksheet, be as judgmental as you were when you were in that situation.

1. In this situation, who angers, confuses, saddens, or disappoints you, and why? *(Example: I'm frustrated with Aiden because he won't listen to me.)*

2. In this situation, how do you want them to change? *(Example: I want Aiden to stop what he's doing, look at me, and listen to me.)*

3. In this situation, what advice would you offer to them? *(Example: Aiden should learn how to listen.)*

4. In order for you to feel better in this situation, what do you need them to think, say, feel, or do? *(Example: I need Aiden to listen.)*

5. What do you think of them in this situation? Make a list. Be petty. *(Example: Aiden is just like his dad - he won't respect me.)*

6. What is it in or about this situation that you don't ever want to experience again? *(Example: I don't ever want to be disrespected by Aiden again.)*

Review what you wrote. Pick one sentence you wrote that feels the most stressful to you right now. Circle it. Rewrite it at the top of Worksheet 2.

Adapted from Byron Katie International, Inc. Rev. 7/2014, with consent.

Self-Inquiry Worksheet 2 of 2

This worksheet is a meditation. When answering the questions, close your eyes, be still, and patiently wait to witness what appears to you. Always give yourself time to let the deeper answers meet the questions.

DIRECTIONS:

A. In the space below, write the thought you circled from Worksheet 1. Then answer questions 1-4.

B. Reconstruct the thought in three new ways. Possibilities are: by directing it inward (number 5 below), exchanging the other person's name with yours (number 6 below), and stating its exact opposite (number 7 below). Examples are provided below. Then, find and record three genuine, specific examples of how each new thought is as true or truer for you in that situation.

C. If you circled the thought from your answer to question 6 on Worksheet 1, you would reconstruct the thought by replacing the words, "I don't ever want to…" with "I am willing to…" and "I look forward to…"

Re-write the thought you circled on Worksheet 1: *(Example: Aiden doesn't listen to me.)*

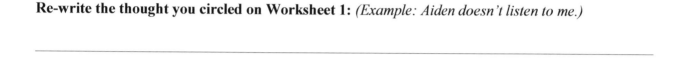

1. In that situation, is this thought true? *(Yes or no only. There are no right or wrong answers. If no, skip to question 3.)*

2. In that situation, can you absolutely know that it's true? *(Yes or no only)*

3. In that situation, how did you *react* when you believed that thought?

4. In that situation, who would you be if you could not believe that thought?

5. Reconstruct the thought by directing it *inward. (Example: I don't listen to me.)* Find and record three genuine, specific examples in that situation how this new thought is as true or truer than the original thought.

6. Reconstruct the thought by *exchanging* the other person's name with yours. *(Example: I don't listen to Aiden.)* Find and record three genuine, specific examples of how this new thought is as true or truer for you in that situation.

7. Reconstruct the thought by stating the *exact opposite. (Example: Aiden does listen to me.)* Find and record three genuine, specific examples of how this new thought is as true or truer for you in that situation.

Adapted from Byron Katie International, Inc. Rev. 7/2014, with consent.

Welcome to Morning 21 - *Your Mother, Your Mirror*

(I invite you to first re-read the Morning Meditation on page 16.)

Dear Present Mother,

Our mothers are not trying to push our buttons. They're just being themselves the best way they know how, given what they're thinking and believing. They have no other choice but to say the things they do and behave the way they do. If they believe their judgments, beliefs, and assumptions that cause disconnection, and haven't yet questioned them, they (and we) have no choice but to act on those beliefs. There is just no other way possible.

What I've found is that no one, not my mom, not my child, not my husband, not my dad, no one can *be* any other way to me, in my eyes, other than the way I see myself. It is an absolutely perfect mirror. There is no other way possible. They are the projected image of how I see myself. I don't expect you to believe this just because you read it or agree with it. I invite you to test it out for yourself. This realization didn't come to me from reading about it. It came from actually *experiencing* it during and after self-inquiry.

What is the one thing that is just so hard to get over when it comes to your mom? Let's go there this morning and find our freedom together.

Notice your breathing. Notice you are being breathed. Notice the in-breath. Notice the out-breath. Notice that you're not doing any of it; it's just occurring. Notice that thoughts are the same way - they're just appearing within the space of the present moment. You're not putting them there consciously.

I invite you to remember a specific moment in time when you were upset with your mother. It could have been last night or twenty years ago. Take in the whole scene. What is she saying, what are you saying, what is her energy like, what is yours like, where are you, what is the situation about, what time of day was it, what time of year? As the images resurface in your mind, what is it that you're feeling? Once you've identified the feeling, identify *why* you are feeling that way. An example might be *I'm angry at Mom because she should not have* _____. *(fill in the blank)*.

When you have a short, simple statement about your mom, I invite you to fill in question number one on Worksheet 1. For now, we'll just complete that first question.

This process is the first part of self-inquiry: identifying the stressful thought. The second half is asking the four questions and reconstructing the thought from new perspectives into new thoughts that are as true as or truer than the original one. I invite you to go slow, as if in meditation, to answer these questions. If you've never meditated, that's okay. It comes very easily when we just slow down and sit with the questions, as if they were our children, and let the answers be shown to us.

Also, I invite you to be a witness of yourself here and just notice if you get caught up in your feelings and your story about your mother. Gently guide yourself back to self-inquiry. Finally, it's important to know, there are no right or wrong answers here. We're just looking inside ourselves to see what's there.

Notice your breathing. Be breathed. Notice you're not doing any of it. Notice that you are the one who is doing the noticing.

If you want, you can fill in Worksheet 2 as we move through it here.

1. Is it true that your *mom shouldn't have* _____? (it's a yes or no question; if no, skip to question 3.)

2. Can you absolutely know it's true, that your *mom shouldn't have* _____? (yes or no only)

3. How do you react, what happens when you believe that thought, *"Mom shouldn't have* _____?"* Please remember to be a witness and notice if you get caught up in your feelings. To answer this question, you could consider how you treat her when you believe that thought, how you treat yourself when you believe that thought, or whether the thought brings you peace or stress. How do you feel in your body specifically when you believe that thought? When was the first time you ever remember believing that thought? Do any addictions or obsessions surface when you believe that thought? What do you get for continuing to believe that thought? What are you not able to do when you believe that thought?

4. Who would you be, in that same situation with your mom, without the thought, *"Mom shouldn't have* _____?"* Please remember to meditate, go slow here, and allow your answers to surface. Let the answers be shown to you, as if you were waiting for your precious child to arrive.

Now, see what the thought would be from new perspectives and then find three specific, genuine examples of how each new thought is as true or truer for you in this specific situation. For instance, the opposite would be: *Mom **should** have* _____. Why should she have? Why might that have been a better thing that happened? Why is it good that she did? How is that statement truer for you than *"Mom **shouldn't** have* _____"*? What are three genuine, specific examples? I invite you to wait patiently for your answers to reveal themselves.

~

Let's see what the thought would be if we direct it toward yourself: *I shouldn't have _____*. Why is this statement true for you in that situation? What are three specific examples that you believe?

~

After you finish the process, I invite you to see what you noticed in yourself as you completed Worksheet 2. What were you aware of? What were you conscious of? When we experience this process and then go back and witness ourselves answering the four questions and reconstructing the thought, our minds begin to loosen their grip on our stressful thinking about our mothers, about our children, about our partners, about anyone, about anything. We're only dealing with thoughts here, not people. So, when you release a thought about your mother through self-inquiry, you release the same thought about everyone else: daughter, sister, friend, son, husband, dad, and the entire world. In so doing, our grip begins to loosen around thoughts of past or future too. New neural connections and new neural pathways are formed, ones that spring from our beautiful, divine presence.

Recently I went to visit my mother for a ten-day visit, or so we thought. After about five days, I noticed that I didn't want to stay any longer. I made plans to leave early and so we did. My mom and I separated sooner than either of us expected, and we separated in the most loving way. We were both happy for the revision in our plans. I love how love moves in our lives when we are present to the beauty in all things. Before self-inquiry we both might have gotten upset about the change in plans. The separation might have been much more challenging. As it was, everyone had a great time together and everyone was happy when we parted as well. It was all good.

Wishing you, dear one, Peace and Presence today,
Catherine

Presence Practice Notes

Your Mother, Your Mirror

Self-Inquiry Worksheet 1 of 2

We've been told all of our lives not to judge others. The fact is we do it anyway. This worksheet allows the mind to see itself, to see the reality of its own thoughts, and to truly consider the thoughts by putting them on paper. This is the time to let those judgments have their own life.

DIRECTIONS:
A. Think of a specific person that is triggering stress in you. It could be your child, partner, ex-partner, mom, or dad. (Not yourself) They could be living or not living.
B. Now, recall a specific stressful situation you had with that person. It might have been a face to face interaction, an event, a phone call, or any situation that caused you any feelings of discomfort. Identify the specific stressful situation, and see it as a *single snapshot* in time.
C. Witness that single snapshot. Notice the time, place, words spoken, body language, and energy of each person. Then, 1) Identify and name the primary uncomfortable feeling you were having, 2) identify why you felt that way, and 3) answer the questions below with *short, simple* statements. *Please do not* try to be psychologically correct, spiritual, or wise now. For the purposes of this worksheet, be as judgmental as you were when you were in that situation.

1. In this situation, who angers, confuses, saddens, or disappoints you, and why? *(Example: I'm frustrated with Aiden because he won't listen to me.)*

2. In this situation, how do you want them to change? *(Example: I want Aiden to stop what he's doing, look at me, and listen to me.)*

3. In this situation, what advice would you offer to them? *(Example: Aiden should learn how to listen.)*

4. In order for you to feel better in this situation, what do you need them to think, say, feel, or do? *(Example: I need Aiden to listen.)*

5. What do you think of them in this situation? Make a list. Be petty. *(Example: Aiden is just like his dad - he won't respect me.)*

6. What is it in or about this situation that you don't ever want to experience again? *(Example: I don't ever want to be disrespected by Aiden again.)*

Review what you wrote. Pick one sentence you wrote that feels the most stressful to you right now. Circle it. Rewrite it at the top of Worksheet 2.

Adapted from Byron Katie International, Inc. Rev. 7/2014, with consent.

Self-Inquiry Worksheet 2 of 2

This worksheet is a meditation. When answering the questions, close your eyes, be still, and patiently wait to witness what appears to you. Always give yourself time to let the deeper answers meet the questions.

DIRECTIONS:

A. In the space below, write the thought you circled from Worksheet 1. Then answer questions 1-4.

B. Reconstruct the thought in three new ways. Possibilities are: by directing it inward (number 5 below), exchanging the other person's name with yours (number 6 below), and stating its exact opposite (number 7 below). Examples are provided below. Then, find and record three genuine, specific examples of how each new thought is as true or truer for you in that situation.

C. If you circled the thought from your answer to question 6 on Worksheet 1, you would reconstruct the thought by replacing the words, "I don't ever want to…" with "I am willing to…" and "I look forward to…"

Re-write the thought you circled on Worksheet 1: *(Example: Aiden doesn't listen to me.)*

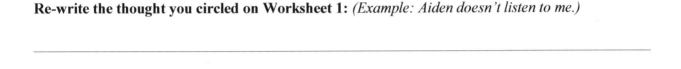

1. In that situation, is this thought true? *(Yes or no only. There are no right or wrong answers. If no, skip to question 3.)*

2. In that situation, can you absolutely know that it's true? *(Yes or no only)*

3. In that situation, how did you *react* when you believed that thought?

4. In that situation, who would you be if you could not believe that thought?

5. Reconstruct the thought by directing it *inward. (Example: I don't listen to me.)* Find and record three genuine, specific examples in that situation how this new thought is as true or truer than the original thought.

6. Reconstruct the thought by *exchanging* the other person's name with yours. *(Example: I don't listen to Aiden.)* Find and record three genuine, specific examples of how this new thought is as true or truer for you in that situation.

7. Reconstruct the thought by stating the *exact opposite. (Example: Aiden does listen to me.)* Find and record three genuine, specific examples of how this new thought is as true or truer for you in that situation.

Adapted from Byron Katie International, Inc. Rev. 7/2014, with consent.

Welcome to Morning 22 - *Living as Love*

(I invite you to first re-read the Morning Meditation on page 16.)

Dear Present Mother,

After self-inquiry, teaching love happens all by itself, simply by the way we live. When we are intent on teaching love, in the traditional definition, we are back to believing thoughts about how people *should* be: loving. Then, we're hooked again. You think your mom isn't acting loving and you're upset with her. This is how wars, small and large, get started. When I reconstruct the thoughts about my mother by directing them back to myself, I see the true way back to love. When we are authentically being loving (our true nature), and when we live *as* love (our true selves), that's where the true teaching is. We *are* the change we wish to see in the world, as Gandhi encourages us to be.

During and after self-inquiry we see, as a witness, our own thoughts, our own awareness of those thoughts, and we experience our own presence emerging. We see, in the present, how our stressful thoughts were what was creating our perceptions of our loved ones, not our *actual* loved ones and not even their behavior or speech. We see that our meanings, stories, and thoughts *about* reality, not reality itself, are what was clouding our mental lens and blocking our presence and the way of love. Getting all our relationships back to love begins and ends with your own relationship with yourself. What stressful thought do you have right now? That's a doorway back.

I didn't realize this until after I actually *did* self-inquiry for a while. True and lasting learning happens through experience. If we're open to being taught (by ourselves) we learn through living our lives. I love reading books, and writing in journals, and meditating. The actual experience of doing self-inquiry is what really stuck with me though. Now, I do self-inquiry significantly more often than I read, or journal, or meditate. It's just more effective and efficient to question the thoughts I believe that are blocking my presence and connection than it is to try and read about doing it, write out the feelings, or try to consciously focus more on the present (meditating),

146

repeating affirmations, or forcing myself to "let it go." Self-inquiry is a form of meditation combined with investigation.

New neural connections (thought patterns), based on experience, take repetition to be reinforced and remembered. "I look *forward* to .... (insert your stressful thought)," is now my genuine truth because every time I get the least bit irritated by anyone's behavior, I get the opportunity again to grow, personally and spiritually, by doing self-inquiry. It's all *for* me, not the other way around. When we commit to growing, developing, and using self-inquiry to get us there (here!), all of these upsets become a welcome addition to our lives since we find our own freedom through them. In that, they seem to dissolve. Before inquiry, the thoughts are there regardless. Why not recognize them and use them for *good*? They're all gifts in disguise.

Learning this new way of thinking and this new way of being present can have its ups and downs. I remember. I hope you're seeing how your time spent on it is so worth it. When you feel confused about something, or angry about it, or upset in any way, just know that it is all part of the learning, all part of your growth. The mind doesn't like to let go of these thoughts that keep you from connecting deeply with your child. It's not an internal war to fight; it's a thought to invite. It's just that it's such a habit to think in our conditioned ways - ways that seemed logical at the time, when we were young, so we could cope with our lives. Now, it's wonderful to use these stressful thoughts to enlighten yourself to your own beautiful presence. Just know that you are doing perfectly with your practice, no matter where you are. I love that you would be the one in your home to live as Love.

Wishing you, dear one, Peace and Presence today,
Catherine

Presence Practice Notes

Living as Love

Self-Inquiry Worksheet 1 of 2

We've been told all of our lives not to judge others. The fact is we do it anyway. This worksheet allows the mind to see itself, to see the reality of its own thoughts, and to truly consider the thoughts by putting them on paper. This is the time to let those judgments have their own life.

DIRECTIONS:

A. Think of a specific person that is triggering stress in you. It could be your child, partner, ex-partner, mom, or dad. (Not yourself) They could be living or not living.

B. Now, recall a specific stressful situation you had with that person. It might have been a face to face interaction, an event, a phone call, or any situation that caused you any feelings of discomfort. Identify the specific stressful situation, and see it as a *single snapshot* in time.

C. Witness that single snapshot. Notice the time, place, words spoken, body language, and energy of each person. Then, 1) Identify and name the primary uncomfortable feeling you were having, 2) identify why you felt that way, and 3) answer the questions below with *short, simple* statements. *Please do not* try to be psychologically correct, spiritual, or wise now. For the purposes of this worksheet, be as judgmental as you were when you were in that situation.

1. In this situation, who angers, confuses, saddens, or disappoints you, and why? *(Example: I'm frustrated with Aiden because he won't listen to me.)*

2. In this situation, how do you want them to change? *(Example: I want Aiden to stop what he's doing, look at me, and listen to me.)*

3. In this situation, what advice would you offer to them? *(Example: Aiden should learn how to listen.)*

4. In order for you to feel better in this situation, what do you need them to think, say, feel, or do? *(Example: I need Aiden to listen.)*

5. What do you think of them in this situation? Make a list. Be petty. *(Example: Aiden is just like his dad - he won't respect me.)*

6. What is it in or about this situation that you don't ever want to experience again? *(Example: I don't ever want to be disrespected by Aiden again.)*

Review what you wrote. Pick one sentence you wrote that feels the most stressful to you right now. Circle it. Rewrite it at the top of Worksheet 2.

Adapted from Byron Katie International, Inc. Rev. 7/2014, with consent.

Self-Inquiry Worksheet 2 of 2

This worksheet is a meditation. When answering the questions, close your eyes, be still, and patiently wait to witness what appears to you. Always give yourself time to let the deeper answers meet the questions.

DIRECTIONS:
A. In the space below, write the thought you circled from Worksheet 1. Then answer questions 1-4.
B. Reconstruct the thought in three new ways. Possibilities are: by directing it inward (number 5 below), exchanging the other person's name with yours (number 6 below), and stating its exact opposite (number 7 below). Examples are provided below. Then, find and record three genuine, specific examples of how each new thought is as true or truer for you in that situation.
C. If you circled the thought from your answer to question 6 on Worksheet 1, you would reconstruct the thought by replacing the words, "I don't ever want to…" with "I am willing to…" and "I look forward to…"

Re-write the thought you circled on Worksheet 1: *(Example: Aiden doesn't listen to me.)*

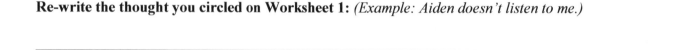

1. In that situation, is this thought true? *(Yes or no only. There are no right or wrong answers. If no, skip to question 3.)*

2. In that situation, can you absolutely know that it's true? *(Yes or no only)*

3. In that situation, how did you *react* when you believed that thought?

4. In that situation, who would you be if you could not believe that thought?

5. Reconstruct the thought by directing it *inward. (Example: I don't listen to me.)* Find and record three genuine, specific examples in that situation how this new thought is as true or truer than the original thought.

6. Reconstruct the thought by *exchanging* the other person's name with yours. *(Example: I don't listen to Aiden.)* Find and record three genuine, specific examples of how this new thought is as true or truer for you in that situation.

7. Reconstruct the thought by stating the *exact opposite. (Example: Aiden does listen to me.)* Find and record three genuine, specific examples of how this new thought is as true or truer for you in that situation.

Welcome to Morning 23 - *Mothering Ourselves*

(I invite you to first re-read the Morning Meditation on page 16.)

Dear Present Mother,

When we are mentally in our mother's business, thinking she should or shouldn't be saying or doing something, we are completely mentally out of our own business. We're not paying any attention to ourselves. We can't be our own best mother to ourselves because we're not even home to ourselves. In addition, we can't be present with our child. It's not unusual to be in our mother's business; it's something we've done for centuries. It's what happens when we don't question our thinking. Now, we have a new way. When we see that we're mentally in our mother's business we can mother ourselves by doing self-inquiry on our thoughts about her to manifest our presence again.

One day I realized I was just so tired of feeling angry with my mother. It took so much energy out of me to keep holding onto those stressful thoughts. So I sort of gave up feeling angry. But then, when I would talk with her or see her, I would get restimulated all over again. Back then I hated that it kept happening yet I didn't know how to prevent it. So, I sort of stopped trying to fix our relationship. I started focusing on my mothering and my kids. Eventually, even with them, I kept getting triggered and frustrated with stressful thoughts that were so similar to the ones I had about my mom. My relationship with my kids meant and means so much to me that I totally committed myself to figuring out how to stop feeling triggered by them *and* by my mom.

Self-inquiry helps us learn how to stop getting our buttons pushed because the buttons disappear after we inquire. We are left to be our true selves; the mother we've always wanted. Finding this compassion for ourselves, within ourselves, fills us up. We start to have more understanding for ourselves, more love for ourselves, and we start to be kinder to ourselves. Then, since everyone else is a projection of how we see ourselves, we begin to see others - our kids, our mothers, everyone - in a more loving light, the light of presence. This is not because they changed but because our perception of ourselves changed. Remember, we project our own thinking about ourselves onto everyone else.

So today, I invite you to judge your mother; we do it anyway. Might as well see if they're true. Get all your thoughts about her down on paper. Then, question every one of them with Worksheet 2. May you find the mother you've always wanted right where you can always find her… inside of you.

If you want to build a fast, deep connection with your mother at this point you might call her and let her know that you've been questioning your thoughts about her, the thoughts that used to cause you to disconnect from her. You might share with her some of your realizations you're making about yourself. I invite you to do this, just for yourself, because it makes you feel better, not because you want anything from your mom.

I saw a movie last night that said something similar to, "Twenty seconds of insane courage could change your life for the better forever." I wonder how that twenty seconds would look if you would share your self-inquiry practice about your mother with her?

Wishing you, dear one, Peace and Presence today,
Catherine

Presence Practice Notes

Mothering Ourselves

Self-Inquiry Worksheet 1 of 2

We've been told all of our lives not to judge others. The fact is we do it anyway. This worksheet allows the mind to see itself, to see the reality of its own thoughts, and to truly consider the thoughts by putting them on paper. This is the time to let those judgments have their own life.

DIRECTIONS:
A. Think of a specific person that is triggering stress in you. It could be your child, partner, ex-partner, mom, or dad. (Not yourself) They could be living or not living.
B. Now, recall a specific stressful situation you had with that person. It might have been a face to face interaction, an event, a phone call, or any situation that caused you any feelings of discomfort. Identify the specific stressful situation, and see it as a *single snapshot* in time.
C. Witness that single snapshot. Notice the time, place, words spoken, body language, and energy of each person. Then, 1) Identify and name the primary uncomfortable feeling you were having, 2) identify why you felt that way, and 3) answer the questions below with *short, simple* statements. *Please do not* try to be psychologically correct, spiritual, or wise now. For the purposes of this worksheet, be as judgmental as you were when you were in that situation.

1. In this situation, who angers, confuses, saddens, or disappoints you, and why? *(Example: I'm frustrated with Aiden because he won't listen to me.)*

2. In this situation, how do you want them to change? *(Example: I want Aiden to stop what he's doing, look at me, and listen to me.)*

3. In this situation, what advice would you offer to them? *(Example: Aiden should learn how to listen.)*

4. In order for you to feel better in this situation, what do you need them to think, say, feel, or do? *(Example: I need Aiden to listen.)*

5. What do you think of them in this situation? Make a list. Be petty. *(Example: Aiden is just like his dad - he won't respect me.)*

6. What is it in or about this situation that you don't ever want to experience again? *(Example: I don't ever want to be disrespected by Aiden again.)*

Review what you wrote. Pick one sentence you wrote that feels the most stressful to you right now. Circle it. Rewrite it at the top of Worksheet 2.

Adapted from Byron Katie International, Inc. Rev. 7/2014, with consent.

Self-Inquiry Worksheet 2 of 2

This worksheet is a meditation. When answering the questions, close your eyes, be still, and patiently wait to witness what appears to you. Always give yourself time to let the deeper answers meet the questions.

DIRECTIONS:

A. In the space below, write the thought you circled from Worksheet 1. Then answer questions 1-4.

B. Reconstruct the thought in three new ways. Possibilities are: by directing it inward (number 5 below), exchanging the other person's name with yours (number 6 below), and stating its exact opposite (number 7 below). Examples are provided below. Then, find and record three genuine, specific examples of how each new thought is as true or truer for you in that situation.

C. If you circled the thought from your answer to question 6 on Worksheet 1, you would reconstruct the thought by replacing the words, "I don't ever want to…" with "I am willing to…" and "I look forward to…"

Re-write the thought you circled on Worksheet 1: *(Example: Aiden doesn't listen to me.)*

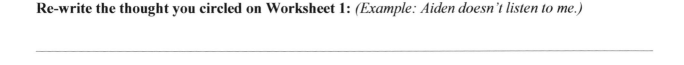

1. In that situation, is this thought true? *(Yes or no only. There are no right or wrong answers. If no, skip to question 3.)*

2. In that situation, can you absolutely know that it's true? *(Yes or no only)*

3. In that situation, how did you *react* when you believed that thought?

4. In that situation, who would you be if you could not believe that thought?

5. Reconstruct the thought by directing it *inward. (Example: I don't listen to me.)* Find and record three genuine, specific examples in that situation how this new thought is as true or truer than the original thought.

6. Reconstruct the thought by *exchanging* the other person's name with yours. *(Example: I don't listen to Aiden.)* Find and record three genuine, specific examples of how this new thought is as true or truer for you in that situation.

7. Reconstruct the thought by stating the *exact opposite. (Example: Aiden does listen to me.)* Find and record three genuine, specific examples of how this new thought is as true or truer for you in that situation.

Adapted from Byron Katie International, Inc. Rev. 7/2014, with consent.

Welcome to Morning 24 - *Our Innocence*

(I invite you to first re-read the Morning Meditation on page 16.)

Dear Present Mother,

If you've been following along on your worksheets and doing self-inquiry this week on your mother, what are you noticing about your experience? What are you aware of that's new for you? What are you conscious of today that you haven't been conscious of before? It's helpful to be aware of those new experiences you're having, and jot down some Presence Practice Notes on the blank page that follows. Being aware of them solidifies them for you and creates those new thought patterns. When you remember them and write them down, they get reinforced. So, I invite you to do that this morning.

When I first started doing self-inquiry, especially on my mother, I noticed that I felt guilty sometimes because I was thinking and writing such negative things about her. Are you experiencing any of that? It is a common experience to feel this way, especially for us, as mothers.

If this is happening with you, I invite you to do some fine tuning in how you're doing your self-inquiry. It's very important to give yourself plenty of time to stay with each of the four questions on Worksheet 2. Go very slowly, meditating with each one and letting answers arise within you to meet them until the answer feels complete. If we skip too fast to reconstructing the thoughts, they sometimes feel painful to read because it feels like we're judging ourselves, and then our mind's first response is a thought that causes guilt. Instead, when we thoroughly complete each question, as if meditating on each one, the reconstructed thoughts feel wonderful, and are full of aha moments. So, notice if you're feeling any judgments or "shoulds" directed at yourself, and if so, just realize what it is and gently bring yourself back.

I found it helpful to consider the reconstructed thoughts in terms of how they could *support me*. For instance, if my original thought was, "*Mom should change,*" then my thought directed inward was "I should change." How does thinking that thought support me? Possible answers are:

~ If I change, then that keeps me in my area of control more, and more in control of my own happiness.

~ If I change, then I stay present to myself, and in turn, I stay present to my child, so this new thought actually *inspires* me.

~ If I change, then I get to be a great example to my child.

It's okay if you've experienced any guilt or any judgment or expectation of yourself. It's just a signal to fine-tune. When we learn anything new, fine-tuning is necessary. Most people have never done self-inquiry before and are very inexperienced when it comes to finding this new way of thinking and deepening our connection to the present (to ourselves). So, please be *ultra-compassionate and ultra-patient* with yourself now because you are learning something that's so new. In the area of presence, we're all like toddlers learning to walk.

Another way that I found compassion for myself - instead of judgment of myself - was to ask, "Where was it that I was completely innocent in thinking what I did?" This is not to find blame in someone else, it is to find and experience compassion and understanding for yourself, which magically creates patience too. One of the sub-questions to "How do you react when you believe that thought?" is "When was the first time you remember believing that thought?" When we look back at when we were a child, there is usually a time when we can remember believing the same thought. We remember the circumstances. Every time I looked, I saw how, when I was young, I was 100% innocent in believing the stressful thought which I was questioning today. Then, I experienced so much compassion for the little girl who felt she needed to protect herself - from some real or imagined future pain - by believing the thought. That little girl did not have self-inquiry so she believed "her" stressful thoughts. There was no other possibility for her.

Self-inquiry is empowering. In the here and now we can re-look at thoughts that used to cause so much suffering because they argued with what was happening in reality. We can now turn those thoughts into *truth*, deepen our connections, and realize our pure presence.

I invite you to continue to judge your mom today by completing the worksheets that follow. In reality, it's actually *you* that you're judging. When you do self-inquiry on those judgments about her, then the judgments will stop about her and about you. Won't it be wonderful when you can stop judging yourself? When you do, you'll be closer to your child, because you'll be closer to *you*.

Wishing you, dear one, Peace and Presence today
Catherine

Presence Practice Notes

Our Innocence

Self-Inquiry Worksheet 1 of 2

We've been told all of our lives not to judge others. The fact is we do it anyway. This worksheet allows the mind to see itself, to see the reality of its own thoughts, and to truly consider the thoughts by putting them on paper. This is the time to let those judgments have their own life.

DIRECTIONS:

A. Think of a specific person that is triggering stress in you. It could be your child, partner, ex-partner, mom, or dad. (Not yourself) They could be living or not living.

B. Now, recall a specific stressful situation you had with that person. It might have been a face to face interaction, an event, a phone call, or any situation that caused you any feelings of discomfort. Identify the specific stressful situation, and see it as a *single snapshot* in time.

C. Witness that single snapshot. Notice the time, place, words spoken, body language, and energy of each person. Then, 1) Identify and name the primary uncomfortable feeling you were having, 2) identify why you felt that way, and 3) answer the questions below with *short, simple* statements. *Please do not* try to be psychologically correct, spiritual, or wise now. For the purposes of this worksheet, be as judgmental as you were when you were in that situation.

1. In this situation, who angers, confuses, saddens, or disappoints you, and why? *(Example: I'm frustrated with Aiden because he won't listen to me.)*

2. In this situation, how do you want them to change? *(Example: I want Aiden to stop what he's doing, look at me, and listen to me.)*

3. In this situation, what advice would you offer to them? *(Example: Aiden should learn how to listen.)*

4. In order for you to feel better in this situation, what do you need them to think, say, feel, or do? *(Example: I need Aiden to listen.)*

5. What do you think of them in this situation? Make a list. Be petty. *(Example: Aiden is just like his dad - he won't respect me.)*

6. What is it in or about this situation that you don't ever want to experience again? *(Example: I don't ever want to be disrespected by Aiden again.)*

Review what you wrote. Pick one sentence you wrote that feels the most stressful to you right now. Circle it. Rewrite it at the top of Worksheet 2.

Self-Inquiry Worksheet 2 of 2

This worksheet is a meditation. When answering the questions, close your eyes, be still, and patiently wait to witness what appears to you. Always give yourself time to let the deeper answers meet the questions.

DIRECTIONS:

A. In the space below, write the thought you circled from Worksheet 1. Then answer questions 1-4.

B. Reconstruct the thought in three new ways. Possibilities are: by directing it inward (number 5 below), exchanging the other person's name with yours (number 6 below), and stating its exact opposite (number 7 below). Examples are provided below. Then, find and record three genuine, specific examples of how each new thought is as true or truer for you in that situation.

C. If you circled the thought from your answer to question 6 on Worksheet 1, you would reconstruct the thought by replacing the words, "I don't ever want to…" with "I am willing to…" and "I look forward to…"

Re-write the thought you circled on Worksheet 1: *(Example: Aiden doesn't listen to me.)*

1. In that situation, is this thought true? *(Yes or no only. There are no right or wrong answers. If no, skip to question 3.)*

2. In that situation, can you absolutely know that it's true? *(Yes or no only)*

3. In that situation, how did you *react* when you believed that thought?

4. In that situation, who would you be if you could not believe that thought?

5. Reconstruct the thought by directing it *inward. (Example: I don't listen to me.)* Find and record three genuine, specific examples in that situation how this new thought is as true or truer than the original thought.

6. Reconstruct the thought by *exchanging* the other person's name with yours. *(Example: I don't listen to Aiden.)* Find and record three genuine, specific examples of how this new thought is as true or truer for you in that situation.

7. Reconstruct the thought by stating the *exact opposite. (Example: Aiden does listen to me.)* Find and record three genuine, specific examples of how this new thought is as true or truer for you in that situation.

Adapted from Byron Katie International, Inc. Rev. 7/2014, with consent.

Welcome to Morning 25 - *Gifts to Yourself*

(I invite you to first re-read the Morning Meditation on page 16.)

Dear Present Mother,

Doing self-inquiry on your judgments about your mother is literally the process of unwrapping your own gift of love for yourself. Before self-inquiry, the depths of this love was hidden from your awareness. You open your gift when your answers to the questions pop out of your own mind, come through the pen and appear on the page. We are wise beyond understanding -- only our wisdom is for ourselves, not for our mothers.

Our answers to questions two, three, and four on Worksheet 1 can give us our own best to-do list for loving ourselves, and in return, our children. When you read what you've written about your mother (or your child, or anyone) and replace her name with your own, you mysteriously get your own prescription for happiness. Today, the last day in the series on our mothers, I invite you to do a very simple, quick exercise with me. Turn to Worksheet 1, judge your mother, and write it down. A beautiful gift is waiting for you at the end. Are you ready?

I invite you to remember a specific stressful incident/conversation/occurrence with your mom. It could be anything, from the smallest irritation to the biggest issue you hold against her. Allow yourself to go back and mentally revisit the whole situation. What are you feeling toward your mother? Is it anger, disappointment, fear, sadness? Identify the feeling. Now, *why* are you feeling that way? Once you've identified your primary feeling and the reason for it, fill in statements one through six on Worksheet 1.

When you've completed the worksheet, I invite you to look at what you wrote in questions two, three, and four, one at a time, and wherever you wrote the word mom/mother/she/her, replace that word with your name/I/me. Now, read it back to yourself, with your name in it instead of hers. It's nice to start a new list, just for you, to record these on.

So, for example, when you filled in question two on your mom, it might read something like, *"I want Mom to treat me more kindly, to stop criticizing me, to say she's sorry, to make it up to me, and to tell me she loves me."* This would now read, "I want *me* to treat me more kindly, I want *me* to stop criticizing me, I want *me* to say I'm sorry to me, I want *me* to make it up to me, I want *me* to tell me I love me." Then, find three specific, genuine examples of how each of these new thoughts, directed inward, are true for you in your specific situation.

~

As you reflect back on doing this exercise, what were you aware of within yourself? What were you conscious of? What did you notice in you? I invite you to write your realizations down. Doing this cements the new neural pathways you just formed in your mind, ones based in the truth and based in the present moment.

I *love* how this works! It's such a simple, magical, easy, efficient, mysterious way to self-realization, enlightenment, awareness, truth, peace, and presence. What results are you starting to see in your life? I invite you to make some Presence Practice Notes about it on the page that follows, and continue to fill in Worksheet 2. I love that you're continuing to deepen your connection with yourself.

When I questioned my thoughts about my mother, I loved how she had nothing to do with it. I literally cannot remember the last time I was upset by anything she said or did or didn't say or didn't do. When I recall situations in the past where I might have gotten upset, it seems like I'm remembering a totally different person, the details are fuzzy, and it seems like a lifetime ago. Before self-inquiry my story of my mom was that she stifled me, cut off my spirit, was emotionally shut-down, was a control freak, and was ultra-critical. Today, that story just doesn't fit my mom. It's not her. Now, I remember the times when she told me it was good to cry sometimes, when she said to blame everything on her if I was ever upset, when she listened to me for hours about how I was doing, and when she was there for me, always, my entire life.

Wishing you, dear one, Peace and Presence today,
Catherine

Presence Practice Notes

Gifts to Yourself

Self-Inquiry Worksheet 1 of 2

We've been told all of our lives not to judge others. The fact is we do it anyway. This worksheet allows the mind to see itself, to see the reality of its own thoughts, and to truly consider the thoughts by putting them on paper. This is the time to let those judgments have their own life.

DIRECTIONS:

A. Think of a specific person that is triggering stress in you. It could be your child, partner, ex-partner, mom, or dad. (Not yourself) They could be living or not living.

B. Now, recall a specific stressful situation you had with that person. It might have been a face to face interaction, an event, a phone call, or any situation that caused you any feelings of discomfort. Identify the specific stressful situation, and see it as a *single snapshot* in time.

C. Witness that single snapshot. Notice the time, place, words spoken, body language, and energy of each person. Then, 1) Identify and name the primary uncomfortable feeling you were having, 2) identify why you felt that way, and 3) answer the questions below with *short, simple* statements. *Please do not* try to be psychologically correct, spiritual, or wise now. For the purposes of this worksheet, be as judgmental as you were when you were in that situation.

1. In this situation, who angers, confuses, saddens, or disappoints you, and why? *(Example: I'm frustrated with Aiden because he won't listen to me.)*

2. In this situation, how do you want them to change? *(Example: I want Aiden to stop what he's doing, look at me, and listen to me.)*

3. In this situation, what advice would you offer to them? *(Example: Aiden should learn how to listen.)*

4. In order for you to feel better in this situation, what do you need them to think, say, feel, or do? *(Example: I need Aiden to listen.)*

5. What do you think of them in this situation? Make a list. Be petty. *(Example: Aiden is just like his dad - he won't respect me.)*

6. What is it in or about this situation that you don't ever want to experience again? *(Example: I don't ever want to be disrespected by Aiden again.)*

Review what you wrote. Pick one sentence you wrote that feels the most stressful to you right now. Circle it. Rewrite it at the top of Worksheet 2.

Adapted from Byron Katie International, Inc. Rev. 7/2014, with consent.

Self-Inquiry Worksheet 2 of 2

This worksheet is a meditation. When answering the questions, close your eyes, be still, and patiently wait to witness what appears to you. Always give yourself time to let the deeper answers meet the questions.

DIRECTIONS:

A. In the space below, write the thought you circled from Worksheet 1. Then answer questions 1-4.

B. Reconstruct the thought in three new ways. Possibilities are: by directing it inward (number 5 below), exchanging the other person's name with yours (number 6 below), and stating its exact opposite (number 7 below). Examples are provided below. Then, find and record three genuine, specific examples of how each new thought is as true or truer for you in that situation.

C. If you circled the thought from your answer to question 6 on Worksheet 1, you would reconstruct the thought by replacing the words, "I don't ever want to…" with "I am willing to…" and "I look forward to…"

Re-write the thought you circled on Worksheet 1: *(Example: Aiden doesn't listen to me.)*

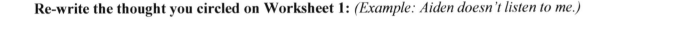

1. In that situation, is this thought true? *(Yes or no only. There are no right or wrong answers. If no, skip to question 3.)*

2. In that situation, can you absolutely know that it's true? *(Yes or no only)*

3. In that situation, how did you *react* when you believed that thought?

4. In that situation, who would you be if you could not believe that thought?

5. Reconstruct the thought by directing it *inward. (Example: I don't listen to me.)* Find and record three genuine, specific examples in that situation how this new thought is as true or truer than the original thought.

6. Reconstruct the thought by *exchanging* the other person's name with yours. *(Example: I don't listen to Aiden.)* Find and record three genuine, specific examples of how this new thought is as true or truer for you in that situation.

7. Reconstruct the thought by stating the *exact opposite. (Example: Aiden does listen to me.)* Find and record three genuine, specific examples of how this new thought is as true or truer for you in that situation.

Adapted from Byron Katie International, Inc. Rev. 7/2014, with consent.

Welcome to Morning 26 - *The Beautiful Flow*

(I invite you to first re-read the Morning Meditation on page 16.)

Dear Present Mother,

I want to know where the unclear places are in my mind. I love getting clear. It's just awesome when I am. Life flows. I am in the river of this flow, seeing all the beautiful scenery as life keeps appearing to me, now, and now, and now. My children are part of the river. We're all happily moving, moment to moment, through life. There is no resistance. When branches hang up a bunch of leaves in the river, and block the flow, it is all part of it, part of what's to love about the river, the flow. When spouse raises voice, when children work out a "conflict," it is all part of the river -- occurrences appearing and disappearing in and out of the present moment. What an amazing trip.

I remember the first stressful thought I ever questioned. It was, "*He's sucking the life out of me.*" This was a judgment I had about my then two-year old son. I believed old stories about how we are supposed to sleep-train our children. I believed that my husband's (and mainstream American society's) way of leaving a two-year old in their rooms to go to sleep by themselves was the way we were supposed to do it. I was sleep-deprived, I felt depressed, I felt furious with my son, and then I felt the deepest guilt and anger from feeling upset with my precious child. My son was crying and crying. He seemed scared of me and my reactions. Seeing that look of fear on his face was *not* what I wanted for him. He was a mess. I was a mess. My perception of what was occurring in those moments was that it should *not* be this way. "*He should not be fighting me to sleep by himself,*" I thought. I was confused too because I thought I was doing all the "right" gentle sleep-training techniques and tricks to help him learn how to fall asleep by himself. He was *not* having it though. I was fighting the river. I was completely exhausted.

During inquiry, when I reconstructed this stress-inducing thought and looked at it from a different point of view, I finally saw all the ways that *I* was sucking the life out of me. Instead of sleeping when he was sleeping, I was talking on the phone or doing dishes or something else that wasn't absolutely necessary. Instead of trusting my own intuition to just hold him and let him fall asleep without trying to force him, I was focusing more on my fear than on my love.

When I started seeing how I – not my son - was causing my own frustrations, I started listening more deeply to my heart than my head. I started being responsible for my own experience, my own feelings. I started noticing how to be at peace with reality and how to be present to the wisdom that emerges from within me when I stopped fighting with reality. Something bloomed and blossomed that day. Something was born. I was aware that I was 100% responsible for my perception of life. It wasn't like saying "Oh, this is good" when I was really thinking it was awful. No, I really believed it *was* good. Thank goodness I had seen what I saw. I felt like things would get much better from then on, and it did. My son and I were in harmony again because my thinking was in harmony with my real life.

After that, I started living differently by sleeping when he slept, carrying him in a sling or backpack and letting him fall asleep on his own, getting some help around the house, eating better, getting fresh air and sunshine more often. Aaaahhhh. It felt so good. My son stopped fighting against me fighting against him. It was perfect: I discovered the real cause and started receiving all the positive effects.

~

Part of me wants to be your cheerleader and encourage you to keep up the good work you're doing by questioning your thoughts and filling in the worksheets. However, me being a cheerleader for you would assume that you *need* one. It's more of a personal motivation thing though, really. Think about it. Do you ever need a cheerleader in order to do something you *really* want to do? Or, do you just seek to do it, no matter if you have a cheerleader or not? Sometimes, a cheerleader for your enlightenment can *distract* you from your own enlightenment. If you rely on me to encourage you then you don't get to encourage yourself. I don't need encouragement to do self-inquiry. I do it because I love being happy and present to my beautiful children and connected to them in a way I've never known before self-inquiry.

That's why I like being a mentor and a guide, not a teacher, and not a cheerleader. I'm the same way with my kids. They are their own cheerleader for themselves. They teach themselves. I mentor them by being an example for them of how to live a happy life. I guide them when they want me to guide them. I answer their questions. I give them the resources they're asking for. I take them places they'd like to go. I'm not their cheerleader. I try not to ever give my opinion of them to them. I want them to look always to themselves for their own opinion of themselves. I don't want to cripple them into always needing others' opinions of them to see if they're doing a "good" job. I want judgments to be left out of the picture and presence to be left in the picture.

I can always pave the way for you if you want to fill in the worksheets and question your thinking, but I would never want it for you if you don't want it. So, even if you're struggling a bit with the worksheets, or with your own thinking, know that you're doing it perfectly, no matter where you are. Remember, you can't do it wrong. If you need any special guidance, you can always find help on http://www.thepresentmother.com/ and every Saturday morning during our mentoring calls, *Morning Walk with the Present Mothers Community* ™. You can even post questions on the website or our private Facebook page and I will do my best to answer them.

For now, may the river of your life with your children show you the places where you're fighting the current, so that self-inquiry can get you back into the beautiful flow.

Wishing you, dear one, Presence and Peace today,
Catherine

Presence Practice Notes

The Beautiful Flow

Self-Inquiry Worksheet 1 of 2

We've been told all of our lives not to judge others. The fact is we do it anyway. This worksheet allows the mind to see itself, to see the reality of its own thoughts, and to truly consider the thoughts by putting them on paper. This is the time to let those judgments have their own life.

DIRECTIONS:
A. Think of a specific person that is triggering stress in you. It could be your child, partner, ex-partner, mom, or dad. (Not yourself) They could be living or not living.
B. Now, recall a specific stressful situation you had with that person. It might have been a face to face interaction, an event, a phone call, or any situation that caused you any feelings of discomfort. Identify the specific stressful situation, and see it as a *single snapshot* in time.
C. Witness that single snapshot. Notice the time, place, words spoken, body language, and energy of each person. Then, 1) Identify and name the primary uncomfortable feeling you were having, 2) identify why you felt that way, and 3) answer the questions below with *short, simple* statements. *Please do not* try to be psychologically correct, spiritual, or wise now. For the purposes of this worksheet, be as judgmental as you were when you were in that situation.

1. In this situation, who angers, confuses, saddens, or disappoints you, and why? *(Example: I'm frustrated with Aiden because he won't listen to me.)*

2. In this situation, how do you want them to change? *(Example: I want Aiden to stop what he's doing, look at me, and listen to me.)*

3. In this situation, what advice would you offer to them? *(Example: Aiden should learn how to listen.)*

4. In order for you to feel better in this situation, what do you need them to think, say, feel, or do? *(Example: I need Aiden to listen.)*

5. What do you think of them in this situation? Make a list. Be petty. *(Example: Aiden is just like his dad - he won't respect me.)*

6. What is it in or about this situation that you don't ever want to experience again? *(Example: I don't ever want to be disrespected by Aiden again.)*

Review what you wrote. Pick one sentence you wrote that feels the most stressful to you right now. Circle it. Rewrite it at the top of Worksheet 2.

Adapted from Byron Katie International, Inc. Rev. 7/2014, with consent.

Self-Inquiry Worksheet 2 of 2

This worksheet is a meditation. When answering the questions, close your eyes, be still, and patiently wait to witness what appears to you. Always give yourself time to let the deeper answers meet the questions.

DIRECTIONS:

A. In the space below, write the thought you circled from Worksheet 1. Then answer questions 1-4.

B. Reconstruct the thought in three new ways. Possibilities are: by directing it inward (number 5 below), exchanging the other person's name with yours (number 6 below), and stating its exact opposite (number 7 below). Examples are provided below. Then, find and record three genuine, specific examples of how each new thought is as true or truer for you in that situation.

C. If you circled the thought from your answer to question 6 on Worksheet 1, you would reconstruct the thought by replacing the words, "I don't ever want to…" with "I am willing to…" and "I look forward to…"

Re-write the thought you circled on Worksheet 1: *(Example: Aiden doesn't listen to me.)*

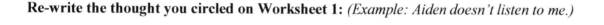

1. In that situation, is this thought true? *(Yes or no only. There are no right or wrong answers. If no, skip to question 3.)*

2. In that situation, can you absolutely know that it's true? *(Yes or no only)*

3. In that situation, how did you *react* when you believed that thought?

4. In that situation, who would you be if you could not believe that thought?

5. Reconstruct the thought by directing it *inward. (Example: I don't listen to me.)* Find and record three genuine, specific examples in that situation how this new thought is as true or truer than the original thought.

6. Reconstruct the thought by *exchanging* the other person's name with yours. *(Example: I don't listen to Aiden.)* Find and record three genuine, specific examples of how this new thought is as true or truer for you in that situation.

7. Reconstruct the thought by stating the *exact opposite. (Example: Aiden does listen to me.)* Find and record three genuine, specific examples of how this new thought is as true or truer for you in that situation.

Adapted from Byron Katie International, Inc. Rev. 7/2014, with consent.

Welcome to Morning 27 - *Judgments*

(I invite you to first re-read the Morning Meditation on page 16.)

Dear Present Mother,

When we start anything new that looks wonderfully life-altering or too good to be true, the mind can easily fall back into old beliefs that could keep us from going deeper with our practice. It might bring up the teensiest bit of pushing against whatever it is - frustration, anger, worry or fear. That's been my experience from doing self-inquiry since 2004. Are you finding it hard to practice? What stressful thought is on your mind now *about* self-inquiry itself?

When I began doing self-inquiry on a regular basis, this mind came up with these judgments:

~ "It's too complicated."

~ "It's too hard."

~ "It takes too much time."

~ "It doesn't honor my feelings."

~ "It isn't as great as it sounds."

~ "It isn't the only way and she makes it sound like it is."

~ "It is too controlling."

~ "It's a cult."

~ "It isn't necessary in my life because meditation (or medication, or affirmations, or fill in other method) does it for me."

~ "It isn't necessary in my life because I've been doing spiritual work for 20 years and I am already present enough for me."

~ "It doesn't work."

and on and on…

~

I decided to do self-inquiry on these beliefs because they all seemed to cause stress for me. When I did, I realized that their opposites are so much truer. I found genuine, specific examples of each one of these in my life which this mind believed. Now I simply don't believe them. Now, I get to realize the power of doing self-inquiry. I experience a deeper connection with my children. I get to be a role model for them to continue to live in the beautiful present moment. I get to remain in the here and now as much as I want to. It's my choice now. When this mind cues up another stressful thought, it is met within seconds with either "Is it true?" or with the exact opposite thought, complete with examples or sometimes even a little laugh. Within seconds I am present again.

For really sticky, old, stressful thoughts from my past - for example, about the way I was raised, how I would raise my children, considering divorce, hormonal swings of menopause, or moving - I always had a simple clear way to realize my own wisdom without getting hooked into my story. It didn't matter to me if I questioned variations of the same thought for a month. I knew that complete freedom and peace waited for me at the end of every inquiry. Absolutely beautiful.

One time I mistook the joy I felt after doing self-inquiry for a new thought that now I didn't *need* to do self-inquiry anymore, like I knew the future. A specific incident comes to my mind. I remember feeling like I was skipping through the tulips after self-inquiry. I felt great for about three days, and then another stressful thought hit me. I fell for it. I believed it. It was about my husband and it was a biggie. I *love* that I came back to self-inquiry and saved my marriage.

Self-inquiry is so simple and powerful because it naturally works the same way our newborn babies' brains work. The brain prunes, all on its own, thoughts that are no longer reinforced. It also cements, all on its own, thoughts that are reinforced. Every time we do self-inquiry on a stressful thought, the synaptic connections that cause stress in the brain literally *die off* a little.[5] The new synaptic connections that we form, grounded in presence, are repeated over and over every time we do self-inquiry and literally become cemented there. We realize what's actually true. We experience our full presence when we answer the question, "Who would you be without that thought?" We are talking about evolutionary biology here, Mom. Doing self-inquiry helps us evolve to the next level of human beings. Literally.

Please don't believe me about any of this; instead test it out for yourself. I invite you to do self-inquiry today on each thought that arises for you *about* self-inquiry. Which one is true for you right now? I invite you to judge the inquiry process itself. Write those judgments down on Worksheet 1. Then do self-inquiry on that judgment using Worksheet 2. Doing self-inquiry about my concerns about the process always took me to the next deeper level of my presence practice. Using self-inquiry, those judgments actually helped me deepen my connection to myself and to my child. I hope it does for you too.

Wishing you, dear one, Presence and Peace today,
Catherine

---

[5] Wikipedia, *Synaptic Plasticity*, http://en.wikipedia.org/wiki/Synaptic_plasticity

Presence Practice Notes

Judgments

Self-Inquiry Worksheet 1 of 2

We've been told all of our lives not to judge others. The fact is we do it anyway. This worksheet allows the mind to see itself, to see the reality of its own thoughts, and to truly consider the thoughts by putting them on paper. This is the time to let those judgments have their own life.

DIRECTIONS:

A. Think of a specific person that is triggering stress in you. It could be your child, partner, ex-partner, mom, or dad. (Not yourself) They could be living or not living.

B. Now, recall a specific stressful situation you had with that person. It might have been a face to face interaction, an event, a phone call, or any situation that caused you any feelings of discomfort. Identify the specific stressful situation, and see it as a *single snapshot* in time.

C. Witness that single snapshot. Notice the time, place, words spoken, body language, and energy of each person. Then, 1) Identify and name the primary uncomfortable feeling you were having, 2) identify why you felt that way, and 3) answer the questions below with *short, simple* statements. *Please do not* try to be psychologically correct, spiritual, or wise now. For the purposes of this worksheet, be as judgmental as you were when you were in that situation.

1. In this situation, who angers, confuses, saddens, or disappoints you, and why? *(Example: I'm frustrated with Aiden because he won't listen to me.)*

2. In this situation, how do you want them to change? *(Example: I want Aiden to stop what he's doing, look at me, and listen to me.)*

3. In this situation, what advice would you offer to them? *(Example: Aiden should learn how to listen.)*

4. In order for you to feel better in this situation, what do you need them to think, say, feel, or do? *(Example: I need Aiden to listen.)*

5. What do you think of them in this situation? Make a list. Be petty. *(Example: Aiden is just like his dad - he won't respect me.)*

6. What is it in or about this situation that you don't ever want to experience again? *(Example: I don't ever want to be disrespected by Aiden again.)*

Review what you wrote. Pick one sentence you wrote that feels the most stressful to you right now. Circle it. Rewrite it at the top of Worksheet 2.

Adapted from Byron Katie International, Inc. Rev. 7/2014, with consent.

Self-Inquiry Worksheet 2 of 2

This worksheet is a meditation. When answering the questions, close your eyes, be still, and patiently wait to witness what appears to you. Always give yourself time to let the deeper answers meet the questions.

DIRECTIONS:
A. In the space below, write the thought you circled from Worksheet 1. Then answer questions 1-4.
B. Reconstruct the thought in three new ways. Possibilities are: by directing it inward (number 5 below), exchanging the other person's name with yours (number 6 below), and stating its exact opposite (number 7 below). Examples are provided below. Then, find and record three genuine, specific examples of how each new thought is as true or truer for you in that situation.
C. If you circled the thought from your answer to question 6 on Worksheet 1, you would reconstruct the thought by replacing the words, "I don't ever want to…" with "I am willing to…" and "I look forward to…"

Re-write the thought you circled on Worksheet 1: *(Example: Aiden doesn't listen to me.)*

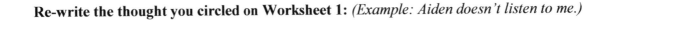

1. In that situation, is this thought true? *(Yes or no only. There are no right or wrong answers. If no, skip to question 3.)*

2. In that situation, can you absolutely know that it's true? *(Yes or no only)*

3. In that situation, how did you *react* when you believed that thought?

4. In that situation, who would you be if you could not believe that thought?

5. Reconstruct the thought by directing it *inward. (Example: I don't listen to me.)* Find and record three genuine, specific examples in that situation how this new thought is as true or truer than the original thought.

6. Reconstruct the thought by *exchanging* the other person's name with yours. *(Example: I don't listen to Aiden.)* Find and record three genuine, specific examples of how this new thought is as true or truer for you in that situation.

7. Reconstruct the thought by stating the *exact opposite. (Example: Aiden does listen to me.)* Find and record three genuine, specific examples of how this new thought is as true or truer for you in that situation.

Adapted from Byron Katie International, Inc. Rev. 7/2014, with consent.

Welcome to Morning 28 - *Your Own Wisdom*

(I invite you to first re-read the Morning Meditation on page 16.)

Dear Present Mother,

The only true rule I have in my house is for me: Question my thoughts if I get hooked. I notice that my children are a perfect reflection of my thinking up until this now moment. All of the things I thought they should do, all of the things I wanted them to do, all of the things I "needed" them to do, I did and do for myself now. They get to stay connected to the present moment and I get to be free to control my own happiness. It's so beautiful the way this works. I cannot imagine a life without it. It wasn't always like this.

I used to think I was pretty good at this thing about giving them freedom and helping them stay connected to the present moment. Then a fear would pop up about something, anything, and I would be sent flying off into my worries, which I would then project on to them. Rule formed. Rebellion started. Lying began. Chaos reigned.

For *years* my kids and I went around and around about rules for screen use. I fretted, inadvertently created conflicts, obsessed about researching the effects, justified my controlling them, tried other people's advice, took away what I had given them as gifts, as well as the opposite - giving them total freedom (with resentment and fear added in), forgetting my view in the process. You name it, we tried it. It caused a lot of disconnection between us.

None of the rules or things I tried worked for us. They all lasted for only a day or two. They all created disconnection between all of us. They all created more drama than any drama you could find on TV. I say it was because I had not dived deep enough into self-inquiry, listening deeply to the wisdom that arises in me when answering the questions on the worksheets. I realized that I was spending way more time watching the stories and movies in my *mind* about their screen-use than they were spending watching or playing anything on any screen! After that realization, my mind, all on its own, dropped *my* addictions to the screens in my mind. Suddenly there was no stress in my mind around screen use in our home. Then - in the beautiful perfect reflection - my son actually asked me to remind him when 30 minutes had passed since he started playing a video game or watching something on YouTube or TV. He told me he wanted to make sure he takes a break and would like my help. Now I lovingly remind him after thirty minutes and then leave it up to him what he does. All he asked was that I remind him; so that's all I do. Self-inquiry is not about which rule about anything will apply in your house and which will not, or which parenting practice to use, or which parenting expert to follow, or about following anyone. It's not about how to raise your children, how to education your children, nor what lifestyle to have. There are no judgments of any of this with self-inquiry. That's another reason I love it so much. When I finally realized this I saw how I could connect with every other mother on the planet because I wasn't judging anyone, since I wasn't judging myself.

Self-inquiry is about finding your *own* wisdom and applying it in your life. It's about allowing yourself the time, the space, the freedom, and the place of non-judgment so you can find your *own* way. That's why I said in the introduction that *here* we are in a place of total acceptance and complete non-judgment, maybe for the first time in your life. We are meeting in the field out beyond ideas of wrongdoing and rightdoing, as Rumi says in his beautiful poem. What a beautiful place it is to be, a place I never want to leave. I love meeting you here.

Wishing you, dear one, Presence and Peace today,
Catherine

Presence Practice Notes

Your Own Wisdom

Self-Inquiry Worksheet 1 of 2

We've been told all of our lives not to judge others. The fact is we do it anyway. This worksheet allows the mind to see itself, to see the reality of its own thoughts, and to truly consider the thoughts by putting them on paper. This is the time to let those judgments have their own life.

DIRECTIONS:
A. Think of a specific person that is triggering stress in you. It could be your child, partner, ex-partner, mom, or dad. (Not yourself) They could be living or not living.
B. Now, recall a specific stressful situation you had with that person. It might have been a face to face interaction, an event, a phone call, or any situation that caused you any feelings of discomfort. Identify the specific stressful situation, and see it as a *single snapshot* in time.
C. Witness that single snapshot. Notice the time, place, words spoken, body language, and energy of each person. Then, 1) Identify and name the primary uncomfortable feeling you were having, 2) identify why you felt that way, and 3) answer the questions below with *short, simple* statements. *Please do not* try to be psychologically correct, spiritual, or wise now. For the purposes of this worksheet, be as judgmental as you were when you were in that situation.

1. In this situation, who angers, confuses, saddens, or disappoints you, and why? *(Example: I'm frustrated with Aiden because he won't listen to me.)*

2. In this situation, how do you want them to change? *(Example: I want Aiden to stop what he's doing, look at me, and listen to me.)*

3. In this situation, what advice would you offer to them? *(Example: Aiden should learn how to listen.)*

4. In order for you to feel better in this situation, what do you need them to think, say, feel, or do? *(Example: I need Aiden to listen.)*

5. What do you think of them in this situation? Make a list. Be petty. *(Example: Aiden is just like his dad - he won't respect me.)*

6. What is it in or about this situation that you don't ever want to experience again? *(Example: I don't ever want to be disrespected by Aiden again.)*

Review what you wrote. Pick one sentence you wrote that feels the most stressful to you right now. Circle it. Rewrite it at the top of Worksheet 2.

Adapted from Byron Katie International, Inc. Rev. 7/2014, with consent.

Self-Inquiry Worksheet 2 of 2

This worksheet is a meditation. When answering the questions, close your eyes, be still, and patiently wait to witness what appears to you. Always give yourself time to let the deeper answers meet the questions.

DIRECTIONS:

A. In the space below, write the thought you circled from Worksheet 1. Then answer questions 1-4.

B. Reconstruct the thought in three new ways. Possibilities are: by directing it inward (number 5 below), exchanging the other person's name with yours (number 6 below), and stating its exact opposite (number 7 below). Examples are provided below. Then, find and record three genuine, specific examples of how each new thought is as true or truer for you in that situation.

C. If you circled the thought from your answer to question 6 on Worksheet 1, you would reconstruct the thought by replacing the words, "I don't ever want to…" with "I am willing to…" and "I look forward to…"

Re-write the thought you circled on Worksheet 1: *(Example: Aiden doesn't listen to me.)*

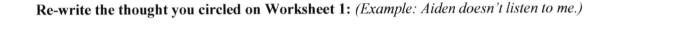

1. In that situation, is this thought true? *(Yes or no only. There are no right or wrong answers. If no, skip to question 3.)*

2. In that situation, can you absolutely know that it's true? *(Yes or no only)*

3. In that situation, how did you *react* when you believed that thought?

4. In that situation, who would you be if you could not believe that thought?

5. Reconstruct the thought by directing it *inward. (Example: I don't listen to me.)* Find and record three genuine, specific examples in that situation how this new thought is as true or truer than the original thought.

6. Reconstruct the thought by *exchanging* the other person's name with yours. *(Example: I don't listen to Aiden.)* Find and record three genuine, specific examples of how this new thought is as true or truer for you in that situation.

7. Reconstruct the thought by stating the *exact opposite. (Example: Aiden does listen to me.)* Find and record three genuine, specific examples of how this new thought is as true or truer for you in that situation.

Adapted from Byron Katie International, Inc. Rev. 7/2014, with consent.

Welcome to Morning 29 - *What Problems?*

(I invite you to first re-read the Morning Meditation on page 16.)

Dear Present Mother,

As I look through my window now, it's so beautiful outside…the leaves are the most amazing spectrum of colors. The air is so clear and crisp. My house is so quiet. Words magically appear on a screen when I move my finger a certain way. Incredible. I completely feel the support of the present moment - nurturing, nourishing. I feel the unmovable strength of the chair beneath me. Beauty in the form of children's paintings surrounds me. What could be more wonderful?

It is equally wonderful to me when a stressful thought arises within this present moment. Last night, the kids and I were all lying down in the bed, ready for sleep. I identified with feeling extremely tired. Both of them were moving around, trying to get comfortable. I was already comfortable. This lasted for about 2 minutes. I was identifying with the thought, *"I want to go to sleep now."* I asked them if they would please stop moving around so much and could they calm themselves down and go to sleep. As I write this right now, I see the projection: "I asked *me* if I would please stop moving around so much - away from the present moment - and could I calm myself down and go to sleep."

Back to the story. They said yes they would calm down and go to sleep, and they did for about *ten* seconds. Then the movement started again: my thoughts wandering away from the present moment and their bodies wriggling in the bed, in perfect reflection. I suddenly sat up and said, "I'm feeling like I'm getting angry." I laid back down in exasperation and started telling the story of how we would all be so tired the next day, et cetera. My daughter softly said, "Mom, you can't know the future." Illusion busted. What an enlightened little girl! Immediately after that, in perfect reflection of my thoughts again (!) my son said, "Mom, pause." I did. Immediately after that I said, "Yes, you're both right. Thank you for pointing those out to me." Then we all went to sleep.

I tell you this story of the past - which now only exists in my mind as a thought pattern, and is therefore not reality - as an example of how there are no problems in my house anymore. I just can't see one. Everything is a gift. The thought, *"I want to go to sleep,"* was a gift. I got to see the brilliance in my children, which I had helped them keep intact. The quiet in the house at this moment is a gift. I got to peacefully share the story with you and have even more realizations about how every action and word our children show us is all *for* us. From this present moment to the next one, they show us what our thoughts are. Amazing! It's a wonderful life. There is ever only this present moment, with thoughts rising and falling within each one.

What stressful thoughts are you attaching to and believing? None of them are true. Really. Even the ones like "It's a wonderful life" are not true. It's all a dream, other than this present moment. Which dream do you like: the dream that there are problems or the dream that it's a wonderful life? The only thing that is truly real is this present moment; everything else is a dream. When I don't believe any stressful thoughts, life is always good.

After you start to do self-inquiry on a regular basis your whole energy begins to shift. Nothing - no thing, and a thought is a thing - is a problem. You just can't see it that way anymore. You're only left with deep appreciation and a deep, constant, gentle energy within you called Love, which is your true nature, as well as your child's. Love moves in life, through you, as you, and you can't stop it.

Wishing you, dear one, Presence and Peace today,
Catherine

Presence Practice Notes

What Problems?

Self-Inquiry Worksheet 1 of 2

We've been told all of our lives not to judge others. The fact is we do it anyway. This worksheet allows the mind to see itself, to see the reality of its own thoughts, and to truly consider the thoughts by putting them on paper. This is the time to let those judgments have their own life.

DIRECTIONS:
A. Think of a specific person that is triggering stress in you. It could be your child, partner, ex-partner, mom, or dad. (Not yourself) They could be living or not living.
B. Now, recall a specific stressful situation you had with that person. It might have been a face to face interaction, an event, a phone call, or any situation that caused you any feelings of discomfort. Identify the specific stressful situation, and see it as a *single snapshot* in time.
C. Witness that single snapshot. Notice the time, place, words spoken, body language, and energy of each person. Then, 1) Identify and name the primary uncomfortable feeling you were having, 2) identify why you felt that way, and 3) answer the questions below with *short, simple* statements. *Please do not* try to be psychologically correct, spiritual, or wise now. For the purposes of this worksheet, be as judgmental as you were when you were in that situation.

1. In this situation, who angers, confuses, saddens, or disappoints you, and why? *(Example: I'm frustrated with Aiden because he won't listen to me.)*

2. In this situation, how do you want them to change? *(Example: I want Aiden to stop what he's doing, look at me, and listen to me.)*

3. In this situation, what advice would you offer to them? *(Example: Aiden should learn how to listen.)*

4. In order for you to feel better in this situation, what do you need them to think, say, feel, or do? *(Example: I need Aiden to listen.)*

5. What do you think of them in this situation? Make a list. Be petty. *(Example: Aiden is just like his dad - he won't respect me.)*

6. What is it in or about this situation that you don't ever want to experience again? *(Example: I don't ever want to be disrespected by Aiden again.)*

Review what you wrote. Pick one sentence you wrote that feels the most stressful to you right now. Circle it. Rewrite it at the top of Worksheet 2.

Self-Inquiry Worksheet 2 of 2

This worksheet is a meditation. When answering the questions, close your eyes, be still, and patiently wait to witness what appears to you. Always give yourself time to let the deeper answers meet the questions.

DIRECTIONS:

A. In the space below, write the thought you circled from Worksheet 1. Then answer questions 1-4.

B. Reconstruct the thought in three new ways. Possibilities are: by directing it inward (number 5 below), exchanging the other person's name with yours (number 6 below), and stating its exact opposite (number 7 below). Examples are provided below. Then, find and record three genuine, specific examples of how each new thought is as true or truer for you in that situation.

C. If you circled the thought from your answer to question 6 on Worksheet 1, you would reconstruct the thought by replacing the words, "I don't ever want to…" with "I am willing to…" and "I look forward to…"

Re-write the thought you circled on Worksheet 1: *(Example: Aiden doesn't listen to me.)*

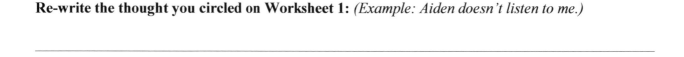

1. In that situation, is this thought true? *(Yes or no only. There are no right or wrong answers. If no, skip to question 3.)*

2. In that situation, can you absolutely know that it's true? *(Yes or no only)*

3. In that situation, how did you *react* when you believed that thought?

4. In that situation, who would you be if you could not believe that thought?

5. Reconstruct the thought by directing it *inward. (Example: I don't listen to me.)* Find and record three genuine, specific examples in that situation how this new thought is as true or truer than the original thought.

6. Reconstruct the thought by *exchanging* the other person's name with yours. *(Example: I don't listen to Aiden.)* Find and record three genuine, specific examples of how this new thought is as true or truer for you in that situation.

7. Reconstruct the thought by stating the *exact opposite. (Example: Aiden does listen to me.)* Find and record three genuine, specific examples of how this new thought is as true or truer for you in that situation.

Adapted from Byron Katie International, Inc. Rev. 7/2014, with consent.

Welcome to Morning 30 - *Pure Love for Your Child*

(I invite you to first re-read the Morning Meditation on page 16.)

Dear Present Mother,

At one point in my mothering journey I believed so many stressful thoughts about my children (without even realizing it) that I spiraled into one of the saddest times of my life. I unconsciously believed so many thoughts about what was "wrong" with them that I felt I couldn't focus on anything else but my worry, fear, sadness, frustration and anger. I didn't know how to shake those feelings. I was almost frantic trying to feel more connected with them. I felt guilty for not feeling more loving. I felt terrified that I *couldn't* seem to find or feel that deeply connected feeling I had before. I became frustrated with myself and my precious children. I felt very confused. Eventually, I began to think, "*Something is wrong with me.*" *How in the world could it be like this*? I cried on and off about it for what seemed like months. Thankfully, I would later find out that all of this had *nothing* to do with my beautiful children.

I can't even describe the elation, utter joy, and overwhelming gratitude I felt during and after doing self-inquiry on those debilitating thoughts about my son and daughter! With its simple, clear structure to ground me, I identified what was coming between me and my love for my children - unconscious thoughts and judgments about them that were simply not my reality, and therefore not even *true*. They were thoughts like, *"They're not supposed to fight with each other, they shouldn't be so mean to each other, they're disobeying me, they won't listen to me, they're lazy, they're violent, I have no influence over them, they're going to have a terrible life, I can't control them.,"* and on and on. There were thoughts and judgments about me too, "*I'm a terrible mother, I don't deserve to be their mom, they're better off without me, I'm a failure,*" and on and on.

I discovered, through self-inquiry, that all of these thoughts were arguments with my reality and that the more I wanted reality to be different the worse my situation got. I was unconsciously believing thoughts that simply were not true, not real, not what was showing itself in the present moment. I eventually realized that the root cause of my disconnection with them, the root cause of my loss of awareness of love was me *believing* these false thoughts and judgments *about* them, and *not* my *actual* children or their behavior. I invite you to read that last sentence again.

~

Slowly, one thought at a time, I began to see how I reacted when I believed these very stressful thoughts. I saw how my belief in these thoughts was the cause of my suffering. Words cannot even point to the happiness I would feel every time after I questioned these thoughts. What I thought was the worst experience I'd ever been through turned out to be the best thing that ever happened to me. I realized so much about myself and I got my relationship back with my kids! I lived in a quiet joy each day. I got the relationship with myself back as well. My awareness of Love was reborn. It was pure bliss.

In the process, I discovered two amazing things:

1. When I was the age that my children were during this time, I believed these same thoughts about *myself*. This was shocking to me and at the same time made so much sense. It was when I was seven, near their ages then, that my parents were divorcing. I thought the divorce was my fault. I believed things like, *"I shouldn't be so mean, I'm disobeying them, they won't listen to me."* Those were the exact same beliefs I had about my children! That's when these beliefs were *born* within me, when I was seven. This is so real and true for me. And it's not the only time I've experienced it. I also experienced it with my husband around this same time, when my oldest child was seven, the same age I was when my mom and dad got divorced and my life changed dramatically. My theory is that this unconscious re-creation of our childhood beliefs, occurring at the same age we were that our child is now, is evident in every other human being on the planet. Until we question those beliefs, they hold us in their grip and *we unconsciously recreate the past.*

~

2. I also discovered that every other person on the planet is thinking (sometimes without their conscious awareness) and believing (sometimes unconsciously) the same stress-inducing thoughts that have been around since the beginning of human existence. *"He should, he shouldn't, she should, she shouldn't, they should, they shouldn't..." Judge, judge, judge.* The only thing we're left with after believing these thoughts that aren't even our *own* thoughts, is disconnection – from ourselves, from others, and from the soul of life. If the thoughts cause stress when we believe them, then I know for sure that they are not personal to me, that I just inherited them from the world that still believes them, and that they are absolutely false when tested against our current reality.

~

When we become mothers it's as if we're dealt a hand of cards with all of the same stressful thoughts on them. If you've ever been a member of a moms group where they talk about stressful thoughts and stories, you'll know this to be true. When you've been doing self-inquiry for a while, you'll know this is true also. If you're involved with a group of mothers who do self-inquiry on these thoughts, you'll also witness that this is true. There are just no *new* stressful thoughts about mothering or anything else. This is *great* news! None of these stressful thoughts are *personal*. None of these stressful thoughts are even *true*. None of these stressful thoughts are *reality*. They're all a big illusion that we've believed for centuries. We don't have to believe them anymore. Thank goodness now we have a new way!

One time, I was with a group of about 300 people who were all practicing self-inquiry. I was surprised and relieved to hear that no one in the room said a *new* stressful thought! It appears that we are all just walking around believing the same stories, coming from the same stressful thoughts. Until we question our stressful thoughts, we are all walking around suffering from some kind of contagious illness or amnesia. I am so glad I have a choice now: suffer, get lost, feel and cause pain *or* question my thinking.

This morning, I invite you to consider - instead of push away or ignore - what stresses you most about your child or your life with your child so that you can free yourself of it. What specific situation comes to your mind? I invite you to do your self-inquiry on that this morning. Put it on paper. It's all in your mind anyway. Why not stop it by writing it down, questioning it, and transcending it? Why not return to your pure love for your child this morning as you do your presence practice?

Calming, relaxing routines while self-inquiry is alive and active in your life can greatly nurture you while in the process. Getting still, being quiet, and being with yourself nourishes the soul. I love Pandora Meditation channel; I play it as much as possible. I invite you to find, remember, or re-commit to your own special rituals and calming routines. I invite you to keep including these in your life as you get to know your true self, your beautiful presence, and your pure Love, through self-inquiry. You and your child will love that you do.

Wishing you, dear one, Presence and Peace today,
Catherine

Presence Practice Notes

Pure Love for Your Child

Self-Inquiry Worksheet 1 of 2

We've been told all of our lives not to judge others. The fact is we do it anyway. This worksheet allows the mind to see itself, to see the reality of its own thoughts, and to truly consider the thoughts by putting them on paper. This is the time to let those judgments have their own life.

DIRECTIONS:

A. Think of a specific person that is triggering stress in you. It could be your child, partner, ex-partner, mom, or dad. (Not yourself) They could be living or not living.

B. Now, recall a specific stressful situation you had with that person. It might have been a face to face interaction, an event, a phone call, or any situation that caused you any feelings of discomfort. Identify the specific stressful situation, and see it as a *single snapshot* in time.

C. Witness that single snapshot. Notice the time, place, words spoken, body language, and energy of each person. Then, 1) Identify and name the primary uncomfortable feeling you were having, 2) identify why you felt that way, and 3) answer the questions below with *short, simple* statements. *Please do not* try to be psychologically correct, spiritual, or wise now. For the purposes of this worksheet, be as judgmental as you were when you were in that situation.

1. In this situation, who angers, confuses, saddens, or disappoints you, and why? *(Example: I'm frustrated with Aiden because he won't listen to me.)*

2. In this situation, how do you want them to change? *(Example: I want Aiden to stop what he's doing, look at me, and listen to me.)*

3. In this situation, what advice would you offer to them? *(Example: Aiden should learn how to listen.)*

4. In order for you to feel better in this situation, what do you need them to think, say, feel, or do? *(Example: I need Aiden to listen.)*

5. What do you think of them in this situation? Make a list. Be petty. *(Example: Aiden is just like his dad - he won't respect me.)*

6. What is it in or about this situation that you don't ever want to experience again? *(Example: I don't ever want to be disrespected by Aiden again.)*

Review what you wrote. Pick one sentence you wrote that feels the most stressful to you right now. Circle it. Rewrite it at the top of Worksheet 2.

Adapted from Byron Katie International, Inc. Rev. 7/2014, with consent.

Self-Inquiry Worksheet 2 of 2

This worksheet is a meditation. When answering the questions, close your eyes, be still, and patiently wait to witness what appears to you. Always give yourself time to let the deeper answers meet the questions.

DIRECTIONS:

A. In the space below, write the thought you circled from Worksheet 1. Then answer questions 1-4.

B. Reconstruct the thought in three new ways. Possibilities are: by directing it inward (number 5 below), exchanging the other person's name with yours (number 6 below), and stating its exact opposite (number 7 below). Examples are provided below. Then, find and record three genuine, specific examples of how each new thought is as true or truer for you in that situation.

C. If you circled the thought from your answer to question 6 on Worksheet 1, you would reconstruct the thought by replacing the words, "I don't ever want to…" with "I am willing to…" and "I look forward to…"

Re-write the thought you circled on Worksheet 1: *(Example: Aiden doesn't listen to me.)*

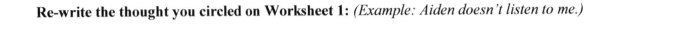

1. In that situation, is this thought true? *(Yes or no only. There are no right or wrong answers. If no, skip to question 3.)*

2. In that situation, can you absolutely know that it's true? *(Yes or no only)*

3. In that situation, how did you *react* when you believed that thought?

4. In that situation, who would you be if you could not believe that thought?

5. Reconstruct the thought by directing it *inward. (Example: I don't listen to me.)* Find and record three genuine, specific examples in that situation how this new thought is as true or truer than the original thought.

6. Reconstruct the thought by *exchanging* the other person's name with yours. *(Example: I don't listen to Aiden.)* Find and record three genuine, specific examples of how this new thought is as true or truer for you in that situation.

7. Reconstruct the thought by stating the *exact opposite. (Example: Aiden does listen to me.)* Find and record three genuine, specific examples of how this new thought is as true or truer for you in that situation.

Adapted from Byron Katie International, Inc. Rev. 7/2014, with consent.

Welcome to Morning 31 - *Noticing*

(I invite you to first re-read the Morning Meditation on page 16.)

Dear Present Mother,

When we're fully present there are very few words being spoken. There are no stories being told. While we are present, if words do get spoken, spontaneously they flow through us, from some divine source, and they are complete perfect Love. There are no conditions placed on love. If we were all completely present, then the phrase "unconditional love" would become extinct. I know this from experience. Imagine, if that were how we all lived, every day. Imagine if that were how all children were raised. What a new world.

One of the most powerful meditations I've ever done helped me see that thoughts come and go, and I don't put them there, they just occur. I can either believe them or identify with them (make them part of my identity) or I can notice them, question them, and then they let go of me. This meditation helped me to know myself as the one who witnesses the thoughts. I am (you are) the one who is aware of the thoughts. It also created in me the act of consciously training my mind to stay in the present moment. I found it to have a very peaceful effect on my state of being.

Our meditation group met outdoors at 7:00 AM for eight mornings in a row. The sunrises were stunning. The air was fresh and cool. Birds could be heard singing their lovely songs. Once we met, warm tea in hand, we were given the meditation instructions: "Silently, slowly walk with each other, following one of the staff. As you're walking and looking around, silently give each thing you notice a first-generation name, slowly and consciously naming each thing. For example, *sun, grass, sky, tree, foot, flower*. When you notice thoughts on your mind that veer from first-generation names (thoughts such as '*beautiful* sky' or 'I'm so sleepy') gently and compassionately guide yourself back to giving only first-generation names." So, I went for it every morning.

Then, silently, after breakfast, we'd meet at the comfortable conference room, overflowing with quiet meditation music and no words being spoken in the room. The first thing that would happen is a version of the meditation you've been using on page 16. I'll try to represent it here as best as I can remember.

The music stopped. Our guide.[6] said, "Breathe. Notice you're being breathed." After about one to two minutes of silence she said, "Notice. Notice the thought on your mind when I said the word *notice*. Label it with a category name like child, mother, money, body. Now, watch it drift, further and further away, until finally it is out of sight." Then about one to two minutes of silence would pass by. Again she said, "Notice. Notice the thought on your mind when I said the word *notice*. Label it with a category name like child, mother, spouse, et cetera. Now, watch it drift, further and further away, until finally it is out of sight." She repeated this about two more times, always waiting the two or so minutes in between. At the end there was a final silence of similar length, and then she would say, "Welcome Family."

Talk about a blank slate! There were no words to utter, no words wanted to be uttered which would break this magical, mysterious, perfect silence. After the meditation, I was in Rumi's field, where the world is too full to talk about. That's why I love being in that field. I feel so young, just learning how to be here now, and stay here, connected to myself and my children.

I hope you enjoy reading the Morning Meditation every morning before each letter. I hope you're experiencing the field where the world is too full to talk about. I love inviting you there (here) every day. If you haven't experienced it yet, that's okay. Remember, it's perfect wherever you are.

Wishing you, dear one, Presence and Peace today,
Catherine

---

[6] This meditation was led by Byron Katie at the Nine-day School For The Work.

Presence Practice Notes

Noticing

Self-Inquiry Worksheet 1 of 2

We've been told all of our lives not to judge others. The fact is we do it anyway. This worksheet allows the mind to see itself, to see the reality of its own thoughts, and to truly consider the thoughts by putting them on paper. This is the time to let those judgments have their own life.

DIRECTIONS:

A. Think of a specific person that is triggering stress in you. It could be your child, partner, ex-partner, mom, or dad. (Not yourself) They could be living or not living.

B. Now, recall a specific stressful situation you had with that person. It might have been a face to face interaction, an event, a phone call, or any situation that caused you any feelings of discomfort. Identify the specific stressful situation, and see it as a *single snapshot* in time.

C. Witness that single snapshot. Notice the time, place, words spoken, body language, and energy of each person. Then, 1) Identify and name the primary uncomfortable feeling you were having, 2) identify why you felt that way, and 3) answer the questions below with *short, simple* statements. *Please do not* try to be psychologically correct, spiritual, or wise now. For the purposes of this worksheet, be as judgmental as you were when you were in that situation.

1. In this situation, who angers, confuses, saddens, or disappoints you, and why? *(Example: I'm frustrated with Aiden because he won't listen to me.)*

2. In this situation, how do you want them to change? *(Example: I want Aiden to stop what he's doing, look at me, and listen to me.)*

3. In this situation, what advice would you offer to them? *(Example: Aiden should learn how to listen.)*

4. In order for you to feel better in this situation, what do you need them to think, say, feel, or do? *(Example: I need Aiden to listen.)*

5. What do you think of them in this situation? Make a list. Be petty. *(Example: Aiden is just like his dad - he won't respect me.)*

6. What is it in or about this situation that you don't ever want to experience again? *(Example: I don't ever want to be disrespected by Aiden again.)*

Review what you wrote. Pick one sentence you wrote that feels the most stressful to you right now. Circle it. Rewrite it at the top of Worksheet 2.

Adapted from Byron Katie International, Inc. Rev. 7/2014, with consent.

Self-Inquiry Worksheet 2 of 2

This worksheet is a meditation. When answering the questions, close your eyes, be still, and patiently wait to witness what appears to you. Always give yourself time to let the deeper answers meet the questions.

DIRECTIONS:

A. In the space below, write the thought you circled from Worksheet 1. Then answer questions 1-4.

B. Reconstruct the thought in three new ways. Possibilities are: by directing it inward (number 5 below), exchanging the other person's name with yours (number 6 below), and stating its exact opposite (number 7 below). Examples are provided below. Then, find and record three genuine, specific examples of how each new thought is as true or truer for you in that situation.

C. If you circled the thought from your answer to question 6 on Worksheet 1, you would reconstruct the thought by replacing the words, "I don't ever want to…" with "I am willing to…" and "I look forward to…"

Re-write the thought you circled on Worksheet 1: *(Example: Aiden doesn't listen to me.)*

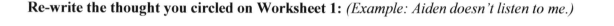

1. In that situation, is this thought true? *(Yes or no only. There are no right or wrong answers. If no, skip to question 3.)*

2. In that situation, can you absolutely know that it's true? *(Yes or no only)*

3. In that situation, how did you *react* when you believed that thought?

4. In that situation, who would you be if you could not believe that thought?

5. Reconstruct the thought by directing it *inward. (Example: I don't listen to me.)* Find and record three genuine, specific examples in that situation how this new thought is as true or truer than the original thought.

6. Reconstruct the thought by *exchanging* the other person's name with yours. *(Example: I don't listen to Aiden.)* Find and record three genuine, specific examples of how this new thought is as true or truer for you in that situation.

7. Reconstruct the thought by stating the *exact opposite. (Example: Aiden does listen to me.)* Find and record three genuine, specific examples of how this new thought is as true or truer for you in that situation.

Adapted from Byron Katie International, Inc. Rev. 7/2014, with consent.

Welcome to Morning 32 - *Peace of Mind*

(I invite you to first re-read the Morning Meditation on page 16.)

Dear Present Mother,

Whenever there used to be some kind of disagreement, argument, or all-out angry push and pull between my two children, I loved saying, "Work it out peacefully." I've always tried to model this to them through my interactions with them and by how I live my life. I was able to remember this most of the time. Sometimes though, which really *shocked* me at first, I reacted in ways I didn't want to. I was definitely not working it out peacefully within myself.

We often hear, as mindful mothers, to stay calm in the face of our children's quarrels. In my experience, this is far easier said than actually done. In reality, how *do* we keep our cool? I was baffled trying to figure this out. I researched and read so much to try to understand how to do this consistently. I tried so many things to try and be calm when they weren't.

It wasn't until I looked deeply *within* and questioned my thoughts *about* their arguments, that I realized how *"work it out peacefully"* was always my own best advice to myself. I now see that their arguing was the best thing that could have ever happened to me in order to assist me in experiencing peace *about* their arguing. Only then, when I was calm enough, could I actually *help* them in any productive way or calmly trust them to work things out for themselves. Arguing in my mind (about their arguing) equaled a third person adding to the argument. Peace in my mind (about their arguing) equaled a calm, peaceful mom to provide support - if needed - and unconditional love. Eventually, my peace was contagious for them.

To demonstrate, I'll share my experience of doing self-inquiry on the stressful thought *"They shouldn't fight!"* My situation is when my two children were arguing right after I was feeling impatient with myself for not eating when I wanted to.

Is it true, they shouldn't fight? Yes! *Can you absolutely know that it's true, they shouldn't fight?* No, not absolutely.

How do you react when you believe that thought? I argue with them about their fighting and then there are three of us fighting! This thought, when I believe it, brings so much stress into my life. I see all the times they've argued in the past and all the times in the future that I think they'll argue again. I feel my throat tighten up. Anger arises. When that happens, I start to believe they should do exactly what I say. I act like they don't have minds of their own. I feel like a roaring lion about to strike in anger. I feel scared that I might actually do that. I feel scared that they're really going to hurt each other. I see images of the future where one of them is really hurt. I'm *so* not present when I see those movies of the future. I give them all the control over my happiness! I see them fighting their whole lives. I see them totally disconnected in their relationship in the future. I'm not able to help them at all. I get angry with myself about not being more present. I say to myself that I'm a bad mother. I am a very harsh judge of myself. I feel guilt, self-condemnation, depression, and sadness after that.

Who would you be without that thought? I would be calm, centered, peaceful, gentle, kind, articulate, aware, skilled, creative, wise, clear, present, connected, loving. I'd have no judgments. I would be the channel for love and compassion to shine through. I would be helpful to both of them.

Reconstruct the thought to a thought that's as true or truer. "They shouldn't fight" becomes:

1. *I* shouldn't fight. Examples are: a) I shouldn't fight with me when I want to eat. I should just go eat! b) I shouldn't fight with them when they're fighting, and with the reality of them arguing and with life. (Life showed me they were arguing, and I fought, in my mind, what I saw). c) I shouldn't fight with me when I want to say no to my kids. I should just clearly, calmly say no to them, and yes to me. It's always a more peaceful result when that happens. d) I shouldn't fight with me when I judge myself about my reaction to their fighting. I should be kinder and more compassionate to me. That would feel good. e) I should make peace within me before I approach them about their fighting. f) I shouldn't be an angry protestor with them when they're arguing. It just makes it worse.

2. They *should* fight. Genuine, specific examples why that's true: a) They're mirroring me: I am still fighting with reality when I see an upset start to build in them and in me. b) Because I was fighting with myself: one of my kids asked me for my attention but I didn't want to give it. Instead I wanted to eat. I said yes anyway, and then immediately got distracted by my hunger and mad at myself for telling her yes and myself no, and not going to eat. That's when the arguing started. c) Another way they're mirroring me is that my daughter said "yes" to my son's request and then she didn't follow through and got distracted instead. Then she said she really didn't want to say yes anyway. Then there was heightened arguing.

3. I look *forward* to them fighting again. Examples are: a) So that I can find more and more peace in my heart about them fighting, through doing self-inquiry on my thoughts about their arguments. b) So that I get to practice projecting that peace out into my life, even when they're fighting. c) So that I can model peace for them, and they'll have an example. d) So they know how to live a peaceful life.

~

I invite you to remember a time when you got upset with your kids for arguing with each other. If you have only one child, try remembering a time when your child was arguing with *you* about something. Remember the time, the place, and all the details. Then, enjoy filling in the worksheets that follow, and discover your own peace of mind.

Wishing you, dear one, Presence and Peace today,
Catherine

Presence Practice Notes

Peace of Mind

Self-Inquiry Worksheet 1 of 2

We've been told all of our lives not to judge others. The fact is we do it anyway. This worksheet allows the mind to see itself, to see the reality of its own thoughts, and to truly consider the thoughts by putting them on paper. This is the time to let those judgments have their own life.

DIRECTIONS:
A. Think of a specific person that is triggering stress in you. It could be your child, partner, ex-partner, mom, or dad. (Not yourself) They could be living or not living.
B. Now, recall a specific stressful situation you had with that person. It might have been a face to face interaction, an event, a phone call, or any situation that caused you any feelings of discomfort. Identify the specific stressful situation, and see it as a *single snapshot* in time.
C. Witness that single snapshot. Notice the time, place, words spoken, body language, and energy of each person. Then, 1) Identify and name the primary uncomfortable feeling you were having, 2) identify why you felt that way, and 3) answer the questions below with *short, simple* statements. *Please do not* try to be psychologically correct, spiritual, or wise now. For the purposes of this worksheet, be as judgmental as you were when you were in that situation.

1. In this situation, who angers, confuses, saddens, or disappoints you, and why? *(Example: I'm frustrated with Aiden because he won't listen to me.)*

2. In this situation, how do you want them to change? *(Example: I want Aiden to stop what he's doing, look at me, and listen to me.)*

3. In this situation, what advice would you offer to them? *(Example: Aiden should learn how to listen.)*

4. In order for you to feel better in this situation, what do you need them to think, say, feel, or do? *(Example: I need Aiden to listen.)*

5. What do you think of them in this situation? Make a list. Be petty. *(Example: Aiden is just like his dad - he won't respect me.)*

6. What is it in or about this situation that you don't ever want to experience again? *(Example: I don't ever want to be disrespected by Aiden again.)*

Review what you wrote. Pick one sentence you wrote that feels the most stressful to you right now. Circle it. Rewrite it at the top of Worksheet 2.

Adapted from Byron Katie International, Inc. Rev. 7/2014, with consent.

Self-Inquiry Worksheet 2 of 2

This worksheet is a meditation. When answering the questions, close your eyes, be still, and patiently wait to witness what appears to you. Always give yourself time to let the deeper answers meet the questions.

DIRECTIONS:

A. In the space below, write the thought you circled from Worksheet 1. Then answer questions 1-4.

B. Reconstruct the thought in three new ways. Possibilities are: by directing it inward (number 5 below), exchanging the other person's name with yours (number 6 below), and stating its exact opposite (number 7 below). Examples are provided below. Then, find and record three genuine, specific examples of how each new thought is as true or truer for you in that situation.

C. If you circled the thought from your answer to question 6 on Worksheet 1, you would reconstruct the thought by replacing the words, "I don't ever want to…" with "I am willing to…" and "I look forward to…"

Re-write the thought you circled on Worksheet 1: *(Example: Aiden doesn't listen to me.)*

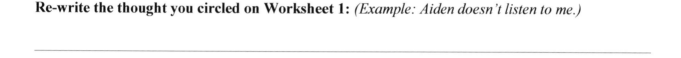

1. In that situation, is this thought true? *(Yes or no only. There are no right or wrong answers. If no, skip to question 3.)*

2. In that situation, can you absolutely know that it's true? *(Yes or no only)*

3. In that situation, how did you *react* when you believed that thought?

4. In that situation, who would you be if you could not believe that thought?

5. Reconstruct the thought by directing it *inward. (Example: I don't listen to me.)* Find and record three genuine, specific examples in that situation how this new thought is as true or truer than the original thought.

6. Reconstruct the thought by *exchanging* the other person's name with yours. *(Example: I don't listen to Aiden.)* Find and record three genuine, specific examples of how this new thought is as true or truer for you in that situation.

7. Reconstruct the thought by stating the *exact opposite. (Example: Aiden does listen to me.)* Find and record three genuine, specific examples of how this new thought is as true or truer for you in that situation.

Adapted from Byron Katie International, Inc. Rev. 7/2014, with consent.

Welcome to Morning 33 - *Setting Yourself Free*

(I invite you to first re-read the Morning Meditation on page 16.)

Dear Present Mother,

This may sound funny (and I'll explain what I mean in a minute) but this whole thing called mothering - and life - is really all about me. For you, you may already realize, it's all about you. There's no other way it can be. But not in the conventional definition of narcissism. I'll explain. It's all a *reflection* of the me I believe myself to be at the time (more precisely, at the time I was the age my children are.) This is how the exact beliefs the parent has about herself are passed down to her child. All of my thoughts about the world are ever always coming through my own mind, so they're *always* about me. It *can't* be any other way if they're only coming through *my* mind. We are bound in this particular body of ours, with this particular mind, seemingly separate from everyone else. However, after I question my stressful thoughts, I see clearly how we are all the same Love when we look underneath our same stressful thoughts.

My life is my personal and spiritual development curriculum. Whenever any feeling arises in me that isn't pleasant - any little irritation, defensiveness, frustration, melancholy, desire to control another, disappointment, guilt, any feeling that we typically don't like - then I know I'm believing a thought that is going against my reality at that moment. I found that reality is actually kinder than my thoughts *about* reality. Sometimes it's just not possible to see that until I do self-inquiry. I love seeing the peace that comes with raising children in a daily environment of so much awareness when there is any kind of suffering in any way. Doing worksheets or self-inquiry in my mind in the morning, or with a friend any time, and the realizations that come with it, set the tone for the whole day in my house.

I didn't sleep as much as I typically do last night. My daughter and her friends really wanted to experience staying up all night and seeing the sun rise. How could I stop them? By trying to control them and being commanding, by manipulating them with a bribe or threat of some kind? No, not here, not now. Instead, we all worked out an arrangement so everyone's sleep needs could be considered and respected.

I was the one who kept me awake, needlessly worrying about them. Each time I had a stressful thought, I responded to myself as a mother would to her own frightened child, taking care of my own worries myself. I had the opportunity to do self-inquiry on some of them that were stickier than others… *"I'll be crabby in the morning," "They'll make a huge mess," "They'll argue and I won't be there to help them," "They'll get sick from not getting enough sleep."* Each time, almost unconsciously, I met each worry with a kind hug from myself, seeing how the opposites were much truer… "I *won't* be crabby in the morning," "*I'll* make a huge mess (if I believe these stressful thoughts)," "*I'll* argue and I *will* be there to help me," "They'll get *well* from not getting enough sleep." I gave my own mind genuine, specific reasons why these new thoughts were truer for me. My mind believed them. The girls are happy. I'm happy. The house is clean. I can write in peace and quiet while they sleep now. The examples of beauty and joy can be seen all over the house. I love this life and all it has given me. What a gift.

What worries are on your mind today? I invite you to do today's self-inquiry on those thoughts. Your life can be your personal and spiritual development curriculum. How can you be a wonderful parent to yourself? Can you listen deeply to yourself, with kindness and compassion, without judgments of right and wrong? The love that you give to yourself could be exactly the love you've been waiting for from your beloved family. I love that you would hold yourself responsible for giving it to you, and set them free from that job. In turn, you set yourself free.

Wishing you, dear one, Presence and Peace today,
Catherine

Presence Practice Notes

Setting Yourself Free

Self-Inquiry Worksheet 1 of 2

We've been told all of our lives not to judge others. The fact is we do it anyway. This worksheet allows the mind to see itself, to see the reality of its own thoughts, and to truly consider the thoughts by putting them on paper. This is the time to let those judgments have their own life.

DIRECTIONS:

A. Think of a specific person that is triggering stress in you. It could be your child, partner, ex-partner, mom, or dad. (Not yourself) They could be living or not living.

B. Now, recall a specific stressful situation you had with that person. It might have been a face to face interaction, an event, a phone call, or any situation that caused you any feelings of discomfort. Identify the specific stressful situation, and see it as a *single snapshot* in time.

C. Witness that single snapshot. Notice the time, place, words spoken, body language, and energy of each person. Then, 1) Identify and name the primary uncomfortable feeling you were having, 2) identify why you felt that way, and 3) answer the questions below with *short, simple* statements. *Please do not* try to be psychologically correct, spiritual, or wise now. For the purposes of this worksheet, be as judgmental as you were when you were in that situation.

1. In this situation, who angers, confuses, saddens, or disappoints you, and why? *(Example: I'm frustrated with Aiden because he won't listen to me.)*

2. In this situation, how do you want them to change? *(Example: I want Aiden to stop what he's doing, look at me, and listen to me.)*

3. In this situation, what advice would you offer to them? *(Example: Aiden should learn how to listen.)*

4. In order for you to feel better in this situation, what do you need them to think, say, feel, or do? *(Example: I need Aiden to listen.)*

5. What do you think of them in this situation? Make a list. Be petty. *(Example: Aiden is just like his dad - he won't respect me.)*

6. What is it in or about this situation that you don't ever want to experience again? *(Example: I don't ever want to be disrespected by Aiden again.)*

Review what you wrote. Pick one sentence you wrote that feels the most stressful to you right now. Circle it. Rewrite it at the top of Worksheet 2.

Adapted from Byron Katie International, Inc. Rev. 7/2014, with consent.

Self-Inquiry Worksheet 2 of 2

This worksheet is a meditation. When answering the questions, close your eyes, be still, and patiently wait to witness what appears to you. Always give yourself time to let the deeper answers meet the questions.

DIRECTIONS:

A. In the space below, write the thought you circled from Worksheet 1. Then answer questions 1-4.

B. Reconstruct the thought in three new ways. Possibilities are: by directing it inward (number 5 below), exchanging the other person's name with yours (number 6 below), and stating its exact opposite (number 7 below). Examples are provided below. Then, find and record three genuine, specific examples of how each new thought is as true or truer for you in that situation.

C. If you circled the thought from your answer to question 6 on Worksheet 1, you would reconstruct the thought by replacing the words, "I don't ever want to…" with "I am willing to…" and "I look forward to…"

Re-write the thought you circled on Worksheet 1: *(Example: Aiden doesn't listen to me.)*

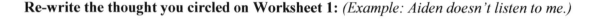

1. In that situation, is this thought true? *(Yes or no only. There are no right or wrong answers. If no, skip to question 3.)*

2. In that situation, can you absolutely know that it's true? *(Yes or no only)*

3. In that situation, how did you *react* when you believed that thought?

4. In that situation, who would you be if you could not believe that thought?

5. Reconstruct the thought by directing it *inward. (Example: I don't listen to me.)* Find and record three genuine, specific examples in that situation how this new thought is as true or truer than the original thought.

6. Reconstruct the thought by *exchanging* the other person's name with yours. *(Example: I don't listen to Aiden.)* Find and record three genuine, specific examples of how this new thought is as true or truer for you in that situation.

7. Reconstruct the thought by stating the *exact opposite. (Example: Aiden does listen to me.)* Find and record three genuine, specific examples of how this new thought is as true or truer for you in that situation.

Adapted from Byron Katie International, Inc. Rev. 7/2014, with consent.

Welcome to Morning 34 - *Our Partners*

(I invite you to first re-read the Morning Meditation on page 16.)

Dear Present Mother,

My husband is coming home today from a week-long business trip and vacation. I love that he's coming home. I also love that he went on his trip when he did. I wasn't always happy about him going on a week-long trip. In fact, I used to feel very resentful. I wanted to go on a week-long trip! The resentment would build. I would start to count all the other ways he had "let me down," adding to my mind's justification for being resentful. He would walk into the room, not saying or doing anything else, and I would automatically feel mad at him! Every little word and action he exhibited fueled my disappointment and anger. I couldn't shake it.

Finally, I began to think, *"I should just leave him."* I saw how it would be better for all of us. Over and over, this thought would come into my mind. And over and over, I knew I was missing something. I'm so thankful that self-inquiry was in my life to invite me back to reality!

I remember one incredibly stressful thought I questioned about my husband (and there were many before that one.) My stressful thought was, *"He isn't there for me, emotionally."* Questioning that belief shifted our entire relationship back to the bliss I felt as a newlywed. This was a very old, repetitive, sticky thought for me. It had lots of nuances, dating back to childhood; I had believed it then, about my mom. I saw how it wasn't even true then, when I first believed it! I just inherited that thought from the world I lived in and didn't ever think to question it.

Now, when I did question it, I knew that *I* wasn't there for me, emotionally, *whenever I wasn't being present*. Oh! The joy, the gratitude, the absolute love I felt for the reality of my beautiful husband was open to me again. (Soon I also realized that questioning this thought about my husband helped me deepen my connection with my mom.)

Today, I love inviting you to question the stressful thoughts you have about your partner or ex-partner. Let's start to unravel the knots in our thoughts about them. Let's find the truth. What is it that your partner or ex-partner has done that you wish they hadn't? Let's do self-inquiry on that wish. Dreams can come true this way.

~

I invite you to close your eyes and allow yourself to travel back to a specific time with your partner where they are doing or saying something you wish they hadn't…

~

What is the situation? What are they doing? What are they saying? When you see it clearly, fill in Worksheet 1, remembering to be as petty and judgmental as you actually felt in your situation. Let it all out. Let those judgments be *seen* on paper – they're there anyway. Let's shine a light on them and really get to know what they are. It's finally time to let them have their life.

Today we're only looking at the judgments we have about our partner or ex-partner. Next time we will shine the light of awareness on them as I walk us through the second half of our self-inquiry. As always, if you're inspired to keep going today and work through Worksheet 2, that's perfect also.

Wishing you, dear one, Presence and Peace,
Catherine

Presence Practice Notes

Our Partners

Self-Inquiry Worksheet 1 of 2

We've been told all of our lives not to judge others. The fact is we do it anyway. This worksheet allows the mind to see itself, to see the reality of its own thoughts, and to truly consider the thoughts by putting them on paper. This is the time to let those judgments have their own life.

DIRECTIONS:

A. Think of a specific person that is triggering stress in you. It could be your child, partner, ex-partner, mom, or dad. (Not yourself) They could be living or not living.

B. Now, recall a specific stressful situation you had with that person. It might have been a face to face interaction, an event, a phone call, or any situation that caused you any feelings of discomfort. Identify the specific stressful situation, and see it as a *single snapshot* in time.

C. Witness that single snapshot. Notice the time, place, words spoken, body language, and energy of each person. Then, 1) Identify and name the primary uncomfortable feeling you were having, 2) identify why you felt that way, and 3) answer the questions below with *short, simple* statements. *Please do not* try to be psychologically correct, spiritual, or wise now. For the purposes of this worksheet, be as judgmental as you were when you were in that situation.

1. In this situation, who angers, confuses, saddens, or disappoints you, and why? *(Example: I'm frustrated with Aiden because he won't listen to me.)*

2. In this situation, how do you want them to change? *(Example: I want Aiden to stop what he's doing, look at me, and listen to me.)*

3. In this situation, what advice would you offer to them? *(Example: Aiden should learn how to listen.)*

4. In order for you to feel better in this situation, what do you need them to think, say, feel, or do? *(Example: I need Aiden to listen.)*

5. What do you think of them in this situation? Make a list. Be petty. *(Example: Aiden is just like his dad - he won't respect me.)*

6. What is it in or about this situation that you don't ever want to experience again? *(Example: I don't ever want to be disrespected by Aiden again.)*

Review what you wrote. Pick one sentence you wrote that feels the most stressful to you right now. Circle it. Rewrite it at the top of Worksheet 2.

Adapted from Byron Katie International, Inc. Rev. 7/2014, with consent.

Self-Inquiry Worksheet 2 of 2

This worksheet is a meditation. When answering the questions, close your eyes, be still, and patiently wait to witness what appears to you. Always give yourself time to let the deeper answers meet the questions.

DIRECTIONS:

A. In the space below, write the thought you circled from Worksheet 1. Then answer questions 1-4.

B. Reconstruct the thought in three new ways. Possibilities are: by directing it inward (number 5 below), exchanging the other person's name with yours (number 6 below), and stating its exact opposite (number 7 below). Examples are provided below. Then, find and record three genuine, specific examples of how each new thought is as true or truer for you in that situation.

C. If you circled the thought from your answer to question 6 on Worksheet 1, you would reconstruct the thought by replacing the words, "I don't ever want to…" with "I am willing to…" and "I look forward to…"

Re-write the thought you circled on Worksheet 1: *(Example: Aiden doesn't listen to me.)*

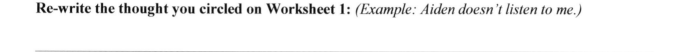

1. In that situation, is this thought true? *(Yes or no only. There are no right or wrong answers. If no, skip to question 3.)*

2. In that situation, can you absolutely know that it's true? *(Yes or no only)*

3. In that situation, how did you *react* when you believed that thought?

4. In that situation, who would you be if you could not believe that thought?

5. Reconstruct the thought by directing it *inward. (Example: I don't listen to me.)* Find and record three genuine, specific examples in that situation how this new thought is as true or truer than the original thought.

6. Reconstruct the thought by *exchanging* the other person's name with yours. *(Example: I don't listen to Aiden.)* Find and record three genuine, specific examples of how this new thought is as true or truer for you in that situation.

7. Reconstruct the thought by stating the *exact opposite. (Example: Aiden does listen to me.)* Find and record three genuine, specific examples of how this new thought is as true or truer for you in that situation.

Adapted from Byron Katie International, Inc. Rev. 7/2014, with consent.

Welcome to Morning 35 - *Waiting for Truth*

(I invite you to first re-read the Morning Meditation on page 16.)

Dear Present Mother,

Today, we're doing the second half of our self-inquiry on our partners or ex-partners. The first half was writing down our real judgments about them. The second half is answering the four questions and reconstructing the stressful thought into three new thoughts that are as true or truer. If you've completed Worksheet 1, then great. If you don't have it completed, I invite you to take a moment now to complete it. Then, circle the thought that's most stressful to you, and write it at the top of Worksheet 2.

I know the pain and suffering of feeling so distant from my partner. It hurt to the core when I believed my stories about him. Eventually I began to see that it wasn't even *my* story that I was believing. I dug out some old worksheets I completed on my husband and I'll share some of those stressful thoughts with you here. The reason I share these is to invite you to see that your stressful thoughts may be very similar to mine. I invite you to see that, until we question our stress-inducing stories about our partners (or anyone else), we're all walking around with our minds re-hashing the same old repetitive thoughts that people have been believing starting from centuries ago. It's like one massively confused mind. I've mentioned earlier that none of these thoughts are *personal* to me or to you. They're inherited from the world we live in that believes its stories of disconnection, strife, and pain. When I realized these thoughts weren't personal to me it lessened their intensity, it lessened my attachment to them, and it lessened the stickiness of the stressful thinking. I knew I could either believe (consciously or unconsciously) these thoughts that caused stress and pain in my family life or I could question them. I didn't put them into my mind on a conscious level; I just believed what I was told or what I assumed. However, now I can investigate and see if these beliefs are valid or not.

I knew intellectually that these thoughts were not true and were just my story, but my mind had not experienced the truth I would give it when I questioned the stressful thoughts I had about him. Here are some of the stressful thoughts I questioned about my husband: *"He keeps on hurting me with his words and won't ever try to understand how to stop." "He keeps tearing me down and making fun of me in front of the kids." "He should grow up spiritually and emotionally." "I need him to change into a more compassionate person." "He is making my life miserable." "I am the one who always has to analyze myself." "I have to question my stressful thoughts in order to be happy." "I want to just be happy without having to work so hard at it." "I can't be my full self with him." "He should love **all** of me." "He doesn't love all of me." "I don't ever want him to reject parts of me." "He hurt me when I was emotional with him."*

It is utter grace and a miracle that we are still happily married. After doing inquiry on him for quite some time, I finally realized that every one of these thoughts was about *me*. I'm the one who *wrote* them. They came out of *my* mind. *None* of them were about him. I was *projecting* them on to him because I was already thinking them about myself and judging *myself* so harshly.

~

Then I would judge him just as harshly as I was judging myself. I hadn't yet learned to understand and love the side of myself that judged him. I didn't yet know how to love the insensitive side of myself. I didn't yet know how to love the part of me that discounted him. I didn't yet know how to love the part of me that didn't love *all* of him. I hadn't yet investigated all of my false judgments of *myself*. I hadn't yet married my *whole* self.

When inquiry led me to face and understand and accept and love *all* of myself, including the parts of myself that I wasn't happy with, then the overwhelming beauty and the divine, gentle, kind, caring, peaceful, purity of Love came shining through. I felt so free to be me in the world! We have a saying in our family that goes, "Olive me loves olive you olive the time." I love that.

Before doing inquiry, I was perpetuating all of the "negative" stories I had unconsciously believed about myself. After inquiry, I finally understood that when I reacted "negatively" toward him, it was because I was believing an untrue story about him (and myself) in the present moment.

I am so grateful for my husband. I understand and am so in love with *all* of him now more than ever before. And he doesn't have any control over that. He didn't change a thing. My story about him changed. *My story of him is always the perfect reflection of my story of myself.*

~

The more we are aware of our own awareness, the more we're cultivating our presence. That's why I love the Morning Meditation coupled with the worksheets after each of your letters. When I would fill in the worksheets, I would become aware of how I would get totally caught up in my story again, sometimes for only a few seconds, and then I would come back to the present moment and see that I was filling out a worksheet on him and looking for the truth. I knew I could find the truth with self-inquiry, so I kept with the process.

If you completed your second worksheet on your partner or ex-partner, what did you notice in yourself as you were writing? What were you conscious of? What were you aware of within your experience of yourself?

If you haven't figured it out yet, self-inquiry is *the real deal*. Your answers to the questions have the possibility of permanently stopping all of your suffering for the rest of your life, no matter what your circumstances. Maybe you don't believe me yet. That's good. You'll only believe it when you test it out for yourself. So I invite you to keep at this. Keep seeing what you see when you look, non-judgmentally, at the thoughts on your mind about your partner or ex-partner. Marriages can be returned to their blissful state with self-inquiry. Divorces can be prevented or they can be amicable. Your child's life can be permanently altered for the better when you do self-inquiry on thoughts about your partner or ex-partner.

As it turns out, in all of its perfection, we'll take more than two letters to complete a sample of self-inquiry on our teachers - our partners. As always, feel free to dig in and do more worksheets today if you're moved to. I'll continue walking us through Worksheet 2 next time. For today,

Wishing you, dear one, Presence and Peace,
Catherine

Presence Practice Notes

Waiting for Truth

Self-Inquiry Worksheet 1 of 2

We've been told all of our lives not to judge others. The fact is we do it anyway. This worksheet allows the mind to see itself, to see the reality of its own thoughts, and to truly consider the thoughts by putting them on paper. This is the time to let those judgments have their own life.

DIRECTIONS:

A. Think of a specific person that is triggering stress in you. It could be your child, partner, ex-partner, mom, or dad. (Not yourself) They could be living or not living.

B. Now, recall a specific stressful situation you had with that person. It might have been a face to face interaction, an event, a phone call, or any situation that caused you any feelings of discomfort. Identify the specific stressful situation, and see it as a *single snapshot* in time.

C. Witness that single snapshot. Notice the time, place, words spoken, body language, and energy of each person. Then, 1) Identify and name the primary uncomfortable feeling you were having, 2) identify why you felt that way, and 3) answer the questions below with *short, simple* statements. *Please do not* try to be psychologically correct, spiritual, or wise now. For the purposes of this worksheet, be as judgmental as you were when you were in that situation.

1. In this situation, who angers, confuses, saddens, or disappoints you, and why? *(Example: I'm frustrated with Aiden because he won't listen to me.)*

2. In this situation, how do you want them to change? *(Example: I want Aiden to stop what he's doing, look at me, and listen to me.)*

3. In this situation, what advice would you offer to them? *(Example: Aiden should learn how to listen.)*

4. In order for you to feel better in this situation, what do you need them to think, say, feel, or do? *(Example: I need Aiden to listen.)*

5. What do you think of them in this situation? Make a list. Be petty. *(Example: Aiden is just like his dad - he won't respect me.)*

6. What is it in or about this situation that you don't ever want to experience again? *(Example: I don't ever want to be disrespected by Aiden again.)*

Review what you wrote. Pick one sentence you wrote that feels the most stressful to you right now. Circle it. Rewrite it at the top of Worksheet 2.

Adapted from Byron Katie International, Inc. Rev. 7/2014, with consent.

Self-Inquiry Worksheet 2 of 2

This worksheet is a meditation. When answering the questions, close your eyes, be still, and patiently wait to witness what appears to you. Always give yourself time to let the deeper answers meet the questions.

DIRECTIONS:

A. In the space below, write the thought you circled from Worksheet 1. Then answer questions 1-4.

B. Reconstruct the thought in three new ways. Possibilities are: by directing it inward (number 5 below), exchanging the other person's name with yours (number 6 below), and stating its exact opposite (number 7 below). Examples are provided below. Then, find and record three genuine, specific examples of how each new thought is as true or truer for you in that situation.

C. If you circled the thought from your answer to question 6 on Worksheet 1, you would reconstruct the thought by replacing the words, "I don't ever want to…" with "I am willing to…" and "I look forward to…"

Re-write the thought you circled on Worksheet 1: *(Example: Aiden doesn't listen to me.)*

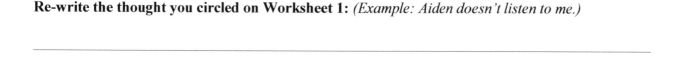

1. In that situation, is this thought true? *(Yes or no only. There are no right or wrong answers. If no, skip to question 3.)*

2. In that situation, can you absolutely know that it's true? *(Yes or no only)*

3. In that situation, how did you *react* when you believed that thought?

4. In that situation, who would you be if you could not believe that thought?

5. Reconstruct the thought by directing it *inward. (Example: I don't listen to me.)* Find and record three genuine, specific examples in that situation how this new thought is as true or truer than the original thought.

6. Reconstruct the thought by *exchanging* the other person's name with yours. *(Example: I don't listen to Aiden.)* Find and record three genuine, specific examples of how this new thought is as true or truer for you in that situation.

7. Reconstruct the thought by stating the *exact opposite. (Example: Aiden does listen to me.)* Find and record three genuine, specific examples of how this new thought is as true or truer for you in that situation.

Adapted from Byron Katie International, Inc. Rev. 7/2014, with consent.

Welcome to Morning 36 - *Our Spouses, Our Teachers*

(I invite you to first re-read the Morning Meditation on page 16.)

Dear Present Mother,

Who would you be without the thought that he or she should be any different than he or she is? The stressful thoughts about the ones we love the most can be the biggest triggers for us in our day-to-day lives. It's possible to meditate on the questions in your self-inquiry for days, even weeks. I invite you to give yourself plenty of time to be with your self-inquiry questions on your partner or ex-partner. I questioned thoughts on my husband on and off for two years. I had believed some of those thoughts since childhood, and they were really cemented in my brain. The easier and more gentle we are with ourselves, the more present we will be when questioning these thoughts and the more self-realizations will come.

We've completed the first half of self-inquiry, which is judging our partners/ex-partners and completing Worksheet 1. Today, I'll continue with the second half of self-inquiry, which are the four questions and your reconstructed thoughts, found on Worksheet 2.

When I was new to self-inquiry, one thought I questioned a *lot* about my spouse was, *"He won't support me."* The situations were usually about our differences in how each of us wanted to raise our children - our seemingly opposite parenting styles. Each time we would get into an argument it would all boil down to that thought in my mind. I'll use that example for today. As you follow along with me, think of a situation in your own life where you thought your significant other would not support you. If you can't find one, see if there are other judgment/blaming kinds of thoughts you have about him. Maybe it's, *"He swears in front of the kids,"* or *"He puts women down,"* or *"He's late with the child support money again,"* or *"He shames the kids."* Pick a thought that you think a lot and that triggers the most stress in you. Then, answer the questions for yourself from that point of view.

~

Question #1: Is it true, that *he won't support me*? (This is a yes or no question, no other answers are required. If it's a no for you, skip to question #3.) *Yes, he won't support me.*

Question #2: Can I absolutely know that it's true, that *he won't support me*? Again, this is a yes or no only question. There are no right or wrong answers. Whichever is the true answer for you at this time is your answer. My answer is "*yes.*"

Questions #3: How do I react when I believe the thought, he won't support me? I get so mad at him, often in front of the kids. Then, I feel awful for letting my children see this. I feel like I'm screwing up my kids doing it this way. I don't know how to get out of this loop I'm in with him. I try to force myself to stop arguing with him in front of our children. I control my speech in front of the kids. I'm not myself. I try to force him to talk to me about parenting when we are alone. We argue almost all the time. I look at my children and think they are complete victims. I see no resilience in my kids. I feel like the kids and I are suffering victims of all this arguing. My house is not peaceful. I am not peaceful. I think the thought that I hate our situation. I think the thought that I want to leave my husband and whisk my kids away to "safety." I'm not able to be the mother I want to be. When I believe this thought it costs me my happiness, it costs me joy, it costs me my marriage, it costs me my relationship with my children. When I believe this thought I see old movies (memories) from my childhood when I believed my mother thought this thought about my father. Then, I go into blaming my mother that I have this thought. Then I go into blaming my father that I have this thought. I make everyone else responsible for my happiness. I keep searching for someone to blame when I believe this thought. My children learn to blame, since I am the teacher of blame, when I believe this thought. My children learn how to argue, since I am the teacher of arguing, when I believe this thought. When I believe this thought I think of all the other times that I've argued with my husband before about this. I view all that time as "wasted" time in my life. I feel so sad and a lot of tears come when I believe this. I feel completely hopeless when I believe this thought.

I'm leaving inquiry for a moment to ask you if you can hear this *story* I'm *perpetuating* when I believe this thought. My story: husbands don't support their wives. Have you ever believed this stress-inducing thought? Have you ever heard this story from another mom? It seems to be a very common theme among mothers. Back to self-inquiry.

Question #4: In this situation, who would I be without the thought, *he won't support me*? I close my eyes, I breathe, I realize I'm being breathed. I watch, ever so trustingly for the answer to this question to surface from this place of stillness inside me. I see the situation but this time I don't have that thought. I see me. I see him. He's still doing and saying what he's doing and saying and I cannot think the thought, "He doesn't support me." Who would I be? Well… I would be kind to him. I would be kind to me. I would be kind to the kids. That kindness would emanate in my energy, in my speaking, and in my behavior. I would confidently and calmly offer my support and my love to the kids and to him. I would express love toward all of us. Life would flow freely and beautifully. I wouldn't have the concern that he's messing up the kids; that would be totally gone. So, I wouldn't worry about the kids… at all. I would be connected with myself, with him, and with the kids. I would be connected to the present moment. I would be present. Words would flow out of my mouth that would meet the present moment with kindness, love, wisdom, and creativity. My kids wouldn't learn how to argue. I would be the teacher of kindness instead. They wouldn't learn how to blame and separate from the ones they love. I would be the teacher of connection instead. There would be no loss of joy or love from my relationship with my partner. I would be the mother I want to be. I would have the kind of marriage I want to have.

~

I invite you to reflect on my answers for a moment. When I reflected on my answers, it solidified my strength for me. It solidified my commitment to my marriage. It solidified my commitment to being present. It solidified my commitment to continue my self-inquiry practice. *My husband was the teacher I learned the most from.* When I remembered that I was rediscovering my true self by questioning the stressful thoughts I had about him, I kept staying in my marriage. When I remembered that I kept finding my love for him when I questioned my stressful thoughts about him, I kept staying in my marriage. I didn't want to be at the whim of these thoughts that caused all of my suffering. I had too much at stake. I had a relationship with a man I've loved for almost half of my life. I had a relationship with a man who was the father of my children. I had to do everything I could to preserve that. When I remembered these glimpses of light that were revealed to me as I answered the question "Who would I be without this thought?" I remembered that I was teaching my kids Love, simply by the way I was *being*.

In your situation, in your home, who would you be without the thought "He doesn't support me"? I invite you to find that situation where you have had this thought this before. Use that this morning, and fill in the worksheets that follow. It's as if miracles start showing up in your life when you do.

Wishing you, dear one, Presence and Peace today,
Catherine

Presence Practice Notes

Our Spouses, Our Teachers

Self-Inquiry Worksheet 1 of 2

We've been told all of our lives not to judge others. The fact is we do it anyway. This worksheet allows the mind to see itself, to see the reality of its own thoughts, and to truly consider the thoughts by putting them on paper. This is the time to let those judgments have their own life.

DIRECTIONS:

A. Think of a specific person that is triggering stress in you. It could be your child, partner, ex-partner, mom, or dad. (Not yourself) They could be living or not living.

B. Now, recall a specific stressful situation you had with that person. It might have been a face to face interaction, an event, a phone call, or any situation that caused you any feelings of discomfort. Identify the specific stressful situation, and see it as a *single snapshot* in time.

C. Witness that single snapshot. Notice the time, place, words spoken, body language, and energy of each person. Then, 1) Identify and name the primary uncomfortable feeling you were having, 2) identify why you felt that way, and 3) answer the questions below with *short, simple* statements. *Please do not* try to be psychologically correct, spiritual, or wise now. For the purposes of this worksheet, be as judgmental as you were when you were in that situation.

1. In this situation, who angers, confuses, saddens, or disappoints you, and why? *(Example: I'm frustrated with Aiden because he won't listen to me.)*

2. In this situation, how do you want them to change? *(Example: I want Aiden to stop what he's doing, look at me, and listen to me.)*

3. In this situation, what advice would you offer to them? *(Example: Aiden should learn how to listen.)*

4. In order for you to feel better in this situation, what do you need them to think, say, feel, or do? *(Example: I need Aiden to listen.)*

5. What do you think of them in this situation? Make a list. Be petty. *(Example: Aiden is just like his dad - he won't respect me.)*

6. What is it in or about this situation that you don't ever want to experience again? *(Example: I don't ever want to be disrespected by Aiden again.)*

Review what you wrote. Pick one sentence you wrote that feels the most stressful to you right now. Circle it. Rewrite it at the top of Worksheet 2.

Adapted from Byron Katie International, Inc. Rev. 7/2014, with consent.

Self-Inquiry Worksheet 2 of 2

This worksheet is a meditation. When answering the questions, close your eyes, be still, and patiently wait to witness what appears to you. Always give yourself time to let the deeper answers meet the questions.

DIRECTIONS:
A. In the space below, write the thought you circled from Worksheet 1. Then answer questions 1-4.
B. Reconstruct the thought in three new ways. Possibilities are: by directing it inward (number 5 below), exchanging the other person's name with yours (number 6 below), and stating its exact opposite (number 7 below). Examples are provided below. Then, find and record three genuine, specific examples of how each new thought is as true or truer for you in that situation.
C. If you circled the thought from your answer to question 6 on Worksheet 1, you would reconstruct the thought by replacing the words, "I don't ever want to…" with "I am willing to…" and "I look forward to…"

Re-write the thought you circled on Worksheet 1: *(Example: Aiden doesn't listen to me.)*

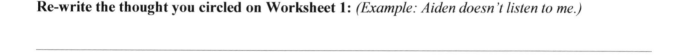

1. In that situation, is this thought true? *(Yes or no only. There are no right or wrong answers. If no, skip to question 3.)*

2. In that situation, can you absolutely know that it's true? *(Yes or no only)*

3. In that situation, how did you *react* when you believed that thought?

4. In that situation, who would you be if you could not believe that thought?

5. Reconstruct the thought by directing it *inward. (Example: I don't listen to me.)* Find and record three genuine, specific examples in that situation how this new thought is as true or truer than the original thought.

6. Reconstruct the thought by *exchanging* the other person's name with yours. *(Example: I don't listen to Aiden.)* Find and record three genuine, specific examples of how this new thought is as true or truer for you in that situation.

7. Reconstruct the thought by stating the *exact opposite. (Example: Aiden does listen to me.)* Find and record three genuine, specific examples of how this new thought is as true or truer for you in that situation.

Adapted from Byron Katie International, Inc. Rev. 7/2014, with consent.

Welcome to Morning 37 - *Supporting Yourself*

(I invite you to first re-read the Morning Meditation on page 16.)

Dear Present Mother,

If I think it's my husband's job to like me, then I know I'm very, *very* confused and I know I haven't questioned my thoughts about him yet. If I think it's my husband's job to do anything for me, when he isn't, I know I'm confused in that area too. So, let's find more truth today.

We're picking up where we left off yesterday, questioning the thought *"He won't support me."* We already questioned that thought and found a beautiful, blissful state of being. We solidified who we would be without that thought, by reflecting on those answers and letting them move through our minds and hearts. It opened us up to love and to presence and to connection.

When we reconstruct the original stressful thought it helps us continue on that same trajectory. The new thoughts you create help you live with an open mind. When you have an open mind, you have an open heart. If you have a closed mind, your heart will be closed. There is no other possibility. So, I invite you to continue with your own self-inquiry on your partner or ex-partner, and follow along as you're following along on your own worksheets for this morning.

~

"He won't support me" directed inward would be: *"I won't support me."* Genuine, specific examples, in my situation, of *"I won't support me"* are: 1) I do things for the kids that I really don't want to do but feel I should do, so I say yes when my truth is to say no or to work out a solution we can all be okay with. 2) I haven't clearly asked him, with no attachment to his answer, for the support I'd like from him. 3) I keep saying yes to him when I really want to say no to him and yes to me; I've ignored myself when I do that.

When I found these examples I saw clearly, in my situation, how "I won't support me" is actually truer to me than "He won't support me." My mind began to believe that the opposite of my original stressful thought was actually truer. My mind began to live with openness. Even just a little crack of openness was enough every time I did self-inquiry. I knew that little crack would open further every time I questioned my thinking *about* him.

Then I began to live my life from that openness. After I did self-inquiry, I began to notice how I naturally started thinking differently about my spouse. I wasn't even trying to think differently about him; it was happening all on its own. I began to notice that when he or my kids or anyone asked me to do something, I was taking my time and really considering if I wanted to say yes or no.

In that way, I was supporting myself. Before, I would have simply responded with a quick yes or no without considering the question they were asking. Space was created in my thought process. Presence had room now to emerge.

Something else I noticed after my self-inquiry about my husband was that although I was still asking him to help me with little things around the house I now had no attachment to his answer - none whatsoever. He said yes if he wanted to and he said no if he wanted to. It was great either way.

Then I started noticing that my husband was always responding either yes or no, to my requests; he wasn't questioning his own beliefs or opinions about what I was asking of him. He wasn't questioning his thoughts. He was unconsciously believing them just like I had done before self-inquiry. Since I found that to be true in myself, I started noticing it in him. I began to have so much compassion for him. I began to feel my love for him even more. I noticed that he said yes to so many of my requests when he really wanted to say no. I noticed how, before self-inquiry, I would *guilt* him into saying yes to my requests. He was feeling forced to say yes. He wasn't supporting himself and his true yes's and his true no's, just like I wasn't supporting mine before self-inquiry. Wow - what a mirror I saw in him.

Then, as I became less attached to his yes or no answer, he became much kinder to me. Why wouldn't he be? I wasn't pressuring him so much anymore. I wasn't forcing him to do things anymore. I kept loving him no matter if he said yes or no. Just like I kept loving me no matter if I said yes or no. Words can't describe how this self-inquiry repaired our relationship.

It's so important to realize that this was happening in my life after self-inquiry, *all on its own.* I was not doing anything to try to improve my situation other than doing self-inquiry. I was not forcing myself to think a certain way. I was not forcing myself to be more loving to him. It was all as if it was emerging from inside me. It was all coming from some internal open space. This new openness was so wondrous and beyond what words can describe. It was presence. It was vast. It was beyond understanding. It was like a huge, loving light emerging from within me.

I began noticing this experience in my life after each time I did self-inquiry. It was like I was becoming this new person every time. It was a pattern. It was a pattern of stress, then inquiry, then bliss. Over the course of the days, weeks, months, and years that I continued my self-inquiry practice, I realized what a profound effect it had on my mind and on my marriage. Now I feel connected to reality. Now I feel present to my husband and my sacred marriage. My husband sometimes says it's like I'm a new person.

I invite you to allow yourself the time to see the examples of where you don't support yourself. The mind sometimes does not want to release very quickly, especially on really repetitive stressful thoughts like *"He won't support me."* That's okay. Just let the examples come to you for "I won't support me." In this situation with your partner/ex-partner, where was that true? Self-inquiry is sometimes like stretching your muscles as you warm up to exercise. You're stretching the muscle of your mind. It's mind yoga! Be gentle and be persistent. It does open. It wants to be at peace with itself. It wants connection and love. It wants happiness. So, hang in there, and wait for your examples to the statement *"I won't support me."*

Once you see the examples in your situation of where you didn't support yourself, I invite you to get very familiar with them. This is where you have all the responsibility and therefore all the control over your happiness. If you find you're starting to judge yourself, or you're feeling sad and you're not liking yourself when you see these examples, that's okay. Just notice the thoughts causing your sadness and write them down to do self-inquiry on them later.

For now, let's return to the next reconstructed thought, exchanging his name with ours. *"He won't support me"* would become *"I won't support **him**."* Some genuine, specific examples from my own experience of *"I won't support **him**"* are: 1) I get resentful when he asks me to do something for him, because I'm thinking he should be supporting me instead, so I don't support him in those moments; 2) I definitely don't support him for not supporting me, that's for sure; 3) not only do I not support him, but I hold a grudge against him for not supporting me. Holding a grudge against someone is definitely not supporting them.

Breathe. Feel these deeply. Feel them to see reality, not to start feeling guilty. Again, if you do start to judge yourself and feel guilty, notice the thoughts that are causing the guilt feelings and write them down on the Presence Practice Notes page that follows. Then, question them the next time you fill in a worksheet. For now, let's return to reconstructing the thought.

"He won't support me" reconstructed to its exact opposite would be *"He **does** support me."* From my own situation, specific examples of *"He **does** support me"* are: 1) he's talking to me, 2) he looks at me, 3) he earns money and supplies it to me for me to use the way I choose, 4) he cooks for me and the kids, 5) he takes the kids swimming, 6) he says he's proud of me, 7) he kisses my cheek. Wow! He really supports me in so many ways.

Can you find more genuine, specific examples in your own life with your partner? Feel and experience them all. Let them sink in deeply. Breathe. There were many more I saw when I looked at my husband from these new perspectives. Tears of happiness and gratitude started to come, too. This may or may not happen with you. Notice if you compare your situation with mine or someone else's-- it takes you out of the present moment. Whatever your experience is now, I invite you to keep looking for more examples today of where he *does* support you. I invite you to keep a running list in your mind. We never know what gems we will discover when we open our minds to the newly reconstructed thoughts. They have a beautiful, peaceful, magical way of opening up our minds, our hearts, and our lives.

I love sharing with you how questioning the thoughts about my husband completely changed me and my marriage. I hope you've found it inspirational. I hope you can now see glimpses of light in your relationship with your partner or ex-partner. I love that you would support yourself this morning by continuing your self-inquiry on every thought causing stress in your relationship with your greatest teacher. The time you spend doing that will be some of the most valuable time you've ever spent in your entire life. In my experience, when I questioned stressful thoughts about my husband it magically repaired every relationship in my family. With your answers to the worksheets that follow, you have that possibility too. I'm sending my love to you as you continue your presence practice.

Wishing you, dear one, Presence and Peace today,
Catherine

Presence Practice Notes

Supporting Yourself

Self-Inquiry Worksheet 1 of 2

We've been told all of our lives not to judge others. The fact is we do it anyway. This worksheet allows the mind to see itself, to see the reality of its own thoughts, and to truly consider the thoughts by putting them on paper. This is the time to let those judgments have their own life.

DIRECTIONS:

A. Think of a specific person that is triggering stress in you. It could be your child, partner, ex-partner, mom, or dad. (Not yourself) They could be living or not living.

B. Now, recall a specific stressful situation you had with that person. It might have been a face to face interaction, an event, a phone call, or any situation that caused you any feelings of discomfort. Identify the specific stressful situation, and see it as a *single snapshot* in time.

C. Witness that single snapshot. Notice the time, place, words spoken, body language, and energy of each person. Then, 1) Identify and name the primary uncomfortable feeling you were having, 2) identify why you felt that way, and 3) answer the questions below with *short, simple* statements. *Please do not* try to be psychologically correct, spiritual, or wise now. For the purposes of this worksheet, be as judgmental as you were when you were in that situation.

1. In this situation, who angers, confuses, saddens, or disappoints you, and why? *(Example: I'm frustrated with Aiden because he won't listen to me.)*

2. In this situation, how do you want them to change? *(Example: I want Aiden to stop what he's doing, look at me, and listen to me.)*

3. In this situation, what advice would you offer to them? *(Example: Aiden should learn how to listen.)*

4. In order for you to feel better in this situation, what do you need them to think, say, feel, or do? *(Example: I need Aiden to listen.)*

5. What do you think of them in this situation? Make a list. Be petty. *(Example: Aiden is just like his dad - he won't respect me.)*

6. What is it in or about this situation that you don't ever want to experience again? *(Example: I don't ever want to be disrespected by Aiden again.)*

Review what you wrote. Pick one sentence you wrote that feels the most stressful to you right now. Circle it. Rewrite it at the top of Worksheet 2.

Adapted from Byron Katie International, Inc. Rev. 7/2014, with consent.

Self-Inquiry Worksheet 2 of 2

This worksheet is a meditation. When answering the questions, close your eyes, be still, and patiently wait to witness what appears to you. Always give yourself time to let the deeper answers meet the questions.

DIRECTIONS:

A. In the space below, write the thought you circled from Worksheet 1. Then answer questions 1-4.

B. Reconstruct the thought in three new ways. Possibilities are: by directing it inward (number 5 below), exchanging the other person's name with yours (number 6 below), and stating its exact opposite (number 7 below). Examples are provided below. Then, find and record three genuine, specific examples of how each new thought is as true or truer for you in that situation.

C. If you circled the thought from your answer to question 6 on Worksheet 1, you would reconstruct the thought by replacing the words, "I don't ever want to…" with "I am willing to…" and "I look forward to…"

Re-write the thought you circled on Worksheet 1: *(Example: Aiden doesn't listen to me.)*

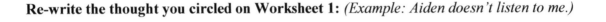

1. In that situation, is this thought true? *(Yes or no only. There are no right or wrong answers. If no, skip to question 3.)*

2. In that situation, can you absolutely know that it's true? *(Yes or no only)*

3. In that situation, how did you *react* when you believed that thought?

4. In that situation, who would you be if you could not believe that thought?

5. Reconstruct the thought by directing it *inward. (Example: I don't listen to me.)* Find and record three genuine, specific examples in that situation how this new thought is as true or truer than the original thought.

6. Reconstruct the thought by *exchanging* the other person's name with yours. *(Example: I don't listen to Aiden.)* Find and record three genuine, specific examples of how this new thought is as true or truer for you in that situation.

7. Reconstruct the thought by stating the *exact opposite. (Example: Aiden does listen to me.)* Find and record three genuine, specific examples of how this new thought is as true or truer for you in that situation.

Adapted from Byron Katie International, Inc. Rev. 7/2014, with consent.

Welcome to Morning 38 - *Gratitude*

(I invite you to first re-read the Morning Meditation on page 16.)

Dear Present Mother,

This morning, gratitude arose in me. I woke up feeling so thankful for the flannel sheets and down comforter. I was so grateful for the sturdy mug I pulled out to hold my warm tea. As our cat rubbed against my leg I felt so thankful for the furry softness on my skin.

What would it be like to be thankful every day of our lives, not just for external things, but for internal ones? On November 1, 2012, in the spirit of Thanksgiving - my favorite holiday - I started a gratitude journal. Each day I wrote at least 10 things I was thankful for. It started out with external things, and then it began to reflect my gratitude for the mother I had previously been, and the mother I was at that time. I started a list of all the things I had done for my children. I noticed all the ways I had loved them over the years. I listed everything, way more than 10 things, from brushing their hair, to thinking of them as I walked down the aisle of the grocery store. Tears of joy began to flow down my cheeks as I reflected on the *endless* love I showed my kids every day of my life. I was in awe of what this woman had done and in awe of the love she had expressed. I felt it deeply. It was absolutely amazing. That's when I began to consider all mothers the same way… I was in complete *awe* of every mother on the planet. Just *look* how we love the children in our lives, every single day of our lives. Do you see it in you?

What stressful thoughts are on your mind that would block your gratitude for yourself? I invite you to actually be grateful for the stressful thought. "What?!" you say? Yes. The stressful thought, in my experience, is part of what to be grateful for. If we have self-inquiry in our lives to meet the stressful thought, and we experience our own answers, we find that the suffering from the thought had a purpose. It has turned into pure gold, alchemy at its finest, something to be so grateful for that we had not even seen yet. Self-inquiry *exponentially* increases my gratitude every single time I do the process.

Gratitude journals are a great way to focus our minds on how precious our lives are. In my experience they are great to do *in conjunction with* self-inquiry; even with our focus on gratitude, the stressful thoughts creep back into our minds. As I was completing my gratitude journal about my husband, I noticed some stressful thoughts came to my mind. This is the same thing that would happen to me when I would recite affirmations, or meditate or pray without doing inquiry: stressful thoughts would keep arising and I would keep unconsciously believing them. However, when I would question those stress-inducing beliefs with self-inquiry, the beliefs would disappear. Doing self-inquiry regularly and consistently creates permanent authenticity. There is no doubt in our minds after self-inquiry. We're *naturally* grateful after self-inquiry. We don't have to try to be grateful. With my focus on gratitude, meditation, affirmations, letting go, and prayer, I could stop paying attention to the stressful thoughts for a while, yet unconsciously I still believed them unless I questioned them. All these methods offered only temporary relief. Any difficult emotion that I experienced was my signal to return to my self-inquiry practice.

Today, I invite you to realize the gifts you bring to your children and family every day. And when difficult emotions come, the ones that take you out of that blissful state of gratitude, I invite you to *catch yourself,* write down who or what you think is causing your pain, and question those thoughts. Gratitude will be waiting for you on the other side.

Wishing you, dear one, Presence and Peace today,
Catherine

Presence Practice Notes

Gratitude

Self-Inquiry Worksheet 1 of 2

We've been told all of our lives not to judge others. The fact is we do it anyway. This worksheet allows the mind to see itself, to see the reality of its own thoughts, and to truly consider the thoughts by putting them on paper. This is the time to let those judgments have their own life.

DIRECTIONS:

A. Think of a specific person that is triggering stress in you. It could be your child, partner, ex-partner, mom, or dad. (Not yourself) They could be living or not living.

B. Now, recall a specific stressful situation you had with that person. It might have been a face to face interaction, an event, a phone call, or any situation that caused you any feelings of discomfort. Identify the specific stressful situation, and see it as a *single snapshot* in time.

C. Witness that single snapshot. Notice the time, place, words spoken, body language, and energy of each person. Then, 1) Identify and name the primary uncomfortable feeling you were having, 2) identify why you felt that way, and 3) answer the questions below with *short, simple* statements. *Please do not* try to be psychologically correct, spiritual, or wise now. For the purposes of this worksheet, be as judgmental as you were when you were in that situation.

1. In this situation, who angers, confuses, saddens, or disappoints you, and why? *(Example: I'm frustrated with Aiden because he won't listen to me.)*

2. In this situation, how do you want them to change? *(Example: I want Aiden to stop what he's doing, look at me, and listen to me.)*

3. In this situation, what advice would you offer to them? *(Example: Aiden should learn how to listen.)*

4. In order for you to feel better in this situation, what do you need them to think, say, feel, or do? *(Example: I need Aiden to listen.)*

5. What do you think of them in this situation? Make a list. Be petty. *(Example: Aiden is just like his dad - he won't respect me.)*

6. What is it in or about this situation that you don't ever want to experience again? *(Example: I don't ever want to be disrespected by Aiden again.)*

Review what you wrote. Pick one sentence you wrote that feels the most stressful to you right now. Circle it. Rewrite it at the top of Worksheet 2.

Self-Inquiry Worksheet 2 of 2

This worksheet is a meditation. When answering the questions, close your eyes, be still, and patiently wait to witness what appears to you. Always give yourself time to let the deeper answers meet the questions.

DIRECTIONS:
A. In the space below, write the thought you circled from Worksheet 1. Then answer questions 1-4.
B. Reconstruct the thought in three new ways. Possibilities are: by directing it inward (number 5 below), exchanging the other person's name with yours (number 6 below), and stating its exact opposite (number 7 below). Examples are provided below. Then, find and record three genuine, specific examples of how each new thought is as true or truer for you in that situation.
C. If you circled the thought from your answer to question 6 on Worksheet 1, you would reconstruct the thought by replacing the words, "I don't ever want to…" with "I am willing to…" and "I look forward to…"

Re-write the thought you circled on Worksheet 1: *(Example: Aiden doesn't listen to me.)*

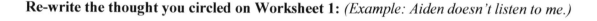

1. In that situation, is this thought true? *(Yes or no only. There are no right or wrong answers. If no, skip to question 3.)*

2. In that situation, can you absolutely know that it's true? *(Yes or no only)*

3. In that situation, how did you *react* when you believed that thought?

4. In that situation, who would you be if you could not believe that thought?

5. Reconstruct the thought by directing it *inward. (Example: I don't listen to me.)* Find and record three genuine, specific examples in that situation how this new thought is as true or truer than the original thought.

6. Reconstruct the thought by *exchanging* the other person's name with yours. *(Example: I don't listen to Aiden.)* Find and record three genuine, specific examples of how this new thought is as true or truer for you in that situation.

7. Reconstruct the thought by stating the *exact opposite. (Example: Aiden does listen to me.)* Find and record three genuine, specific examples of how this new thought is as true or truer for you in that situation.

Adapted from Byron Katie International, Inc. Rev. 7/2014, with consent.

Welcome to Morning 39 - *No More Nightmare*

(I invite you to first re-read the Morning Meditation on page 16.)

Dear Present Mother,

When I choose to question the thoughts that cause my disconnection with my child, there are no more nightmares in my mothering life. This mind I am one with is a peace zone. I do self-inquiry and it's as if my children, husband, Mom, Dad, and friends do it also. I cannot see anything in them other than what I see in my own mind about myself. They're a perfect reflection, a perfect mirror of my thinking, whether I believe that or not or whether I choose to do self-inquiry or not. It's an absolute truth.

I am so grateful that my children do not have to suffer any more. I am so thankful that I know the way out, so that now they do too. Self-inquiry is so deep and so sustainable and so permanent. I have the power now to instantly "heal old wounds," to inoculate my children from any future "problems," and to be so deeply connected with them that nothing can separate us – not nightmares, not video games, not junk food, and not even death.

In the middle of the night last night, my daughter came into my bed and said she was so scared. She was shaking. Her voice had a high-pitched sound. When I asked her what was going on, she said she was so frightened by the Halloween movie she saw. Since we were not watching the movie at that moment, I knew she was seeing the images of the past, the images of the movie in her mind, covering up the still, quiet, peaceful present moment. It was all in her imagination. She was just confused. She was scaring herself over and over again by continuing to re-watch the movie from the past. Right when I pointed out to her what I noticed was happening, she completely calmed down, present again. She asked me to sing her a lullaby. Then she fell right to sleep. I love how self-inquiry moves in my life.

This immersion in my understanding of the workings of the mind has affected every area of my life. The peace zone that now exists in my head is reflected back out into the world as peace. Peace in the mind, peace in the world. I understand war now because I've seen the war in my own mind that argued with my mothering reality. Those arguments I had in my mind about the apparent reality "out there" were what caused all the stress and negative feelings I've ever had in my entire life. When I love what is, and I see every thought I would superimpose on top of the perfect present moment as the illusion that it is, then I am my kind, loving self, my true self. Let me always see my fight with reality for what it truly is - my unquestioned thoughts that oppose it.

Most anyone can *do* peaceful things. Have you ever tried to *be* peaceful when you don't truly *feel* peaceful? It's not possible because it's a doing, a trying, a pretend act, not a way of being, not authentic. Being doesn't require any trying. If I want the real thing, and I always do, then I question my thinking. In the process, new neural pathways are created, which are completely at one with the only reality there ever is: the present moment. Then I am one with reality, and I work *with* reality only, and not against it. I'm not separate from it. I am one with it. I am the present moment – wise and kind, and pure love. I am in awe of the power of this simple, profound process to turn lives around.

This morning, I invite you to see all the ways that self-inquiry has affected your life. What beauty do you see now that you didn't see before? What view of yourself are you projecting out as your view of your child? If you find anything there that causes discomfort in you, wonderful. That's your divine self seeing the next door to walk through with your self-inquiry practice. You are walking through that door, into the light and out of the nightmare, and I love that for you.

Wishing you, dear one, Presence and Peace today,
Catherine

Presence Practice Notes

No More Nightmare

Self-Inquiry Worksheet 1 of 2

We've been told all of our lives not to judge others. The fact is we do it anyway. This worksheet allows the mind to see itself, to see the reality of its own thoughts, and to truly consider the thoughts by putting them on paper. This is the time to let those judgments have their own life.

DIRECTIONS:

A. Think of a specific person that is triggering stress in you. It could be your child, partner, ex-partner, mom, or dad. (Not yourself) They could be living or not living.

B. Now, recall a specific stressful situation you had with that person. It might have been a face to face interaction, an event, a phone call, or any situation that caused you any feelings of discomfort. Identify the specific stressful situation, and see it as a *single snapshot* in time.

C. Witness that single snapshot. Notice the time, place, words spoken, body language, and energy of each person. Then, 1) Identify and name the primary uncomfortable feeling you were having, 2) identify why you felt that way, and 3) answer the questions below with *short, simple* statements. *Please do not* try to be psychologically correct, spiritual, or wise now. For the purposes of this worksheet, be as judgmental as you were when you were in that situation.

1. In this situation, who angers, confuses, saddens, or disappoints you, and why? *(Example: I'm frustrated with Aiden because he won't listen to me.)*

2. In this situation, how do you want them to change? *(Example: I want Aiden to stop what he's doing, look at me, and listen to me.)*

3. In this situation, what advice would you offer to them? *(Example: Aiden should learn how to listen.)*

4. In order for you to feel better in this situation, what do you need them to think, say, feel, or do? *(Example: I need Aiden to listen.)*

5. What do you think of them in this situation? Make a list. Be petty. *(Example: Aiden is just like his dad - he won't respect me.)*

6. What is it in or about this situation that you don't ever want to experience again? *(Example: I don't ever want to be disrespected by Aiden again.)*

Review what you wrote. Pick one sentence you wrote that feels the most stressful to you right now. Circle it. Rewrite it at the top of Worksheet 2.

Adapted from Byron Katie International, Inc. Rev. 7/2014, with consent.

Self-Inquiry Worksheet 2 of 2

This worksheet is a meditation. When answering the questions, close your eyes, be still, and patiently wait to witness what appears to you. Always give yourself time to let the deeper answers meet the questions.

DIRECTIONS:
A. In the space below, write the thought you circled from Worksheet 1. Then answer questions 1-4.
B. Reconstruct the thought in three new ways. Possibilities are: by directing it inward (number 5 below), exchanging the other person's name with yours (number 6 below), and stating its exact opposite (number 7 below). Examples are provided below. Then, find and record three genuine, specific examples of how each new thought is as true or truer for you in that situation.
C. If you circled the thought from your answer to question 6 on Worksheet 1, you would reconstruct the thought by replacing the words, "I don't ever want to…" with "I am willing to…" and "I look forward to…"

Re-write the thought you circled on Worksheet 1: *(Example: Aiden doesn't listen to me.)*

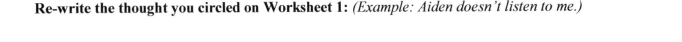

1. In that situation, is this thought true? *(Yes or no only. There are no right or wrong answers. If no, skip to question 3.)*

2. In that situation, can you absolutely know that it's true? *(Yes or no only)*

3. In that situation, how did you *react* when you believed that thought?

4. In that situation, who would you be if you could not believe that thought?

5. Reconstruct the thought by directing it *inward. (Example: I don't listen to me.)* Find and record three genuine, specific examples in that situation how this new thought is as true or truer than the original thought.

6. Reconstruct the thought by *exchanging* the other person's name with yours. *(Example: I don't listen to Aiden.)* Find and record three genuine, specific examples of how this new thought is as true or truer for you in that situation.

7. Reconstruct the thought by stating the *exact opposite. (Example: Aiden does listen to me.)* Find and record three genuine, specific examples of how this new thought is as true or truer for you in that situation.

Adapted from Byron Katie International, Inc. Rev. 7/2014, with consent.

Welcome to Morning 40 - *Returning to Love*

(I invite you to first re-read the Morning Meditation on page 16.)

Dear Present Mother,

There is a bumper sticker I love that says, "Motherhood: The shortest and steepest path to enlightenment." In my experience, that is the absolute truth only when we *let* motherhood grow and develop us. Only when we are the student can we be enlightened. Otherwise, the "I know" part of our mind - which is our fearful illusory ego - will always control us. I invite you to commit to always seeing past this illusion.

When my children were born, I had never been so in love with any other human beings in all of my life. With each child, tears of joy streamed down my face on and off the whole first month after giving birth. It was pure bliss.

It was only when I started believing thoughts that they should be any different than how they were that my joy turned to frustration. Then, it turned into sporadic, surprising moments of anger. Then it turned into guilt and deep sadness. I had periods where I would think everything was okay, and then all of a sudden my reactions told me that everything was not okay, within me. The judgments and worries I believed about my kids - really about me - blocked my awareness of love and connection.

I agreed with all the conscious parenting books I read. It all made sense. Yes, I would treat my kids that way. Yes, I would stay conscious. I used all of the parenting advice that I'd read and thought was good. I used all the "right" words, methods, and tactics. I tried to memorize and emulate all the things I thought would work to raise our kids in the best way I knew possible. I did all the "right" things they recommended I do. Yet none of them could help me with these sudden, surprising uncomfortable thoughts and reactions I kept having.

My full awareness of love didn't return until I fully embraced all of my mothering "challenges" and questioned the stressful thoughts behind them. Now, there is a whole new beautiful relationship between my children and me. Now, I parent in the here and now, without the grip of fears of the future or guilt over the past. Now, I love them fully, all of them, because I love me fully, all of me.

Each time I questioned my thinking, I created new thoughts in my mind. Each time those new thoughts would manifest in my life as a new way of being with my children. For example, the tone of my voice would be gentler and the energy in my demeanor calmed down. Before self-inquiry I would say things like "I would prefer" or "I would like" to them when I wanted them to do something they were not doing. There was an energy I was exuding with my words that was like, "You should do this because I'm asking in such a nice way." So, even when I would say the words that I had read and memorized and tried to apply from "healthy" parenting communications skills books, I was still attached to the belief that they *should* do what I was asking because I was asking in the "right" way. When they wouldn't do whatever it was that I was asking, I would energetically oppose them, and would feel and appear slightly upset. I was doing and saying what I thought I "should" do and say because I read that was the best way to talk to children so they would listen to me and do what I said. I was awkwardly trying to apply "healthy" parenting communication suggestions I had memorized. I noticed that even when I said the exact words that the parenting experts suggested there was still some suffering in the situations where I tried to apply these phrases because I was attached to the belief that they *should* comply. My energy did not match my words.

Then, I began to question those thoughts that they *should* do what I said, lost my attachment to whether they did or didn't, and now there is no suffering. Now the words "I would prefer" or "I would like" come out of my mouth the same as before, however the energy of my words is a lot more peaceful and accepting of the possibility that they may not do what I say. Now, my kids either do or don't do what I'd like, and I am totally happy either way. (I'm not talking about a situation where there *is* eminent danger, as I mentioned before. Every situation is different and specific. I only give you this example to show you how doing inquiry regularly and consistently clears the way for your authenticity, clarity, happiness, peace, perfect action, and presence.)

I truly treat them how I would like to be treated. I don't have to think about doing that; it just happens naturally. I trust them, not as an act or a doing of something, but as a way of naturally being with them. I respect them as I would respect you, and again not as a thing I do, but as a natural way of being. I end up guiding them using only the way I live my life as their curriculum. They learn by watching me and my husband and by their own experiences. I stay in my own business so I stay present. This teaches them to stay in their business, to not worry about me or my husband, nor to try to control us. If they stay in their business, then *they* stay present.

I treat them differently now. Before, fears for their future safety would lead me to do things like hide or secretly give away the things I thought were bad for them, like a plastic toy or something with sugar in it. Now, we have conversations about their requests and I let them know my preferences. After we talk through it, I say yes most of the time as long as I really feel like saying yes. I do this not because I want them to learn a lesson about how something is bad for them but because I'm supportive of them testing out what real consequences their actions cause.

And I've questioned my fears about their future. Now, I want what they want. That's what love does.

I used to want to control their path, a *lot*. Now, I honor their path. If something makes them happy, I want that for them. And, I don't expose them to things I'd prefer they not have; I do expose them to things I think or hope they might enjoy. I'm always open to not knowing what's good for them to experience or not to experience. If they do ever get exposed to something I don't want for them, I question my thinking, instead of getting upset like I used to do. I get clarity. I understand myself. I get quiet. I use it all for my own growth and development. This teaches my children to listen to *themselves*. They listen to their own internal guidance system, as I listen to mine. They are able to stay in touch with their bodies, minds, and spirits. They can hear themselves and act accordingly when they aren't attracted to something or someone. They trust themselves because I reflect that trust back to them. Every time there is what used to be called a "problem" situation, new solutions appear to come out of nowhere (now here) because I question my thinking.

Before self-inquiry, if my kids were ever sad or disappointed, I would listen and validate because I read that was the best thing to *do*. After a while, this would backfire because I wasn't being authentic. I wasn't *being* trusting as the background to this *doing* of listening and *doing* of validating. Now, if they're ever sad or disappointed, I listen to them, *knowing* - from experience - that they are believing a thought that isn't true, and I patiently wait for their storm to pass. I have faith in myself that this is true, so I have faith in them. I have faith in them from my own experience of transcending negative thoughts. They have the same power to do the same thing now.

I help them follow their passions as much as I can. I don't force them to bend to my will. I question my thoughts when I feel like it but don't want to bend theirs. When a thought like *"We shouldn't stay inside all day and play on the computer"* crosses my mind, I question it. It argues with my reality, so I just can't believe it. I'm calm about it then, and I sit with them and watch and play together, or I calmly do things I love while indoors, or I go outside myself, or I encourage us all to do something outside but it's in a calmer unattached way. We might talk about it and come up with something else we'd all like to do. My daughter or son might tell me they're so bored of watching YouTube and they can't wait to go play outside with their friends or with me. Then we're so happy to spend time together outside. They're outside because they authentically *want* to be, not because I forced them to be. They've stayed true to themselves. We all work things out so that everyone's apparent needs are considered and met. I also question any stressful thoughts that might arise that say we "need" something when we clearly don't have it, since that's also an argument with our reality.

My son knows I love it when spring comes and the leaves and flowers start to bloom. Just now he called to me from the other room. "Mom, come here!" I did. "Look straight that way." I looked in the direction he was pointing and saw bright green new leaves sprouting from a tree in our backyard. I looked at him and said, "Thank you for showing me that!" and gave him a kiss.

He smiled. Precious moments like these happen spontaneously and authentically in a home filled with non-judgment, connection, and presence.

This is how presence looks in our lives. It could look totally different in yours. Only you will experience what it will look like in your family when you create space for presence to live through you, as you.

Self-inquiry is not about what children should or shouldn't be doing or how you should or shouldn't do certain things in your parenting. It's about *being*. It's about deepening your connection to love, to presence, and to your precious child. It's about realizing you are love; you are the present moment. It's about relieving your own suffering so you can be your true self again, for good. It's about loving all of you, and loving your entire child. In my experience, it's about returning to love.

When you practice self-inquiry, you'll never have to feel upset, worried, or frustrated about your child ever again. You'll never unintentionally disconnect from your child again. Your child will trust herself. Your child will trust her wings to fly. This has been my experience with self-inquiry. It's possible for you, too.

I invite you to sit with yourself today - and always - and see how you are able to realize a deeper connection to the present moment, to yourself, and to your child. When you question the thoughts that take you away from it, I love that you would be the one to return to Love.

Wishing you, dear one, Presence and Peace today and always,
Catherine

Presence Practice Notes

Returning to Love

Self-Inquiry Worksheet 1 of 2

We've been told all of our lives not to judge others. The fact is we do it anyway. This worksheet allows the mind to see itself, to see the reality of its own thoughts, and to truly consider the thoughts by putting them on paper. This is the time to let those judgments have their own life.

DIRECTIONS:

A. Think of a specific person that is triggering stress in you. It could be your child, partner, ex-partner, mom, or dad. (Not yourself) They could be living or not living.

B. Now, recall a specific stressful situation you had with that person. It might have been a face to face interaction, an event, a phone call, or any situation that caused you any feelings of discomfort. Identify the specific stressful situation, and see it as a *single snapshot* in time.

C. Witness that single snapshot. Notice the time, place, words spoken, body language, and energy of each person. Then, 1) Identify and name the primary uncomfortable feeling you were having, 2) identify why you felt that way, and 3) answer the questions below with *short, simple* statements. *Please do not* try to be psychologically correct, spiritual, or wise now. For the purposes of this worksheet, be as judgmental as you were when you were in that situation.

1. In this situation, who angers, confuses, saddens, or disappoints you, and why? *(Example: I'm frustrated with Aiden because he won't listen to me.)*

2. In this situation, how do you want them to change? *(Example: I want Aiden to stop what he's doing, look at me, and listen to me.)*

3. In this situation, what advice would you offer to them? *(Example: Aiden should learn how to listen.)*

4. In order for you to feel better in this situation, what do you need them to think, say, feel, or do? *(Example: I need Aiden to listen.)*

5. What do you think of them in this situation? Make a list. Be petty. *(Example: Aiden is just like his dad - he won't respect me.)*

6. What is it in or about this situation that you don't ever want to experience again? *(Example: I don't ever want to be disrespected by Aiden again.)*

Review what you wrote. Pick one sentence you wrote that feels the most stressful to you right now. Circle it. Rewrite it at the top of Worksheet 2.

Adapted from Byron Katie International, Inc. Rev. 7/2014, with consent.

Self-Inquiry Worksheet 2 of 2

This worksheet is a meditation. When answering the questions, close your eyes, be still, and patiently wait to witness what appears to you. Always give yourself time to let the deeper answers meet the questions.

DIRECTIONS:

A. In the space below, write the thought you circled from Worksheet 1. Then answer questions 1-4.

B. Reconstruct the thought in three new ways. Possibilities are: by directing it inward (number 5 below), exchanging the other person's name with yours (number 6 below), and stating its exact opposite (number 7 below). Examples are provided below. Then, find and record three genuine, specific examples of how each new thought is as true or truer for you in that situation.

C. If you circled the thought from your answer to question 6 on Worksheet 1, you would reconstruct the thought by replacing the words, "I don't ever want to…" with "I am willing to…" and "I look forward to…"

Re-write the thought you circled on Worksheet 1: *(Example: Aiden doesn't listen to me.)*

1. In that situation, is this thought true? *(Yes or no only. There are no right or wrong answers. If no, skip to question 3.)*

2. In that situation, can you absolutely know that it's true? *(Yes or no only)*

3. In that situation, how did you *react* when you believed that thought?

4. In that situation, who would you be if you could not believe that thought?

5. Reconstruct the thought by directing it *inward. (Example: I don't listen to me.)* Find and record three genuine, specific examples in that situation how this new thought is as true or truer than the original thought.

6. Reconstruct the thought by *exchanging* the other person's name with yours. *(Example: I don't listen to Aiden.)* Find and record three genuine, specific examples of how this new thought is as true or truer for you in that situation.

7. Reconstruct the thought by stating the *exact opposite. (Example: Aiden does listen to me.)* Find and record three genuine, specific examples of how this new thought is as true or truer for you in that situation.

Adapted from Byron Katie International, Inc. Rev. 7/2014, with consent.

Index of Stressful Thoughts

250

251

Recommended Reading

Adyashanti. *The Way of Liberation: A Practical Guide to Spiritual Enlightenment.* Campbell, California: Adyashanti, 2012. Print.

Brown, Resa Steindel. *The Call to Brilliance: A True Story to Inspire Parents and Educators.* Thousand Oaks, CA: Fredric Press, 2006. Print.

Byrne, Rhonda. *The Secret Gratitude Book.* New York: Atria Books, 2007. Print.

Byrne, Rhonda. *The Magic.* New York: Atria Books, 2012. Print.

Chopra, Mallika. *100 Promises to My Baby.* Rodale, 2005. Print.

Clarke, Jean Illsley, and Connie Dawson. *Growing Up Again, Parenting Ourselves, Parenting Our Children.* 2nd ed. Center City, Minn.: Hazelden, 1998. Print.

Eliot, Lise. *What's Going On in There?: How the Brain and Mind Develop in the First Five Years of Life.* New York, N.Y.: Bantam Books, 1999. Print.

Ginott, Haim G.. *Between Parent and Child: New Solutions to Old Problems.* New York: Macmillan, 1965. Print.

Grayson, Henry. *Mindful Loving: 10 Practices for Creating Deeper Connections.* New York: Gotham Books, 2003. Print.

Hay, Louise. *Inner Wisdom: Meditations for the Heart and Soul.* Carlsbad, Calif.: Hay House, 2000. Print.

Hendrix, Harville, and Helen Hunt. *The Parenting Companion: Meditations and Exercises for Giving the Love That Heals.* New York: Pocket Books, 1999. Print.

Holt, John Caldwell. *How Children Learn*. New York: Pitman Pub. Corp., 1967. Print.

Hunt, Jan, Jason Hunt, and Nanda Gestel. *The Unschooling Unmanual*. Salt Spring Island, B.C.: Natural Child Project, 2008. Print.

Jenkins, Peggy Davison. *Nurturing Spirituality in Children: Simple Hands-On Activities*. Hillsboro, OR: Beyond Words Pub., 1995. Print.

Katie, Byron, and Stephen Mitchell. *Loving What Is: Four Questions That Can Change Your Life*. New York: Harmony Books, 2002. Print.

Katie, Byron, and Stephen Mitchell. *Byron Katie on Parents and Children*. Marina Del Ray, CA: Byron Katie International, 2006. Print.

Kiloby, Scott. *Love's Quiet Revolution: The End of the Spiritual Search*. Charleston, SC: BookSurge, 2008. Print.

Laricchia, Pam. *Free to Learn: Five Ideas for a Joyful Unschooling Life*. Erin, Ontario: Living Joyfully Enterprises, 2012. Print.

Leo, Pam. *Connection Parenting: Parenting Through Connection Instead of Coercion, Through Love Instead of Fear*. 2nd ed. Deadwood, OR: Wyatt-MacKenzie Pub., 2007. Print.

Lipton, Bruce H.. *The Biology of Belief: Unleashing the Power of Consciousness, Matter and Miracles*. Santa Rosa, CA: Mountain of Love/Elite Books, 2005. Print.

Martin, William. *The Parent's Tao Te Ching: A New Interpretation: Ancient Advice for Modern Parents*. New York: Marlowe, 1999. Print.

McClure, Vimala Schneider. *The Tao of Motherhood*. Novato, CA: New World Library, 1997. Print.

McGowan, Dale. *Parenting Beyond Belief: On Raising Ethical, Caring Kids Without Religion*. New York: American Management Association, 2007. Print.

McGrath, Sara. *Unschooling: A Lifestyle of Learning*. Ed. 4 ed. Duvall, WA: S. McGrath, 2010. Print.

McKee, Alison. *Homeschooling Our Children, Unschooling Ourselves*. Madison, WI.: Bittersweet House, 2002. Print.

McGrath, Sara. *The Unschooling Happiness Project: A Guide to Living a Happy and Fulfilling Life Through Love and Creativity*. North Charleston, SC: CreateSpace, 2010. Print.

Mongan, Marie F.. *Hypnobirthing: A Celebration of Life: A Definitive Guide for a Safer, Easier, More Comfortable Birthing in the Way That Most Mirrors Nature*. Expanded ed. Concord, NH: Rivertree Pub., 1998. Print.

Neill, Alexander Sutherland, and Albert Lamb. *Summerhill School: A New View of Childhood*. New York: St. Martin's Press, 1993. Print.

Nirmala (Daniel Erway). *Nothing Personal: Seeing Beyond the Illusion of a Separate Self*. Sedona, AZ: Endless Satsang Foundation, 2001. Print.

Pieper, Martha Heineman, and William Joseph Pieper. *Smart Love: The Compassionate Alternative to Discipline That Will Make You a Better Parent and Your Child a Better Person*. Boston, MA: Harvard Common Press, 1999. Print.

Rosenberg, Marshall B.. *Raising Children Compassionately, Parenting the Nonviolent Communication Way*. Encinitas, CA: PuddleDancer Press, 2003. Print.

Rosenberg, Marshall B.. *Nonviolent Communication: A Language of Life*. 2nd ed. Encinitas, CA: PuddleDancer Press, 2003. Print.

Rosenberg, Marshall B.. *The Surprising Purpose of Anger: Beyond Anger Management: Finding the Gift*. Encinitas, CA: PuddleDancer Press, 2005. Print.

Sanders, Leigh. *Being Enough*. Newnan, GA: Fair's Arbor Press, 1997. Print.

Tolle, Eckhart. *A New Earth: Awakening to Your Life's Purpose*. New York: Plume, 2006. Print.

Tolle, Eckhart. *The Power of Now: A Guide to Spiritual Enlightenment*. Novato, CA: New World Library, 1999. Print.

Tolle, Eckhart. *Eckhart Tolle's Findhorn Retreat: Stillness Amidst the World*. Novato, CA: New World Library, 2006. Print.

Tolle, Eckhart, Robert S. Friedman, and Frank Riccio. *Milton's Secret: An Adventure of Discovery Through Then, When, and the Power of Now*. Charlottesville, VA: Hampton Roads Pub., 2008. Print.

Tolle, Eckhart, Byron Katie, Stephen Mitchell, and Michele Penn. *Peace in the Present Moment*. Charlottesville, VA: Hampton Roads Publishing Company, Inc., 2010. Print.

Tsabary, Shefali. *The Conscious Parent: Transforming Ourselves, Empowering Our Children*. Vancouver: Namaste Pub., 2010. Print.

Walsch, Neale Donald. *Conversations with God: An Uncommon Dialogue*. Norfolk, VA: Hampton Roads Pub. Co., 1997. Print.

Weil, Zoe. *Above All, Be Kind: Raising a Humane Child in Challenging Times*. Gabriola Island, B.C.: New Society Publishers, 2003. Print

The Present Mothers Community

The Present Mothers Community is a personal and spiritual development group for mothers who are passionate about being present - in mind, body, and spirit - for the sake of their children.

Dear Present Mother,

I invite you to join us every Saturday morning for a *Morning Walk with The Present Mothers Community*. Our walk is a one-hour conference call which I facilitate. You'll be with mothers like you, who have either done the 40-day presence practice in *The Present Mother*, are currently reading and working through the book, or who found out about us through the internet.

Our call starts with a meditation similar to the one you've been using from page 16. That's followed by me facilitating you in your self-inquiry on one of your stressful thoughts about mothering (anonymously if you like). We end with questions and answers.

This hour of personal reflection is intended to help you question the thoughts that cause all of the suffering in your mothering life and return you to your true, peaceful, present nature. To learn more about the structure, costs, and how to sign up, visit our website at

www.thepresentmother.com.

Love,
Catherine

About Catherine Weiss

As a child, Catherine pondered the depths of what it was that inspired people to say the things they said or didn't say. This propelled her into an intensive, 20-year, self-directed study of self-actualization, neuroscience, presence, mindfulness, and transpersonal psychology. She has had a life-long interest in epigenetics, the study of inheritable changes in gene activity that are not caused by changes in our DNA. She views our inheritance of belief systems as the main driver in the evolution of consciousness and that mothers can make a huge difference toward that. In 2007, shortly after she became a mother she began a regular practice of self-inquiry, questioning literally hundreds of stressful thoughts, because of its transformational effect on her mothering. She is a Certified Facilitator Candidate of the self-inquiry process called The Work, a Certified Children's Grief Support Group Facilitator for Rainbows, a Certified Adult Facilitative Trainer, and a Certified Coach Candidate from Coach University. She holds a Master's degree from Florida State University. She is not a parenting expert; she helps mothers become aware of and trust the expert they always have within. She lives near Portland, Oregon with her husband and two children.

Made in the USA
Middletown, DE
16 November 2016